MUSIC THERAPY

MUSIC THERAPY

EDITED BY

EDWARD PODOLSKY, M.D.

Department of Psychiatry, Kings County Hospital, Brooklyn, N. Y.

PHILOSOPHICAL LIBRARY · NEW YORK

ACKNOWLEDGMENT

The Editor is grateful to the editors of the following periodicals for generous permission to reprint papers originally published in their journals.

American Journal of Psychiatry
American Journal of Psychology
American Journal of Psychotherapy
Educational Music Magazine
Journal of Abnormal and Social Psychology
Journal of Nervous and Mental Diseases
Journal of Social Psychology
Journal of Speech Disorders
Mental Hygiene
Occupational Therapy and Rehabilitation
Plastic and Reconstructive Surgery
Psychiatric Quarterly
Sociometry
West Virginia Medical Journal

CONTENTS

CONTRIBUTORS

ALESSI, Salvatore L., M.S., Psychologist, Connecticut State Hospital, Middletown, Conn.

ALTSHULER, Ira M., M.D., Wayne County General Hospital, Eloise, Mich.

ARRINGTON, George E., Jr., M.D., Huntington, W. Va.

BRADLEY, Harold, B.M., Music Therapist, Brooklyn, N. Y.

BRIGHOUSE, Gilbert, Occidental College, Los Angeles, Calif.

BROADBENT, T. Ray, M.D., National Cancer Institute, Bethesda, Md.

BROWN, Louis M., M.A., Music Therapist, Brooklyn, N. Y.

BROWNE, Hermina Eisele, Director, Music Therapy Dept., New Jersey State Hospital at Marlboro, N. J.

EATON, Merrill T., Jr., M.D., Dept. of Psychiatry, University of Kansas Medical Center, Kansas City, Kansas

EDWARDS, Benjamin F., M.D., Duke University, Durham, N. C.

ELLIS, Douglas E., Iowa State College, Ames, Iowa

FISHER, Rhoda Lee, Elgin State Hospital, Elgin, Illinois

FISHER, Seymour, Elgin State Hospital, Elgin, Illinois

GARRITY, Daniel A.

GIRARD, James, M.A., Psychologist, Boston, Mass.

GRUNEWALD, Marta, Ph.D., New York, N. Y.

HANSON, Howard, Mus.Bac., Mus.Doc., LL.D., F.A.A.R., Rochester, N. Y.

HASLERUD, George M., University of New Hampshire, Durham, N. H.

HERMAN, E. P., M.S., Clinical Psychologist, Brooklyn, N. Y.

HILLIARD, Bernard, Ph.D., Clinical Psychologist, New York, N. Y.

HOLZBERG, Jules D., Ph.D., Clinical Psychologist, Connecticut State Hospital, Middletown, Conn.

KNOUSS, Ruth, Occupational Therapy Department, Sheppard and Enoch Pratt Hospital, Towson, Maryland

METZGER, James T., M.D., Duke University, Durham, N. C.

MOUNTNEY, Virginia, Occupational Therapy Department, Sheppard and Enoch Pratt Hospital, Towson, Maryland

MURDOCK, Harry M., M.D., Medical Director, The Sheppard and Enoch Pratt Hospital, Towson, Maryland

PALMER, Martin F., Sc.D., Director, Institute of Logopedics and Head, Department of Logopedics, Municipal University of Wichita, Wichita, Kansas

xi

PAPERTE, Frances, Music Research Foundation, Director of Applied Music, Walter Reed General Hospital, Washington, D. C.

PEPINSKY, Abe, Ph.D., Head of Dept. of Psychology, Haverford College, Haverford, Pa.

PICKRELL, Kenneth L., M.D., Duke University, Durham, N. C.

PODOLSKY, Edward, M.D., Department of Psychiatry, Kings County Hospital, Brooklyn, N. Y.

PRESTON, Mary Jane, Supervisor of Recreation, Pilgrim State Hospital, West Brentwood, New York

PRICE, Henrietta G., O.T.R., Occupational Therapy Department, Sheppard and Enoch Pratt Hospital, Towson, Maryland

REESE, Hans H., M.D., Professor of Neuropsychiatry, University Hospital, Madison, Wisc.

SIMON, Benjamin, M.D., Ring Sanatorium, Arlington Heights, Mass.

SKELLY, Clyde G., University of New Hampshire, Durham, N. H.

SUGARMAN, Paul, Ph.D., Mus.M., Music Therapist, Chicago, Illinois

WALTERS, Lawrence, Music Therapist, New York, N. Y.

WILDE, N. John, D.D.S., M.D., Duke University, Durham, N. C.

ZERBE, Louis E., M.M., formerly Professor of Violin, University of Wichita, Wichita, Kansas

MUSIC THERAPY

INTRODUCTION

The ancient men of medicine were wise in the ways of nature. Very early they became acquainted with an astonishing variety of methods to heal the mind and body. Before long they learned that music was a definite healing force. Four thousand years ago the priest-doctors of Egypt had a favorite incantation in music which purported to have a favorable influence on the fertility of women. This incantation is still preserved in the most ancient of all Egyptian papyri. The Egyptians called music the "physic of the soul." The Persians, who regarded music as an expression of the good principle Ohura-Mazda, are said to have cured various illnesses by the sound of the lute.

The ancient Hebrews employed music in several recorded cases of physical and mental illness, perhaps the most famous being that of King Saul who when he felt that his reason was disintegrating was benefited by listening to music. "When the evil spirit from God was upon Saul, then David took up a harp and played with his hands so that Saul was refreshed and well, and the evil spirit departed from him."

Confucius was a great lover of music; it was his belief that music was a definite aid to harmonious living. Plato also regarded music very highly. In his THE REPUBLIC he expressed his belief that health in mind and body could be obtained through music. Aristotle ascribed the beneficial effects of music to an emotional catharsis. Cassidorus attributed marked powers to music in promoting emotional hygiene. He stated that "it doth extenuate fears, furies, appeaseth cruelty, abateth heaviness, and to such as are watchful it causeth quiet rest; it takes away spleen and hatred—it cures all irksomeness and heaviness of soul." Pythagoras also regarded music as a valuable therapeutic agent in mental and emotional health and he recommended that it be used more often.

The ancient Greeks have left us a great many examples of the remarkable powers of music. Polybius, a well known Greek author, speaking of a musical race of Arcadia, contrasted the gentleness of their manners with the cruelty of the Cynetes, who neglected the cultivation of music. Terpender restored a rebellious people to their allegiance through his melodies. On the other hand, the Spartan, Tyrtaeus, by means of certain verses which he sang to the accompaniment of flutes, so inflamed the courage of his countrymen that they achieved a great victory over the Messenians, to whom they had lost battles on several previous and musicless occasions.

A similar incident is related by Plutarch in his biography of Solon. He tells us that the celebrated legislator succeeded in inciting the Athenians to invade and capture the Isle of Salamis by singing a song of his own composition. Empedocles is said to have actually prevented the murder of his father by playing on his lyre. The fierce and murderous temper of Achilles (of the vulnerable heel) was moderated and quite nicely controlled only by soothing music.

The harp later became a popular instrument for moderating outbursts of excessive temperament. Damon, by playing on his harp, was said to have been able to pacify the alcohol-maddened play-boys. Music was the first medicine for a hangover. Asclepiades who also had a harp was able to use it to good advantage in restoring seditious armies to reason and order.

The first use of music as a regular therapeutic modality is attributed to Zenocrates, Sarpender and Arion, ancient Greeks with modern ideas, who used harp music to curb the wild outbursts of the violently mentally disturbed. Celsus, a leading early medical authority, was an enthusiastic user of music instead of brutality to treat the insane. He pointed out different methods of influencing the minds of the mentally ill, depending upon the nature of their illness. He said, "We must quiet their demoniacal laughter by reprimands, and soothe their sadness by harmony, the sound of cymbals and other instruments."

It was learned quite early that soft music has a soothing effect and that lively music has a stimulating effect. Antigenides, the first exponent of swing, played a very fiery, highly rhythmical composition before Alexander the Great and so inflamed him that he leaped from his chair, drew his sword and began attacking those about him.

Centuries later one of the greatest plagues of history swept across Europe. Following closely upon its horrors, in 1374, a curious phenomenon was observed in Germany. This was known as the Dancing Mania. Entire communities joined hands, screamed and shook for hours on end until they dropped from exhaustion. It was thoroughly infectious and no medicine was known at that time that had any effect on the addicts. Music was found to be the only means of checking it. The authorities of many towns ordered soft, slow, soothing music to be played in the streets and market places; gradually the dancers became normal and the strange contagion was arrested.

It is quite remarkable that music can act either as a calming influence or as a stimulant. Napoleon is alleged to have attributed his defeat in Russia to the combination of the Russian winter and the Russian military music. The weird, barbaric tunes of "those monstrous Cossack regiments" incited the Muscovites to furious attacks in which they wiped out the best regiments of the French army. Probably there have been many similar incidents in other wars. Music is as necessary to an army as food and ammunition.

Some individuals are particularly susceptible to music, especially stimulating music. It is said that Claude le Jeune, the favorite musician of Henry III, once played a very lively tune at a wedding, "which so animated a gentleman who was present that he clapped his hands on his sword and swore that it was impossible for him to refrain from fighting with the first person he met; upon which Claude caused another air to be performed, of a soothing kind, which immediately restored him to his natural temperament."

The soothing effects of music have, from time to time, been put to the most practical use. The most surprising of all instances —if it does not strain our credulity—is recorded in the life of Fillipe Palma, the singer. Palma was always falling into debt. For this reason his house was continually besieged by creditors. One day an enraged creditor stormed into his house and the singer at once realized that no soft-spoken words would have any effect on him. He decided to try music. Accordingly, he sat down at the harpsichord and began to play a very soothing tune. In a short time the angry creditor was thoroughly pacified. It is also noted that not only did he cancel Palma's debts, but that he even gave him money to pay off his other creditors.

A similar but more dramatic story is told of the Sultan Amurath, who having laid siege to Baghdad and taken it, gave orders that some 30,000 Persians were to be put to death, notwithstanding the fact that they had put their arms down. Among the intended victims was a musician. He begged the officer in charge to spare him but for a moment that he might be permitted to speak to the Sultan. He was granted this favor and brought before the conqueror. He then began to play the saddest and most heart-rending tune that he could think of. After a half hour of this the Sultan could bear up no longer. He lost all restraint and broke down, weeping hysterically. He countermanded the order for the massacre.

The case of Philip V of Spain is famous. He suffered severely from spells of melancholia, which nearly ended in insanity. The court physician tried in vain to cure him and as a last resort determined to try music. Carlo Broschi Farinelli, a famous singer and a former favorite of the unhappy king was sent for to take part in this experiment. He was placed in a room adjoining that in which Philip sat in melancholy solitude. He sang a number of lively tunes. No results were perceptible on the first day, but when the experiment was repeated, the king began to show signs of returning interest. He listened and gradually he became absorbed in the exquisite solo concerts. His interest grew daily. He became more discriminating, until finally, his attention once more thoroughly aroused, he showed a definite improvement in his condition.

George II of England was also subjected to terrible spells of depression, and the only solace he received was from music. He would often ask for it when he sensed his melancholia coming on. In time music was successful in permanently freeing him from this mental affliction.

Another case is recorded in the archives of the Academy of Sciences in Paris. A well-known musician and composer was subjected to occasional seizures of severe mental depression which no drug in the materia medica could cure. His doctor thought that music might prove of value. Bernier's Cantata was sung. As soon as he heard the first notes his nervous tension relaxed. In another hour his depression was gone. As soon as the music ceased he had a relapse, but after ten trials of this treatment a complete cure was effected.

King Ludwig of Bavaria, who was subjected to fits of melancholia, came in time to know that music was the best medicine he could obtain. He was continually being plunged into the blackest depths of depression; for these attacks there were two melodies which were more precious than any drug. They were the DREAM SONG from Auber's MASANIELLO and HYMN from von Flotow's STRADELLA. They helped him tide over his melancholic episodes.

It was only toward the end of the 18th century that any serious effort to evaluate the precise effects of music on the human mind was made. Among the first investigators was Dr. Brocklesby, who conducted a series of experiments on a child of two, born of musical parents, "who was one day remarkable for mirth and good humor upon hearing sprightly airs of music; this gave occasion to the father and Mr. Stanley to try the effects of different measures when they had raised the infant's spirits very high by these means. But as the chromatic and the graver strains began, the child grew melancholy and sad, which temper was removed as soon as the pleasanter strain was played. Thus as I am informed they could, solely by this art, raise and allay grief and joy in terms of this infant's mind."

In 1890 Dr. D. T. Wimmer described the results of experiments with music conducted in mental hospitals. The piano was played for half an hour to fourteen hundred mentally ill women. It was found that all responded to the rhythm. In some cases the pulse rate rose; others became restless and beat time. Melody without emphatic rhythm had no effect at all except when it happened to be an air which awakened memories. Through slow music the worst cases were soothed and sometimes went to sleep. After several experiments all showed improvement.

Since then scores of practical applications of the beneficial effects of music in mental cases have been made. Thus, the Guild of St. Cecilia toward the end of the last century and the beginning of this, organized curative concerts for mental hospitals. About the same time Dr Bechinsky, a Russian physician of note, attended a three-year-old child who suffered from insomnia due to night terrors. He advised the child's mother to play one of Chopin's waltzes. The effect was immediate and most satisfactory.

Within more recent times the Hospital Music Committee of the New York Visiting Committee has been taking music into city hospitals and state hospitals for the mentally ill for a score of years. It is a subcommittee of the State Charities Aid Association and it has been doing very valuable work in musical therapy.

The music provided by the Hospital Music Committee is especially valuable for mentally disturbed patients and it is quite often the means of bringing about recovery. Many interesting stories have been told by the committee members. Here is a typical instance of the value of music in an emotionally upset patient in Lincoln Hospital, New York. One ward was being disturbed by the moans of a patient, who, the nurse declared, was not so much in pain as he was extremely nervous. The members of the Music Committee went close to the bed and kept playing and singing softly. It was not before long that the man ceased to moan. Music had helped him to get a better grip on himself.

Not so long ago, Moissaye Boguslawski, the famous pianist, conducted a series of novel experiments in a Chicago hospital for the mentally ill. Boguslawski played a group of Italian melodies before an Italian mother who was so mentally disturbed that she refused to have anything to do with her baby. The woman showed no reaction until the pianist began to play an aria from IL TROVATORE. This aroused sufficient interest in her to pay attention to her baby and to look after it.

Dr. L. S. Bender, of Bellevue Hospital, reports cases of deranged children whose fits of violence were quickly terminated by music. In a state hospital in Illinois one hundred patients were treated with marked success by piano playing. Playing for each one individually, the pianist began with nursery pieces and continued through adolescence and adulthood, until some tune established a chain of associations with the world of reality.

Among these patients was a young mother whose mind had become deranged at childbirth. She, too, would have nothing to do with her newly born infant. Her mind was restored to normal with music, particularly Brahms' LULLABY. An Italian who had not spoken for three months was able to get a better grip on herself and began to talk once more after a course of musical therapy. A woman who could not remember where she lived regained her memory after a course of psychotherapy in which music was used consistently.

There was also the case of a man who went blind because of hysteria following the sudden death of his wife. A pianist was called who played slow, soothing music at first. Later the patient requested gay, lively tunes, and after a week of treatment his nerves relaxed and he regained his sight.

There is no doubt that there is a bright outlook regarding research in music as a means of alleviating certain types of mental and emotional illness. The physiological and psychological effects of music, its social, educational and aesthetic attributes, place music in a sphere that is quite unique. There is still a great deal of work to be done with music in diseases of the mind and severe emotional disturbances, and the future holds much of promise in this direction.

E. P.

MUSIC AND MENTAL HEALTH

By EDWARD PODOLSKY, M.D.

Dept. Psychiatry, Kings County Hospital, Brooklyn, N. Y.

Physicians whose sole task is caring for the mentally ill have long realized that music is one of the best medicines for the mind. Several years ago Dr. Egbert Guernsey said: "If every hospital or asylum inducted in its medical staff a musical director, and if every physician and trained musician understood the nature and action of music, there is no telling the good that might be accomplished, the lives brightened and the tangled brains restored to harmony."

Of a similar mind was Dr. Emmett Dent, for many years Superintendent of the Manhattan State Hospital. After segregating a number of patients for a time and recording the effect of especially selected music upon them Dr. Dent became an enthusiastic user of music as a means of alleviating some of the symptoms of the unsound mind. Many years' trial with music in mental cases have only furthered his opinion. He said: "Music is responsible for cures among the insane and improvements of patients seemingly in a hopeless condition that are little short of marvelous."

Some time ago the Superintendent of the State Hospital in Middletown, Connecticut, organized an orchestra in that institution which provided music for patients at meal time. He stated: "The effects of that orchestra music on the thirteen hundred patients assembled during meals in the dining room, afflicted with every grade of mental derangement, is satisfactory to the highest degree. Under its influence those patients are quiet, self-controlled

[11]

and observe as complete decorum as could be found in the dining room of any large hotel, and I believe the influence to be not only pleasing but of lasting benefit. While the scheme is to a large degree experimental, the results are so gratifying that we would be extremely loath to discontinue."

The scheme was not discontinued. The doctor carried on this experiment with music in his institution for many years. At the end of that period he made another interesting statement: "We have continued to maintain an orchestra in our dining room, where fourteen hundred insane patients take their meals, ever since its organization ten years ago, and we have never seen the time when we deemed it possible to dispense with it. Of course, it is very difficult to estimate the amount of possible value music has for the insane; nevertheless, we have no doubt that whatever that may be it has a distinct, excellent, curative influence. Time and experience have only served to confirm the attitude I assumed in the matter ten years ago. We are able to bring fourteen hundred patients of both sexes together for their meals and keep them quiet, amiable, cheerful and orderly during the meal hour with the aid of music of a high-class orchestra. I am ready therefore to re-affirm the opinion expressed ten years ago as to the salutary influence of music on the insane."

These are not isolated instances. Physicians throughout the world are beginning to realize that music is of definite value in keeping the mind healthy. Henry Phipps' magnificent gift of $500,000 for the advanced scientific treatment of mental disorders has made possible the equipment of a musical department in the Phipps Psychiatric Clinic of the Johns Hopkins Hospital in Baltimore, one of the finest institutions of its kind in the world. In that now famous clinic music is being tested as a means of treating mental disorders of various types and degrees, with encouraging results. It has been found that music lessens the fury of the most violent cases and in general is providing a valuable aid to the methods in use at the clinic.

Let us consider some individual cases in which music has proved to be of great benefit. A dementia praecox case is reported of a woman who spent all day talking about her teeth. Nothing could get her mind away from this subject. Finally music was tried. She listened to music without once speaking or apparently thinking of her fixation. As the musical treatment continued she drew further away, in the intervals without music, from her delusion. Her mind gradually became more normal.

Another interesting case is that of a boy of ten who, several years ago, was a patient in the wards of the Whitmouth Hospital in Dublin. He was abnormally overactive. His mother stated that he would stand for hours listening to the phonograph. The only thing that would keep him quiet was music in one form or another. He was a normal boy only when he listened to music.

Still another case was reported in the *American Journal of Psychiatry* by Drs. Willem van de Wall and Earl D. Bond of the Institute for Mental Hygiene, of the Pennsylvania Hospital. It will be given here in detail as an example of what may be accomplished with music as a curative agent in psychoneurosis.

Miss C., aged 29, was referred on April 13, 1932, to the Institute because her physician, after a thorough physical examination, had been unable to discover the cause of her symptoms, which she described as "excruciating pains at menses, requiring bed for days; tightness and pain on both sides of the neck; pains in the face and head." The patient while at the Institute complained of three types of pain: in her face and neck, in her abdomen and in her legs.

The history given by the patient, her mother and a friend showed that these pains were of long standing and that invalidism had begun at the age of nine. At this age she had had fever with some delirium. After this, and not before, she was nervous, easily frightened, insecure and sensitive. Fatigue and, later, menstrual pains, made her schooling irregular. She thought that she was never understood. Nevertheless, she graduated from college and taught for a while with some success, according to pupils and fellow teachers but with no satisfaction to herself.

Because of the distrust of her own ambitions, she always accepted too much work and was always tired. She held an important secretarial job in a college and did very well until she had to give it up because of severe pains. Before any coming event she wore herself out with worry. At the time of her coming and treatment she was most undecided and self-centered, and she spent hours in daydreaming and in watching herself in the mirror. She was conscious of a lump and metallic taste in her throat.

Her musical history is of extreme interest. Her first contact with music came through her mother, whose father, in turn, had fostered musical interests in her home. This man, the patient's maternal grandfather, was an immigrant, and he never lost his longings to return to his native land. He had a great love for music and organized his seven children into a home orchestra, which for many years performed every night.

The patient had a great admiration for her mother's vocal abilities and power of improvisation. Her mother taught her at an early age little songs to be performed in Sunday school. She was reared in the country. During the grammar school period, hymns of the rural church were about her only music literature. At home she spent hours with an older sister improvising melodies and practising two-part singing. The two girls sang for church programs. She described this as follows: "We ran and sang to the wind, climbing the trees, swinging and singing, washing dishes, pasting labels, singing about it, happy and living with melodies bubbling up as an inseparable part of the moment."

When she was thirteen she suddenly became interested in the piano. She taught herself from an old organ book to play two-part melodies with two fingers. She acquired ability to read the melody from the page, but "the tune I fitted to the ear." She states: "I was exalted over my ability to play my first hymn with two hands. I learned to play awful-sounding dramatic interludes and accompaniments on the organ for the entertainments and dramatic presentations of the church."

During her high-school period the patient's experiences in which music was an important factor increased. She spent the year singing in a glee club, parts with very high notes. She helped to perform an oratario. "This enchanted me. The changes in time I loved most. I was charmed by some of the beautiful chorus movements and modulations." When she was sixteen, she joined the choir of what she termed "an emotional revival-meeting session." She tells us that she found "a new depth of appeal in the hymns ALMOST PERSUADED and WHERE HE LEADS ME I WILL FOLLOW."

She loved to listen to music, but she felt more and more the necessity to produce music. Thus she organized a home orchestra— violin, trombone, alto horn and piano. Music-making had become the dynamic factor in her life.

For a month the patient stayed near the Institute and talked to the psychiatrist three or four times a week. Physio-therapy of various sorts was tried but with little success. The doctors decided to try music as a curative method. This consisted of three periods of treatment.

The first period was one of closely supervised study and living in a controlled environment. An expert vocal teacher was secured and a suitable inexpensive home was secured with two women of the patient's own age. These women had always earned their own livelihood, a task which had not always been easy for them; they were understanding and welcomed the patient.

The first method adopted was to focus her immediate attention on her vocal work and to eliminate the idea of being a patient who did her work for the purpose of treatment. She received three or four vocal lessons per week and was instructed to exercise and rest each day as prescribed by the vocal instructor. These lessons consisted of relaxation exercises of the throat, mouth and body muscles and of practice in tone and breathing. The instructor found the patient to be extremely tense and stiff. Efforts by the patient to undertake the simple exercises resulted in contraction of the throat, mouth and neck muscles and a stiffening of the entire body.

It took the patient seven weeks of daily exercise to come gradually to a state of being able to relax the neck, throat and jaw muscles and to produce a free and open tone. She said that each new exercise caused tenseness and pain. As soon as she had opened one tenseness another was experienced. By conscious effort and experiment she learned to develop confidence in relaxing before undertaking to produce tones. The initial attempt to release the jaw caused her severe pain around the nose, eyes and throat and quivers in the shoulders and arms. She was told to rest and start again. After five weeks of practice she was able to relax her jaws for singing exercises without pain. She stated: "I see that I have been thinking that I would never learn to sing again and made myself stupidly tense."

Breathing exercises led in two months to an extension of the inhalation time from ten to eighty-four seconds and vocalization by humming ten tunes to three octaves. Toward the end of the second month she was able to relax her jaw completely and to produce the high C with ease.

In the first week the vocal teacher found the patient rather distracted, dreamy and fearful as well as inhibited. As early as the fourth week this condition had changed to an attentive, concentrated, confident and projective attitude.

During the sixth week the patient began to talk less and less about herself and to discuss spontaneously the musical needs of small rural children and also what could be done to fulfill these needs. At the close of the first period she wanted nothing so much as to continue her training.

After a vacation of three weeks the second period began. As the young woman progressed her pains and muscular stiffness began to disappear. She had become quick and vivacious in movement, but remained somewhat insecure in rhythmical control and expression.

At the end of the second month she said: "I am free, twenty-one and a case no longer. I want to work and be of use." The third and final period of musical training completed her education in music and relaxation.

Upon completion of this treatment with music the patient's mother reported: "It is wonderful to see the change in a year. Instead of wandering pitifully about the house with a hot-water bottle for her pains, she is busy every minute and cheerfully trying to help others." The patient herself said: "I am growing happy from the inside—and I think I begin to manage instead of allowing a stampede of forces within me. I am alive with ambition."

In this case music proved to be the one great means of saving the patient from a life of mental invalidism. Fortunately, she had this marked interest in music, and musical training in her case proved the solution of her troubles. But almost every person is to some extent interested in music and will enjoy an active participation in it.

The next case is that of Horace F. which Dr. Ira Altshuler studied and reported in some detail and which attracted a great deal of attention in the press. Horace was suffering from the catatonic type of schizophrenia. He had lost contact with his environment and was completely withdrawn and living within himself in a world of fantasy. He had been in the hospital for nine years and had been treated with insulin, electroshock, prolonged sleep with no improvement in his condition. Horace had been a pianist before coming to the hospital and Dr. Altshuler determined to see what musical therapy would do in this case.

At this time Horace was 45 years of age; his mental illness had begun when he was thirty-four and it had continued ever since. He had begun the study of piano when he was twelve and continued until he had become mentally ill. During these years he had received a rather thorough musical education and training.

Horace had been a sensitive, easily offended, irritable, nervous child. He grew up under the domination of his mother, who over-protected him. He never played games with the boys in the neighborhood and did not care for boys' games. He had no close contact with men at any time in his life and was shy of girls. He feared animals except cats. His schoolmates considered him a "sissy" but admired his musical ability. The boys were somewhat protective of him but the girls were aloof and inclined to be less friendly.

When Horace was thirty-four things began to happen to his mind. The first of his symptoms was suspicion—people making personal comments about him, questioning his masculinity. He became uncertain of his own identity. He could not sleep. He became nervous and cried a great deal. Next came a half wish and a half fear that people were going to kill him. This led to brooding and cutting himself off from all social life.

Horace retreated more and more from reality. He became confused, refused to eat, to talk and to dress himself. Then he was brought to the hospital. He was given all the latest treatment and all of them produced no improvement in his condition. It was after this series of treatments that Dr. Altshuler decided to try musical therapy.

Horace had been particularly fond of Chopin's music. It was felt that exposing Horace to Chopin's music, especially such works as he had played before might attract his attention and find an emotional echo. Accordingly Horace was given daily doses of Chopin's works. After a few days of this a faint smile came to his face. He had begun to awaken, slowly, gradually. At times he stopped and listened for a few minutes. There was a definite response. It became more and more sustained. Weeks and months went by. Progress was slow. Horace's interest in music gradually awakened. He sat down at the piano and played a few notes.

As time went on Horace spent more and more time at the piano playing first simple melodies and later all the pieces he had learned before he became mentally ill. He played the works of

Chopin, Mendelssohn, Schumann, Debussy, Bach, Liszt and Beethoven. He played them correctly and with the proper emotional evaluation. He began to display poise in body and head movement and in fingering.

Further improvement was noticed when Horace began to take notice of things around him. He was returning to his environment. He was able to go home on weekends. He recognized old familiar streets, parks and buildings. He began to regain his social amenities. Occasionally he uttered coherent sentences. He became conscious of his appearance and began to take some pride in it.

Horace has not recovered his mental health entirely. It is not known if he ever will. Music has not brought Horace back to his old self, but it has, in this case, definitely arrested further mental deterioration. During the time Horace plays he apparently acts and feels normally—though when he finishes playing he plunges back again into mental darkness. The very significant thing is that music has prevented Horace from slipping into the world of a complete and final mental blackout.

The potential value of music as a resocializing agent in treating mental patients is immeasurable. Music is capable of changing mood; it overcomes depressed feelings and calms over-active patients. It can change a dissatisfied and destructive mood to a satisfied and constructive one. Since music has this power it is being used quite widely on mental patients to bring them out of seclusion, relieve tensions and afford contact with reality by relaxation and the creation of an emotional outlet.

Dr. W. Simon in 1945 organized a program of music therapy which was carried out with great success in one of the Veterans Hospitals. Mental patients were exposed to the sound and rhythm of music and some of them later became actual performers. In time the hospital had a band in which 25 patients participated. Musical entertainment was provided in the dining-room during the Sunday noon meal and on the wards for the benefit of infirm patients. Individual patients practiced for their own enjoyment in small groups, in addition to playing at regularly scheduled rehearsals.

The response to music as a therapeutic agent for those patients participating, and for the large number of patients who comprised the audience, was very gratifying. Those listening to the music had been observed reacting to familiar melodies by tapping their feet, drumming their fingers, etc. The concerts aided in distracting the patients' thoughts from abnormal mental states, replacing them with normal emotional feelings. Those who participated in these performances were given an emotional outlet for their repressed feelings and at the same time were encouraged in an art of self-expression. Frequently a change of mood was observed in un-friendly and hostile patients, resulting in the establishment of an atmosphere conducive to a closer and more harmonious relation-ship between patients and employees. The interest of depressed patients was stimulated and channeled into purposeful activity with the result that better contact with reality was thus achieved.

Dr. Simon found that by playing instruments the patients prac-ticed co-ordination of nerve and muscle and developed new means of self-expression. They derived a great sense of accomplishment from playing and showed signs of relaxation, achieving momen-tary release from their anxieties, emotional conflicts and mental confusion.

Dr. Leonard Gilman conducted a three and a half years con-stant study of the use and effects of specific music in relation to mental patients at the Army Medical Center in Washington, D. C. Music was specially selected to produce predetermined change, utilizing whenever possible pertinent background facts from the patient's associative experiences. Patients were grouped homo-geneously according to medical and musical needs. The piano was the instrument chiefly used, although violin, cello, harp and solovox attachments were also employed.

Musical treatment sessions were divided into three parts: 1. Introductory or mood determination and development period.

2. A brief interim period for the patients to talk things over with the musicians. 3. A period of patient participation on a voluntary basis, or arrangements for private instruction.

Patients were assigned to small groups of three to six, to meet regularly five days a week for music. All patients were benefited to some degree by musical therapy, some more than others, quite a few making a complete recovery, and others receiving only slight benefit.

Frances Paperte, Director of the Department of Applied Music at Walter Reed Army Hospital, and a music therapist of note, has been in charge of the musical therapy department at the Walter Reed Hospital for some years now and has had considerable experience with music as a therapeutic agent. Music like drugs varies in action. She has helped to establish a system of general classification of music as follows:

I. All music for use in hospitals should be first generally classified as follows:

> A. Music of solely rhythmic interest.
> B. Music of solely harmonic interest.
> C. Music of solely melodic interest.

II. Of the first group (I), each subheading (A, B, C) should then be divided into two groups (slow, fast) as follows:

> A. Music of modal nature—slow, fast.
> B. Music of classic nature—slow, fast.
> C. Music of a romantic nature—slow, fast.
> D. Music of impressionistic nature—slow, fast.
> E. Music of modern modal nature.

III. Of the second group (II), each subheading (A-E) should finally be divided as to key, length of piece, tempo and character.

Miss Paperte, after many hundreds of cases treated with music at the Walter Reed Hospital recommends the following:

[21]

Diagnosis	Type of Music
Psychoneurosis, conversion hysteria	Stimulating
Psychoneurosis, anxiety type	Soothing, relaxing
Schizophrenia, paranoid type	Soothing
Schizophrenia, hebephrenic type	Stimulating
Manic depressive psychosis	Soothing
Psychoneurosis, mixed type	Relaxing

Mary Jane Preston, music therapist at the Pilgrim State Hospital has had several years experience with music in the rehabilitation of mental patients. At the Pilgrim State Hospital music has an important place in the treatment of the mentally ill, and it is employed in a variety of ways. Thus it has been found that group singing is important in any musical program, as patients who will not talk will frequently sing with a group. Songs are selected in accordance with the variety of tastes represented. From ward singing groups patients are selected for singing in choirs, chorus or glee club, or playing in the band or orchestra.

Small rhythm bands provide enjoyable activity for low grade and regressed patients. Individual musical therapy, in the form of private instruction in voice, piano, instrumental music and composition is often helpful in awakening old interests and instilling self-confidence.

Musical work with regressed patients stresses the effort to develop rhythm, awaken interest and increase initiative by means of stimulating tunes, action songs and rhythmical instruments. Music for disturbed patients emphasizes soft, soothing melodies, while group singing is helpful with anti-social or difficult patients. Older patients enjoy old, familiar songs.

Miss Preston described three experiments carried out at the Pilgrim State Hospital with music in a report to a medical journal. The first was concerned with the use of music before and after electroshock therapy, and showed that patients are soothed and relaxed and the general atmosphere is improved by the use of music. The second experiment was designed to show the effects of music periods on individual patients. In a group of 23 patients definite improvement in behavior and appearance was observed. The third experiment consisted of a series of concerts, which were enthusiastically received by all the patients.

Dr. Ira M. Altshuler who has been doing some very important work with music in the treatment of mental patients at Eloise Hospital in Michigan is of the opinion that bringing music into the minds of patients means to bring into it basic realities in the form of feelings, perceptions and imagery. Such material is capable of replacing states of phantasy, hallucinations, illusions and fears.

Dr. Altshuler employs the "iso" principle. He has found that the "iso" principle—using music identical to the mood or mental tempo of the patient—has been found useful in facilitating the response of mental patients to music. Depressed patients are readily aroused with andante tempo in music and maniacal patients with allegro. The mobilization and prolongation of attention can be more easily achieved by beginning with music which appeals to the lower brain levels. Musical rhythm which has a strong relationship with bodily rhythm is used first. It stirs and stimulates the kinesthetic sense because the feeling of bodily rhythm goes through kinesthesis. The child, the feeble-minded and the mentally sick person respond to rhythm. Melody which is played next, is a succession of musical tones felt as a psychological entity. Mood-modifying music follows melody. Its purpose is the arousing of emotion and modifying the mood. Harmony is the highest form of musical evolution and has a general integrating influence. Pictorial-associative music stimulates imagery and association of higher intensity.

THE PAST, PRESENT AND FUTURE
OF MUSICAL THERAPY

By IRA M. ALTSHULER, M.D.

Wayne County General Hospital, Eloise, Michigan

Any factor or agent that helps to prevent an illness, alleviates or cures disease or aids physical or mental health can be regarded as a therapy. Indeed, promotion and preservation of life, as practiced by nature itself, is a form of biological therapy. Nature, constantly improving the tools and facilities to maintain and promote life, practices prophylactic treatment, the basic form of therapy.

Minerals, herbs, water, electricity, the power of the spoken word and music are potential therapies. They all possess the common property to arouse or suppress living cells. No medication with the exception of glandular products is capable of imparting new function into the human organism. Most of the remedies act on the basis of either stimulating or suppressing. Music shares in this capacity with the other therapeutic agents.

Radical treatment is the most ideal form of therapy. It is based on the precise knowledge of the disease process, as well as the thorough appreciation of the dynamics of the remedy. Radical therapy is, however, the exception and not the rule. The treatment of diphtheria with anti-toxin is a good example of radical therapy. Most therapies treat symptoms only because the nature of many diseases is still obscure.

If the medical man had waited for the pathologist and pharmacologist to clear the way for radical treatment, he could not have dared to make out a medical prescription until the latter half of the nineteenth century; that is the time of the beginning of scientific pharmacology. Yet medical prescriptions have been written for the past 4000 years.

EMPIRICAL USE

The fact that radical therapy cannot be executed with music should not make us abandon it as a remedy. The utilization of a therapeutic agent cannot and should not be postponed to a time when its exact mode of action, avenues of attack and precise dosage are known. The history of medicine shows that many agents have been used empirically and advantageously as remedies without precise knowledge as to the acting principles involved. An example is the treatment of heart diseases with Digitalis, or fox-glove. A long time ago an elderly lady in Shropshire, England, was in possession of a secret herb recipe for the treatment of dropsy. This recipe had in it among other things Digitalis, which upon subsequent investigation by medical men proved to be one of the best remedies for heart conditions. Thus from a vague appreciation of its therapeutic potence in the past, this drug became one of the best known and can now be given in precise dosages.

WORDS VS. MUSIC

Psychotherapy is the utilization of words, their meanings and the dynamics behind them for the purpose of bringing about the proper attitude toward life. The meanings of words appeal primarily to the cerebral hemispheres, the master brain. There must be no resistance or inhibition on the part of the master brain to initiate action. After they are passed by the master brain, emotional reactions and organ functions follow. If someone calls me names, I become emotional and am perhaps ready to fight. My glands and organs participate in this, but only after the master brain has made the situation clear to the organism.

The powerful verbal form of therapy, so skillfully and successfully developed by the psychiatrists, was long ago used by the poet, philosopher, writer, educator, and preacher. Its "therapeutic" influence before its elevation into a scientific doctrine had made itself felt in education, religion, social and political life, and in propaganda.

Analyzing the powers of music, one should keep in mind that music has always been an important factor in the instinctual, emotional, intellectual, cultural and spiritual life of people, and as such, from time immemorial, exercised a sort of therapeutic influence.

Music, even more than the spoken word, lends itself as a therapy because it meets with little or no intellectual resistance and does not need to appeal to logic to initiate action. It is more subtle and more primitive and therefore its appeal is wider and greater.

Rhythm and Man

Man, a product of nature, cannot remain aloof to music because tone and rhythm, of which music is composed, have a strong affinity for living organisms. The whole animal kingdom is conditioned to sound and rhythm, and such vital processes as propagation and protection depend upon them. In lower forms of life the vibration sense takes on the job of hearing, a sense which, by the way, man still retains. The compulsion to respond to sound is seen in the evolution of various devices to capture them. The fish, for instance, has a primitive ear, a "lateral line" organ which runs the whole length of its body, from head to tail. This registers difference of pressure of water and thus acts as a warning of the proximity of an enemy or of the presence of prey. All fish produce sounds which we can now detect with sensitive electric devices. Some species produce pure and longdrawn sounds which range nearly an octave.

Many species of insects and birds turn some of their body

parts into "musical instruments." Even external objects are utilized by some creatures to produce music. These "instruments" no doubt are intended to attract attention, to arouse emotion, to create a mood and to evoke a response. In a sense it is a form of biological "therapy" which nature practices to safeguard and promote life. Some insects make loud music, so that it can be heard at a considerable distance, as is the case with beetles. The musical sounds produced by various creatures are highly specific, that is, each male animal produces its own tone which is identified by the female. The mother bird uses special signals for her young and the young for the mother bird. Some insects show amazing musical skill. In ancient times certain insects were carried around in cages to supply music for entertainment. The male Katydid—a grasshopper species—and the common cricket are great insect musicians. Singing or making music by the birds is well-known. They improvise all kinds of instruments. They give us the tone colors discernible in the flute, the drum, the trumpet, and the violin.

In the course of evolution, hearing devices continued to evolve, through the sensitive ear of the mammal, which orients sound in space, to the highly perfected ear of modern man, which while it has not the same range of pitch as the dog, can distinguish tones more finely and combine them for his pleasure and entertainment. Man, unlike the lizard, does not live in a world of vibrations from which he must scurry away, but has learned to master sound, and turn it to his own advantage; next to the eye, it is the most valuable of his senses. Sound waves to man are not one's signals of alarm, or gross mating stimuli, but through the intercession of the brain literally convert matter into mind. From vibrations to neural impulses, to sensations, to feelings, to emotions, to aesthetic, spiritual and social appreciations.

The element of rhythm in music enters intimately into the problem of music therapy. Man is essentially a rhythmical being. There is rhythm in respiration, heart beat, speech, gait, etc. The cerebral hemispheres are in a perpetual state of rhythmical swing

—day and night. Even the slightest change in the body, such as opening or closing of the eye-lids causes a change in brain rhythm. These brain waves differ in emotional states, fever, intoxication, infections and such conditions as epilepsy.

The Davises of Harvard some time ago observed "instances in which tones initiated special waves (Beta Rhythm) and also abolished them." Living in a rhythmical universe adds more responsivity to music rhythm. Man-made rhythm is a replica of cosmic and bodily rhythm. Descartes' "I think, therefore I exist" perhaps should read "I rhythm, therefore I exist" . . . .

The study of folk legends, fairy tales and the myth—products of the collective unconscious—indicates that man has always attributed great powers to music. Music, according to those beliefs, was so omnipotent that it could restore the dead to life, cure the sick, and even affect the course of nature itself. It is interesting that the antipode of the primitive man—the philosopher—maintained similar beliefs regarding the powers of music. The ancient Greek philosophers were keenly conscious of the influence of music upon social and political life. Plato thought that no change could be made in music without profoundly affecting the policies of a state. Malice, insolence, and their opposite, could be brought about by music, he believed. Aristotle concurred in this opinion.

The study of Greek culture reveals that they recognized the value of music as mental hygiene. One of the seven muses, Euterpe, was in charge of music prophylaxis and promoting civilization. The therapeutic properties of music were keenly appreciated by the Greeks. Apollo, the God of the Sun, exercised a double function—that of God of Medicine and Music, while his mythical son, Aesculapius, was the patron of medicine.

OBJECTIVE APPROACH

In the eighteenth and nineteenth centuries, and especially with the arrival of the experimental method, a new orientation ensued concerning the influence of music upon the human organism. An attempt was made to an objective approach. Interesting reports appeared in Europe and in our own country in which the effect of music upon metabolism, muscular energy, blood pressure, respiration, and pulse, was described. Cannon, the eminent Harvard physiologist, believes that music arouses emotions and releases adrenalin and perhaps other hormones. Clinical reports dealing with observations made on groups of mental patients also appeared. All these experiments and observations, however interesting and valuable, failed to take into consideration two fundamental factors, namely, the role of the central nervous system in musico-dynamics and the structural elements of music.

Various brain centers, viz. hypothalamus, thalamus, cerebellum, in addition to the cerebral hemisphere, the master brain, take part not only in metamorphosing tone and rhythm into music, but giving it an emotional and mental content. The understanding of the anatomy and physiology of these brain centers is therefore indispensable. The hypothalamus exercises influence upon such physiological processes as metabolism, sleep, rhythm, etc. It is connected by nerve pathways with the thalamus and through it with the other brain centers. One can see thus how music can influence the body, that is via thalamus, hypothalamus.

The thalamus is a subcortical brain center made up of gray matter, lying below the master brain. It is the main relay station of emotions, sensations and feelings. It is believed that even aesthetic feelings are relayed by the thalamus to the master brain. The thalamus is connected with the master brain by nerve pathways, and the stimulation of the thalamus almost simultaneously arouses the master brain. Once the master brain is aroused, it sends impulses back to the thalamus and so a reverberating circuit is set in motion. Now this is an important finding. There are nervous and mental patients who cannot be reached through the spoken word (that is, through the master brain), because these patients are either inattentive, distractible, confused, depressed, hallucinated or in a state of anxiety which makes verbal contact next to impossible. It is precisely here that music makes itself useful. Music, which does not depend upon the master brain to gain its entry into the organism, can still arouse by way of the thalamus— the relay station of all emotions, sensations and feelings. Once having been able to reach the thalamus, the master brain is automatically invaded, and if continued for some time, a closer contact between the master brain and world of reality can be thus established.

CONTACT THROUGH MUSIC

In the management of nervous and mental patients this is important. In order to be able to initiate psychotherapy, the removal of states of inattention, anxiety, tension and morbid moods is essential. That temporary contact with the patient through music can be established is seen from the fact that patients considerably disturbed or confused will respond to music by either tapping of a foot, swaying the body or nodding the head. Such responses are known as thalamic reflexes. When the music tempo is changed one can observe that the tempo of the tap, even in the most confused and disturbed patients, is correspondingly affected. The phenomenon of the thalamic reflex is important in another respect; it can be utilized in objective study of the effect of music upon nervous and mental patients. Clinical experiences indicate that the mood and the mental tempo of psychotic patients can be influenced more readily by music if a special approach is employed. Thus when a patient is depressed, sad music (in minor keys) will capture his mood more readily than gay music. Gay music may in the beginning even irritate him. Hypomaniacal patients, whose emotional tone is raised and who think fast, talk fast and walk fast, can be more easily "captured" by music with a fast tempo.

Only after one has worked himself "musically" into the mood or tempo of the mental patient, a shift to a different mood or tempo can be made; this, of course, by the employment of special music. This maneuver is known as the "iso" principle. "Iso" simply means "equal"; that is, that the mood or the tempo of the music in the beginning must be in "iso" relation with the mood or tempo of the mental patient. The "iso" principle is extended also to volume and rhythm. In a noisy ward, for instance, sometimes, the volume of music is raised to overcome the noise.

In clinical work with ward patients, where one finds all kinds and degrees of psychoses, it is important to have some arrangement whereby as many patients as possible can be reached at one time. The practice at Eloise Hospital is therefore to make a survey of the ward prior to the initiation of group-music therapy. Among other things, in such surveys the number of patients, sex, their mean age, the percentage of different nationalities, the number of violent, depressed and preoccupied is noted. The purpose of the survey is to suit the music to the patients on the ward. Thus, for instance, if there are 15% Poles and 10% Italians, and 70% Americans, music is dispensed accordingly. If there are, for instance, 30% depressed and 70% hyper-active, the music again is proportionately allocated according to the "iso" principle. Where it is convenient, depressed patients can be segregated in one place; similar arrangements can be worked out with nationalities, age groups, etc.

Every possible therapeutic property inherent in music should be utilized. The instrument or tone color possesses a given therapeutic property. Its nature and effect should be further studied. Stringed instruments lend themselves better in dispensing sad music and should be used in the work with depressed patients in the initial musical attack. Brass instruments are not suitable with patients who are sensitive to noise or suffering from anxiety states. Combinations of instruments can also be used. We have found the trio (violin, cello and piano) a good combination in the work with mental patients.

ORDER OF PRESENTATION

In addition to the "iso" maneuver, the strategy of "level" attacks is also practiced at Eloise Hospital in an attempt to arouse attention, to modify the mood, to stimulate imagery and association—steps essential in launching psychotherapy. For some time we have pursued the following order in exposing our patients to music: We begin with music in which there is a predominance of rhythm; this because rhythm as known has a strong appeal to the instinctual and primitive spheres. Rhythm, with its stress, duration and pause, exercises a specific physiological and psychological effect, which differs from that of melody; the latter is apprehended as an entity, and exercises therefore an entirely different effect than rhythm. Melody is followed by harmony which has an integrating effect and is linked with cerebellar influences. The cerebellum, as mentioned, is the center of integration and coordination, receiving impulses from the ear and all peripheral muscles. The "accord" felt in harmony is due to the influence of the cerebellum primarily and to the cortex in the second place. The next music played has a predominance of mood—sad or gay. It is intended to catch the mood of the patients and then shift it into the emotional tone desired. This can be accomplished by playing first sad and then gay music. Pictorial associative music is played next to stimulate imagery and associations. Through such music the calling up of various past experiences is facilitated. Music leaves not only a "memory" in the mind but in the emotional sphere in movements and muscles. It is more easily recalled by the mental patient than anything else for it is more firmly implanted in his system. Calling up of past experiences means bringing back into the mind of the mental patients basic realities. These bits of realities act as pontoons, bridging the patient's mind with the outer world. It thus exercises a special therapeutic effect, even if the effect is short-lived. The temporary effect can be overcome by repeating such music every day. At Eloise Hospital we have daily sessions on some wards in which the sequence, Rhythm, Melody, Harmony, Mood, Pictorial-association music is included in the musical prescription.

Prior to the administration of the above recipe, a theme song is played. The purpose of this theme song is to lure and induce the patients to join the group which meets in the ward.

Composers, who wrought music, naturally did not know that their compositions might be used for therapeutic purposes. There are no musical designs therefore which are purely rhythm, melody or pictorial-associative, but there are compositions which have a predominance of one or the other element. Thus, for instance, the march is rhythmically dominant, while the intermezzo is melodically dominant. At Eloise we have catalogued musical designs according to the principal predominance of a structural element. The use of level attacks is not only intended to affect various psychoses, but the same patients on their various mental levels.

Music is pleasurable because it is one of the few arts which helps to relieve instinctual and emotional tensions. This capacity of music can be traced in the lower animals. On this level of life, sounds produced in the mating season are of a more "socializing" nature—luring, inducing, suggesting, instead of forcing. Both the male and female, as mentioned, have an opportunity to relieve their emotional tension through making rhythm and sounds. In a sense the creature finds considerable self-reassurance in the process of making musical overtures. Biologically, the singing of the bird is the first step in the mating process and thus is self-encouraging. In human beings this process, although more disguised, nevertheless pursues the same intent. Singing of a love song by a young man, even if not in the presence of his loved one, offers some emotional relief. The love-prone individual first must be reassured inwardly that there is a love object and singing or making or listening to music strengthens this hope.

The ego, while singing or making music, expands and through

listening and singing identifies itself with the outer world, reality, with the aesthetical. The attacking soldier by shouting "Hurrah" expands his ego, makes himself feel a part of his group, and, thus relieves his fear.

Music has always been a great factor in helping to sublimate the sensual, the aggressive and the destructive. Sublimation is easier with the help of music because listening to music offers more opportunity than any other art for muscular action and motion—processes not far removed from natural patterns of instinctual relief. There is no social restriction imposed and no feeling of guilt in jitter-bugging or boogie-woogie, the nature and manifestations of which are unmistakably sensual. Even when listening to a symphony, the libido has ample room for expression and relief; this without the person being aware of it. Shakespeare's "If music be the food of love, play on, give me excess of it" . . . . gains additional meaning.

The Narcissistic urge (loving one's own body) finds ample relief through music, especially through its rhythm. Music rhythm, which stimulates body rhythm, gives human beings the opportunity to feel themselves not only more integrated and organized but capable of easy and graceful expression.

Music has the added capacity to reconcile the most contrasted and foreign feelings. It can arouse and calm at the same time. Bringing us nearer to the spiritual it does not, however, separate us from the instinctual.

Music in addition to the physiological and psychological properties possesses properties which no other agents or media have. It has in it the aesthetic and the spiritual and through the performer, the artistic. Music as a pure art has always exercised beneficial influence upon normal people. This influence is not lessened in nervous and mental patients. Bringing to the patient good music means added therapeutic power. We insist, therefore, whenever it is possible, that the music be administered by skilled and talented musicians. The purity of music is even more essential than the purity of drugs and chemicals.

In the future the musician is destined to play a very important role in the care and treatment of nervous and mental diseases, as well as in mental hygiene. The musical therapist will have to be trained in psychology and related subjects so he can be closer integrated into this work. Michigan State College has already made steps in this direction. It offers courses in musical therapy and a three months' internship at Eloise Hospital upon graduation.

The musician of the future will be able to understand and fill musical prescriptions written by the psychiatrist. He will combine the role of chemist and pharmacist. He will adhere to his traditional role of artistic performance by bringing to the patient the therapeutic properties of music clothed in art.

HOW MUSIC PRODUCES ITS EFFECTS
ON THE BRAIN AND MIND

By LAWRENCE WALTERS

Music Therapist, New York, N. Y.

Music very definitely produces measurable effects on the brain and mind. It is quite logical to maintain that when measurable results are produced on the brain, the mind is also in some way influenced. Toward the close of the last century, in 1896, to be exact, Dr. M. L. Patrici, an Italian physiologist, conducted a series of experiments to determine the influence of different kinds of music on the circulation of the blood in the brain. A thirteen year old boy named Emanuel Favre, a native of Savoy, while acting as an assistant to his employer, a woodcutter, was severely wounded in the head by a glancing blow of his ax. Through careful treatment in the hospital he was restored to health, although the wound was more than three inches in length, cleaving the bone of the skull for the entire distance. When the wound was healed the bones did not fully cover over the brain, but left a small section exposed. It was possible to measure accurately changes in the blood circulation in the brain. The boy was bright and fully willing to undergo these experiments. Dr. Patrici set out to ascertain first, if the circulation of the brain in general is influenced by music, and second, if the circulation in the brain is more or less influenced than that of other parts of the body.

An apparatus was devised which consisted of a closed cylinder of glass for holding the arm in water and a registering apparatus connected with the needle of a galvanometer. For registering the pulse in the brain a cap of gutta-percha was made, with an electrical connection capable of showing the slightest modification in blood volume as well as in pulsation.

It had already been claimed by former observers that any excitement of the brain by musical sounds increases the flow of blood in other parts of the body. Accordingly two tracings were made simultaneously, the one of the pulsation of the blood in the brain and the other of the pulse in the arm.

During the course of these experiments three phenomena were observed:

1. The volume of the pulse in the arm was elevated in the same proportion as that of the brain.
2. At times it was found that the circulation of the blood in the brain was increased while that of the arm was slowed down.
3. There were instances in which the amount of blood in the arm was not in the least influenced while the circulation of blood in the brain was increased.

Lively music was found to cause an increase of blood in the brain as well as a livelier pulse. The *Marseillaise* was used with very definite effects. This reaction indicated a purely physiological explanation as to how, for instance, the stirring music of the national anthem will arouse love of country and other strong emotions.

The increase of blood in the brain together with the speed of circulation also explains why more work can be accomplished when lively music is being played. We have here the basis of using music to arouse one from a depressive mood.

We have also here the explanation of why agitated individuals can sometimes be soothed by soft, slow music. Dr. Patrici demonstrated that such music has the effect of slowing the blood circulation in the brain and decreasing its volume. Some degree of cerebral anemia is therefore necessary to control over-active and over-emotional people. Just as lovely music stimulates the brain to greater mental activity, slow music is necessary to rest the brain after too much activity.

Dr. J. P. Shepard in 1906 had a similar opportunity to study the effects of music on the circulation of blood in the brain. He confirmed the findings of Dr. Patrici. It is thus established that moods have biological foundations. They depend to a great extent on the activity of the brain and blood. Depression and exaltation are actuated by speed or sluggishness of the blood in the brain and blood vessels as well as by nervous tension. The "blues" for example, are accompanied by sluggishness of heart and circulation.

Within recent years it has been ascertained that the brain functions in rhythm. In 1923 Professor Hans Berger of Jena, Germany, was the first to demonstrate in his physiological laboratory the presence of rhythm in the human brain. He made a great many tracings on strips of film and found that these brain waves were constant in frequency and that they were influenced by various physical and mental states.

It has been found that musical rhythm has a profound effect on brain rhythm and thus on brain function. However, this is but one of several theories. One of the most recent is that of Dr. Ira M. Altshuler, the psychiatrist who has been using musical therapy in the treatment of the mentally deranged for quite a few years now.

It is Dr. Altshuler's belief that the therapeutic principle of music rests upon the close affinity between the human organism, and rhythm as well as upon the symbolism inherent in musical sounds. The chief significance of music as a means of healing lies in the mechanics of the human brain and the way musical sounds reach and affect it. Music, according to Dr. Altshuler, is first perceived by that part of the brain known as the thalamus. The thalamus is one of the older portions of the brain and it is the seat of all sensations, emotions and esthetic feeling. This is one of the reasons that music is so important as a therapeutic agent.

Stimulating the thalamus automatically incites the cortex of the brain, the seat of higher elements which are involved in thinking and reasoning. Thus, through the help of music physicians are able to reach the innermost mental life of the mentally deranged person. Music in addition to its capacity to replace various morbid states such as delusions, hallucinations, depressions and fears, definitely commands attention. Once attention has been gained the patient usually can be taken out of his morbid mental state.

Dr. Sigmund Freud divided the human personality into three different parts: the *Id,* the *Ego* and the *Superego.* The Id is the most primitive stratum of the personality; it is fed by instincts and is identified with the unconscious. It has no direct contact with reality and thus has no awareness of the outer world and people. Its drives are directed toward the pursuit of pleasure and the avoidance of pain. Time and space do not exist in the Id.

The second level in the personality is the Ego, the rational part of man's self. It is in the Ego that man's thoughts exist. The grown-up individual is always aware of his Ego. The Ego sees and compares; it makes judgments and reasons. The Ego is aware of the existence of other human beings and it checks ideas and concepts against reality. It uses the spoken word to clarify and appreciate self and the world.

The third stratum of the personality is the Superego. The Superego is our conscience. It not only separates good from evil, and right from wrong, but dictates to the Ego what to do and what not to do. The Superego constantly supervises the Ego; here feelings of guilt take their origin. If the Ego does not want to conform with the code of morality, ethical standards and tradition, the Superego retaliates. A good example of the Id is the animal; of the Ego without the Superego is the savage and infant. The three must be in complete harmony in the same person.

How are these three strata of the personality related to music? The Id, otherwise oblivious to the world, heeds music. The Ego, which is threatened by reality does not remain immune totally for in the realm of music there are no sharp conflicts, and thus music is acceptable to the Ego. The Superego, too, is accessible as far as music is concerned because, unlike the sphere of thought and speech, music creates no feelings of guilt.

The Id and Superego admit music freely but are affected by it in their own special way. While the Id, which is identified with the instincts, is affected by music on the biological level, the Superego is affected on a higher social and cultural level. The effect is similar, just as in the case of human beings—some are affected by jazz while others by great symphonies. The Superego is not aware of the sensuality in music to the same degree and extent as it is aware through the spoken word. Thus music can still serve erotic needs to the civilized person without arousing a feeling of moral guilt.

Music can serve even further—offering physical relief by making the whole musculature rhythm react to sensual music. Sensuality, conveyed through music, arouses no opposition and no resistance, even in the most moral person because it infiltrates man through the emotional sphere in which there is no delineation, no contrast regarding good, bad, hostile or friendly; it causes no feeling of guilt. Thus music has access to the Id, Ego and Superego even if these are not integrated and are not working in accord as in cases of severe mental illness. Indeed, music tends to reconcile all these. This fact is most important in understanding the general principle of music therapy.

Thus, music can work upon the mentally disturbed mind and upon its various dynamic spheres (Id, Ego and Superego) as if the mind had not lost its emotional stability and mental functions. Music tends to reintegrate, to bring together these various spheres which have gone astray.

These are the theories of Dr. Altshuler, one of the most careful of the modern students of musical therapy. In addition, he has also thoroughly analyzed musical design and has found it to consist of various components which variously affect the listener. He has found that different instruments have different effect on the listener, a violin and flute having the greatest appeal. He also found that a trio of stringed instruments is more effective than a single instrument when used in hospitals for treating the mentally ill.

Dr. Altshuler has also found that such elements of music as tone, rhythm, and tempo, contrasts in shading (fast-slow; high-low; loud-soft) and volume and intensity, each plays a role in influencing the listener. In addition to music's capacity to attract attention, it is also capable of modifying the mood, stimulating the imagination and intellect. Physiologically, the response of the nervous system to long-short music is quieting, to short-long, stimulating. Loud sounds are stimulating because they are associated with danger. Soft tones are quieting because they are associated with the gentle tones of nature.

Together with Dr. Bessey H. Shebesta, Dr. Altshuler conducted a series of experiments with music on mentally deranged patients at the state hospital at Eloise, Michigan, and succeeded in producing a quieting effect. They found that soft music was 35 per cent more effective than the wet pack sheet which is used routinely in quieting disturbed patients.

Music therapy was begun at Eloise in 1938. At the present time several thousand patients have been treated with music. They receive music in their wards for half-hour periods five times a week. For each ward there is specially selected music; for the violent patients soothing music is played. For the depressed and lethargic patients, lively, stimulating music is prescribed. Music was furnished by 24 musicians paid from the funds of the Federal Music Project. These musicians worked in units of three, usually violin, 'cello and piano.

When music is played it has been observed that these patients as well as normally healthy men and women react to it by tapping their feet, drumming their fingers or swaying their bodies, in time with the music. This is a definite indication that music is breakng through the barrier of mental blocking.

Dr. Altshuler enumerates the following chief attributes of music for mental and emotional difficulties:

1. Capacity to produce changes in metabolism, respiration, blood pressure, pulse and endocrine and muscular energy.
2. Ability to command attention and increase its span.
3. Power of diversion and substitution (as distracting from morbid states and replacing with wholesome feelings and ideas).
4. Capacity to modify moods.
5. Capacity to stimulate pictorially and intellectually.

THE RELATION OF MUSIC TO DISEASES OF THE BRAIN[1]

By HANS H. REESE, M.D.

Professor of Neuropsychiatry, University Hospitals
Madison, Wisconsin

At the Wisconsin Psychiatric Institute in 1943 on "Music as Therapy," the experiences cited led to the belief that the thalamus was the seat of sensations and emotions, and that by musical rhythms we could stimulate unconscious automatic responses.[2] That is, a person might tap his fingers or sway in time to the music at the thalamic level and appreciate music consciously at the cortical level. The withdrawn, depressed, or even the elated person may be retarded on a cortical level of response, but may be aroused with appropriate musical stimulation at the thalamic level and thereby, let us say, we may reach him through the "back door" at the unconscious level.

During our investigations pulse rate, blood pressure, and respirations were studied and we are ready to postulate that the pulse rate becomes accelerated in most patients under musical stimulation. In a catatonic schizophrenic girl with a pulse rate of 80 the pulse increased to 96 when she heard a waltz; it increased to 100, at times to 162, when she heard a waltz tango. It is believed that these fluctuations in pulse rate are caused by emotional stim-

---

[1] Presented at "Music in Therapy" Institute, University of Wisconsin, August 1947. Condensed for publication.

[2] Experiments conducted by Lucille Schreiber, OTR.

uli acting through the autonomic nervous system and/or by means of normal controls.

Music is closely allied to language functions, therefore defects in the musical functions appear almost invariably with incapacities in other psychomotor functions, of which the foremost is speech. The study of the pathology of language and of musical functions in cases of detectable brain disease supports the theories that had been postulated regarding anatomical areas of the brain. Cerebral lesions, such as hemorrhages, infections, tumors, or degeneration may influence our motor, sensory and special senses in widely differing ways, and in the latter in conjunction with cerebral hemispheric speech disorders also affect the musical capacities. Dysphasia or aphasia are the terms commonly applied to all language disorders, whether motor or sensory; they are not used to denote disturbances caused by faulty innervation of the musculature necessary for speech. The peripheral disturbances are called dysarthrias and interfere with vocal expressions. If the peripheral speech mechanism is impaired, we differentiate lip, tongue, pharyngeal, and laryngeal phases which are the result of special cranial nerve paralyses and only occasionally result from a brain lesion in the major hemisphere. In a right handed person we call the left brain the major hemisphere and the right brain the minor hemisphere. The expressive speech faculty is localized in the motor speech area of the brain and the ability to sing, to perform, and to write music is localized in similar and nearby areas; there are also perceptive areas in which music seen or heard is interpreted. We associate words, sounds, and musical symbols with pleasant or disagreeable emotional memories. Not uncommonly there is a definite overlapping of the motor and sensory dysfunctions even in localized small lesions of the brain. It is obvious that diffuse brain lesions cannot be utilized for a study of speech and music disturbances. Before an investigation is begun a study of the pre-morbid personality, that is, the total personality reaction pattern of any case under investigation, must be evaluated. It is of the utmost importance to separate factual clinical observations from speculations. Do we recognize personalities with inborn prominent musical talents who possess extreme or unusual acoustic sensory-receptive and acoustic motor creative sensitivity? The musico-esthetic literature is vague in postulating special musico-psychological traits in the composer, in the reproductive musician or in the appreciative listener. Is meter a cortical function and is rhythm a subcortical one? Is executive instrumental skill determined by any demonstrable inborn tendencies or natural musical abilities? These are questions which are difficult to answer because no uniformity of opinion is at hand. If we have a lesion in the upper temporal brain lobe on each side (Wernicke's area) it produces sound deafness, a loss of power to recognize spoken verbal symbols; but if such lesions extend anteriorly into the tips of the temporal lobes, they cause sensory amusia in addition. In other cases with a destroyed left lower frontal brain lobe lesion (Broca's area), motor expressive language difficulties, especially in the ability to name objects, is seen. If such a localized lesion extends anteriorly, expression of musical tones is abolished—motor amusia (aphaemia). At times the minor hemisphere takes over the function of the destroyed major area on the left side as a compensation phenomenon; this fact explains the interesting observation that an otherwise motor aphasic person can, upon being properly irritated, produce words which cannot be expressed or uttered without stimulation. The fact that the right brain can compensate for the destruction in the left hemisphere explains the finding that aphasic patients may swear and sing upon adequately strong emotional stimulation, indicating that the emotional language is not always inhibited by left sided major lobe lesions. Music is perceived mainly by the auditory route but also by the visual pathways, i.e., reading notes or scores. It is expressed as we all know, by vocal articulations, by tactile reproductions, or by total compositions. As I have stated, there are many points of correlation between speech and music. Today we assume that music is a much more primitive function than speech, and that the ability to perceive music is much less well developed in humans than is the ability to perceive words. The literature on the subject is complicated since many have reported an isolated case without elaborating on the premorbid personality of the patient, and most of the musical studies were not conducted by critical observers. We assume that there may be an optical and an acoustic center for note reading and for tone hearing; and that there are two motor centers, one for singing and the other for instrumental playing. There is some evidence that these centers are independent anatomically from the much better known speech centers. Henschen analyzed 200 cases with post-mortem studies in 100 and found that among 120 motor dysphasics two-thirds could not speak, but 84 could sing; that among 56 cases showing word deafness, 45 also suffered from tone deafness; and that among 12 patients having word blindness, four could read and interpret notes. Why and how patients react differently to musical stimuli and why some cannot differentiate the tone scale, the meter, or have no rhythmical sense has been explained by some through the use of the acoustic tonal theory of Helmholtz, and by others on the basis of faulty affective symbolization. We question whether music utilizes symbols in the same sense that speech utilizes them. Epileptic aura with acoustic hallucinations or with humming and singing impulses have been accepted as evidences of organic temporal lobe irritations; however, in the case of the acoustic-motor epileptics in whom a sudden unexpected sound startles the patient and produces an epileptic seizure, other strong auditory irritations or sensory precipitations will not illicit epileptic phenomena. We do not know the nature of the irritation or what unpleasant quality in the sound excites in some epileptics profound cortical discharges with obvious convulsive seizures. We do know, however, that brain wave studies localize irritation in the cerebral cortex and that the brain wave rhythm can be influenced by drugs, stimulation, or injuries. Musicogenic epilepsy is a term indicating that the association between musical stimuli and an epileptic attack is close, and that epileptic seizures are precipitated only by specifically irritating music. An attack does not usually follow the onset of music at once, but the music creates an uneasiness and the nervous system irritation ushers in physical signs which culminate in convulsions of various magnitudes, from mild transient blackouts of consciousness to major epileptic seizures. Cases of musicogenic epilepsy are very rare. Only twenty cases have been reported in the world literature. Reviewing the specific character of epileptogenic stimuli indicated that in some cases classical music was involved and in others "old time" or "reminiscent" melodies were more powerful. A well punctuated rhythm is the most dangerous quality in music for epileptics. Instrumental music is much more potent than is vocal music; slow music is more endurable than are lively melodies. Dance and march music have been shown to be alarming and unbearable in some of these cases. The age at which the epileptic phenomena first make their appearance in cases of musicogenic epilepsy is later than is found in patients with idiopathic epilepsy. Usually the onset is after the age of 35. Since no cases have been reported previously in the American medical literature, I wish to present two cases.

A 42 year old housewife was referred to the Wisconsin General Hospital April 22, 1942. The patient had been ill since the age of 29 at which time a thyroidectomy was performed. She complained of fatigue, of pain in the legs and arms, of frequent fronto-temporal headaches with vertigo, and a sing-song sensation in the head. She became irritable and depressed. Her past medical history was unimportant. At the age of 31 she noticed for the first time, uncontrollable emotionalism upon hearing funeral music. At the age of 33 she became aware of uneasiness and crying spells upon hearing choral or sentimental pieces and these emotional attacks were preceded by a queer humming sensation, by a sing-song sound and at times by a repetitious word formation in her mind. She could not sing or carry a tune, and therefore did not enjoy school or church music. Because she could not keep time to music, she disliked dancing.

[47]

The patient was left-handed and without hearing, reading, writing, or speech dysfunctions. She was sluggish and had suggestive old age features in posture and in facial expressions but was well informed, oriented, and comprehended quickly and retained well. The pre-morbid personality investigation was negative. Her childhood and married life had been happy. There was no familial history of epilepsy or migraine. Her speech was rather toneless, quavering, and monotonous. The physical examination was essentially negative except for a dry, thin skin, sparse hair development and moderate hypertension.

X-rays of the skull revealed a single bone rarefaction in the right parietal region (a benign bone cyst). All laboratory findings were normal except for a low basal metabolic rate (—11 to —25). The encephalogram showed the subarachnoidal spaces and the channels over both hemispheres to be definitely dilated indicating generalized cortical atrophy with an associated dilatation of the ventricular structures.

The Rorschach inventory revealed a personality within normal limits, with a well-developed inner life, poise, and with excellent emotional contact with the environment.

The patient was submitted to many musical and vocal stimuli and it was found that the melodious tunes of Stephen Foster would immediately create forward and backward swaying. Then the patient would stare into space—her eyes quivering. She would slump backwards into a chair or against the wall, and would not respond to commands. Her pupils became dilated and did not react to light. At this phase a tremor of the left hand would begin with irregular to and fro movements of the fingers followed by a rhythmical jactation of the left fingers and hand and abductive movements of the arm and mild jerking of the left shoulder. These Jacksonian-pattern attacks would last from one to four minutes and were followed by amnesia. Frequent repetitions of seizures did not increase the amplitude of movements and never precipitated a generalized convulsion. The seizures described were induced by music on different days with equal success, but finally the experiments created apprehension and crying spells.

Readmitted for further study six months after discharge: she had improved in strength and was more assertive. The Rorschach, however, revealed a marked change showing a complete loss of the formerly good adjustment to emotional responses. In their place was considerable anxiety, apprehension and perhaps what might be described as "touchiness." The responses indicating a satisfactory inner life as recorded previously had been lost and the general shrinkage of mental horizons concomitant with some type of organic cerebral condition had become evident.

A sodium amytal analysis revealed no deviation from the given history and no further information as to instability or psychic trauma could be elicited. While she was under drug narcosis, the playing of "Jeannie With the Light Brown Hair" precipitated the same reactions as observed in the wakeful state. Postural gravity studies demonstrated a definite to and fro movement in the vertical position (fig. 1) and a marked shift of the center of gravity of the feet (fig. 2) when stimulated by the music.

The College of Music submitted this patient to the Seashore tests and studied specific musical and memory functions as well as expressive faculties with the conclusion: Amusicality.

Professor A. W. West of the Speech Department studied this patient with us on several occasions. Reading poems of a sentimental nature by Matthew Arnold, Thomas Hood, or Oscar Wilde with great emotional feeling and vocality produced no changes. Submitting her to a series of pure tones from the beat-frequency of an Audio-Oscillator covering the entire audible scale sometimes arranged in rhythmic melodic patterns and at other times merely as sliding tones similar to sirens brought forth the remark from the patient, "It is something like what brings it on," but only when rhythmic patterns were played in the low frequencies did the patient express uneasiness, and even then she had no seizures. Experiments involving the human female voice, low, medium and high humming with no pitch variation or with a pronounced vibrato and great changes in the pitch level had no effect.

One had to consider the cultural background, life interests, and experiences of our patient. The pre-menopausal period suggested no psychoneurotic tendencies but there were physical setbacks in the way of illnesses. After her menopause her reactions had been those of anxiety and tension. Like a stutterer in whom the situation in which the stuttering appears grows constantly broader, we had here anxieties which by musical stimulation expressed themselves in psychosomatic manifestations.

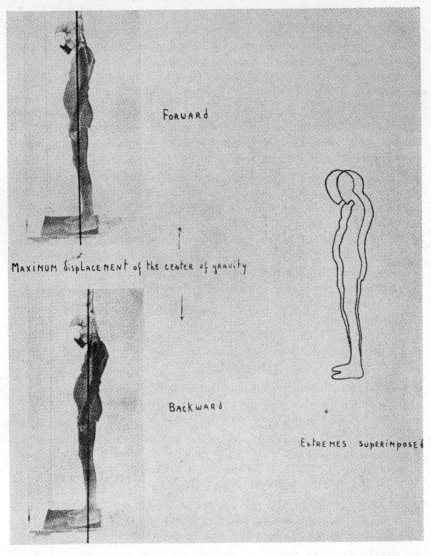

Fig. 1

Our patient had been amusic in the broad sense of the word. She could not sing at home, in school, or in church so she became indifferent to music. She could not get any pleasurable sensation from a melodious rhythm. The normally inherent faculty of emotional response to melodic acoustic association was absent and, therefore, any basic rhythm or tempo such as the music of Lohengrin's Bridal March or the lively Tarantella or the nerve-racking boogie-woogie would not raise her pulse beat, until she developed at the time of her menopause definite reactive changes in the thalamus-cortex relationship. Did the cortical atrophies with the alteration in the basal ganglia create greater psychic lability with pronounced emotional excitability? and did the overflow of thalamic responses cause local irritation in her right major cortex with seizures of the Jacksonian type?

From the constant pattern of the epileptic seizures with involvement of the left hand, one must suspect an epileptogenic focus no doubt in the cortex of the right temporal lobe. The electro-encephalographic record also evidenced more abnormal activity from the right temporal region. Several patients in whom epileptic seizures began with an aura of music have been found to have neoplasms in the temporal region (Penfield and Erickson, 1941). Penfield has also produced hallucinations of music by stimulation of the superior temporal gyrus in one patient. Although it is apparent that these latter seizures characterized by an aura of music are not the same as in this case of musicogenic epilepsy, it is possible that music acts as a precipitating factor by an effect upon some specific locus in the auditory area of the temporal lobe which is primarily concerned with music. The very fact that the pattern of the attacks in our patient was so constant suggests that the music produced a spread from the epileptogenic focus in the cortex rather than at some other level of the nervous system. If this concept is correct, musicogenic epilepsy should be regarded as a highly integrated form of reflex epilepsy due to sensory irritation rather than as an example of psychic precipitation of the seizures alone.

The second case is a white woman 57 years of age who was admitted to the Wisconsin General Hospital on March 18, 1946 with the complaint of "spells." The objective history revealed that she had been well until four years before admission. At that time she had had a sudden onset of unconsciousness accompanied by clenched fists and jaws, rolling of the eyes, and generalized shaking of her body of a few minutes duration. The attacks recurred slightly more often at night than during the day.

The seizures that were seen by the family were almost all pre-

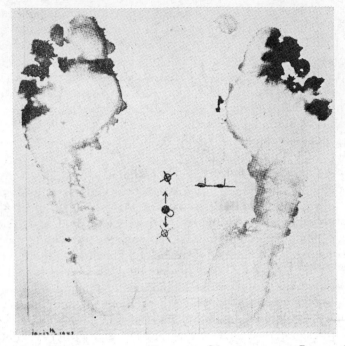

Fig. 2. Vertical Projection of the Center of Gravity into the Base of Support ⊕ = Maximum displacement of the C. of gravity forward. ● = Average position of the C. of gravity during the total period of observation. This comes close to the geometric center of the base, disregarding the toes which do not always contribute actively to the A-P diameter of support. ⊕ = Maximum displacement of the C. of gravity backward. ○ = Morton's center disregarding toes.

cipitated by music of some sort. One attack occurred at church while the minister sang; at times she had complained of a crawling sensation in the hands the day of an attack. She had also periods of "blankness" during which she would suddenly stare unseeingly for 15-45 seconds and just as suddenly arouse from the "spell." The patient had begun to fear music. The patient stated that she had *never* had an attack during the day without musical stimulation. She had always enjoyed music previously although she could never carry a tune. Anything that tired her out or upset her emotionally made her more susceptible to an attack. In the past the patient had had severe one-sided headaches which disappeared at the menopause. The patient had ten children, living and well. No family history of epileptic seizures was elicited.

[52]

Physical examination was essentially negative except for cardiac enlargement and blood pressure of 150/100. Laboratory findings were normal. A pneumoencephalogram was normal. The electroencephalogram revealed slower than normal waves prior to exposure to music. Three minutes of "Irish Lilt" had no observable effect. After about 2½ minutes of "It Might as Well Be Spring" the patient had a grand mal attack with development of slow waves in all leads followed by spikes in all leads, then slow stupor waves in all leads. A Wechsler-Bellevue test showed an I.Q. of 79.

This is a patient in whom a cortical sensitivity to music has been established, resulting in epileptic seizures, and the electroencephalographic correlation leaves no doubt that this is a true case of musicogenic epilepsy.

The two cases reported permit the study of musical functions, since in them, these functions are not subordinated to any speech disturbances. Words produced normal response. In both patients certain specific music stimulations produced the same reaction pattern. In each instance the individual's capacity for appreciating music seems to have been defective and the development of such capacities as existed was faulty. Then illness came into the picture and created hypersensitivity to music which expressed itself in seizures.

I consider musicality a complex term in which inborn tendencies or talent is a prerequisite. But this core must be linked up by training with other cerebral centers and emotional reactions.

Therefore, in our efforts to utilize music as a therapy we must observe the effects of music upon the patients' emotional responses and study patients at programmed musical activities carefully and select equally sick groups for therapeutic music sessions afterward to obtain resocializing effects by emotional outlets.

Diminished capacity to memorize music, defects in the ability to comprehend melodic figures, and mutism are common among psychiatric patients. The power to sing with words is more often impaired than is the power to hum a melody or to whistle a tune.

The functional capacity and the location of musical aptitudes are obscure but they are most probably located in the left major hemisphere in right handed persons. However, in conclusion, I want to emphasize the fact that cerebral functions, whether they be cortical or subcortical, are not isolated but are interconnected.

THE ORGANISM-AS-A-WHOLE AND
MUSIC THERAPY

By IRA M. ALTSHULER, M.D.

Wayne County General Hospital, Eloise, Michigan

William White's "organism-as-a-whole" concept is helpful in understanding the therapeutic properties of the fine arts. It conceives a human being as a compact entity, sealed by nature, time and habit—even if composed of many opposing tendencies. "Organism-as-a-whole" does not reject the idea of "mind and body," but relates them as inseparable and having a common purpose. The viewpoint organism-as-a-whole is particularly enlightening in dealing with nervous and mental patients.

Although the arts have never been seriously mobilized for therapeutic attacks as have herbs, chemicals, electricity and numerous other agents, yet they made themselves keenly felt in the field of mental hygiene and as useful social vitamins.

The arts, more than other agents, arouse the organism-as-a-whole, not only because of their aesthetic appeal, but because they accent human experience. As Dewey says: "In art as an experience, actuality and possibility, or ideality, the *new*, the *old*, objective material and personal response, the individual and universal, surface and depth, sense and meaning, are integrated in an experience in which they are transfigured from the significance that belongs to them when isolated in reflection." Art penetrates man's senses and arouses emotions, feelings, the glands and intellect. It affects his entire past, his rites, ceremonies, his religion, his morale and his conduct. The Greeks understood that art reflects the emotions and ideas associated with the chief institutions of social life. Plato's demand for censorship of poetry, music and drama shows how strongly they believed in the influence of the arts upon man.

Always in the vanguard of science, the arts foreshadow human progress, even in technical endeavor. A substantial number of discoveries and inventions were vaguely conceived in the fertile minds of poets and writers long before the blueprints were drawn. The idea of submarine and transatlantic aeroplane slumbered in the imagination of Jules Verne and in the story of the "Magic Carpet." Science, which proceeds more slowly and cautiously needs the inspiration and prophetic spark of the arts.

Long before Sigmund Freud untangled some of the mysteries of the mind and conceived the conscious and sub-conscious, Goethe, Nietzsche and Hartmann with rare insight grasped its workings. Dr. Faust, the conscious, and Mephistopheles, the sub-conscious mind, portray the eternal struggle between the two. The influence of the arts upon man's life and emotions is no less effective than that contributed by the academic deliberations of Freud. By gratifying man's unconscious need for affection, for aggression and narcissism, they are, in their own way serving a "therapeutic" purpose. Moreno's dictum:—"A true therapeutic procedure cannot have less an objective than the whole of mankind," becomes more concrete if one thinks of the effects of the arts.

The arts not only please and enlighten but they assist in relieving emotional tension. In "Brothers Karamazov," Dostoyevski through Mitja not only relives his own patricidal impulses, but helps vicariously to alleviate similar impulses in the readers in whose bosoms such impulses may lie dormant. The introvert, Don Quixote, and the extrovert hypomanic, Sancho Panza, foretold Kretshmer's constitutional types.

Music, even more than prose or drama, presents an opportunity for stifled emotions to find vent, by means of voluminous body rhythm and motion. Listening to Rimsky-Korsakov's "Ivan The Terrible," for instance, is bound to have some effect in relieving sadistic impulses, even if the listener may not be aware of the plot. And one can mourn the death of a dear friend with less grief listening to "Asa's Death." Mood music has the capacity to objectify personal sorrow; to shift it into "world sorrow" which is, of course, easier to bear. The music of Richard Wagner, who had himself been disappointed in love, provides an example of this. The groping, morbid, unsatisfied phrases, building towards tremendous climaxes which never arrive, represent extreme frustration, thus providing an outlet for those in similar situations. Also, happiness and gayety can be accented by mood music.

The selective action of the arts is the organism-as-a-whole and not that of a special tissue or organ as is the case with medicaments, viz. digitalis or pituitary extract, which affect the heart and water diuresis respectively. In whatever motive power the arts may reside—a product of the unconscious, a suppressed sexuality, or an attempt to counteract the fear of nature's mysterious forces— they inspire, socialize and educate.

The arts have always served as a medium for bringing people together and uniting them. And of them all, there is no equal to music as a cementing force, a force which at once creates unity and intimacy, even in the most heterogeneous congregate. Racial and lingual barriers, differences in creed or education are easily surmounted by the musical message. One cannot hate the one with whom one is singing, provided the voices are modulated to blend. John Dewey's observation that "Art breaks through barriers that divide human beings and which are impermeable to ordinary association" is very applicable to music.

A given composition not only helps to sublimate the instincts of the composer, but serves a like purpose to the performer and to the listener. Each may be affected by the same composition in his own way and each may be benefited to a greater or lesser degree. A talented performer will deliver the original message of the composer, preserving its emotional content and meaning so that the listener will get the full impact of it.

Beethoven's statement, "Music is the mediator between the spiritual and sensual life" finds strong substantiation in clinical observation. The socialization of the sexual instinct is effected by means of music. Lower species of animals use brute force to do the work of procreation. There are female insects which devour the partner in the process of love-making. Others force coitus by superior strength. Pursuit and capture are gradually replaced by sexual advertisement, through rhythmic movements (the dance), sounds and colors. The evolution from killing during coitus, forcing coitus by superior strength, to luring and inducing it through rhythm and sound represents quite a progress. Thus the enlarged limbs with which a certain species of crustacea seizes and holds the female, evolve into the chirping of the cricket, croak of the frog, the charming song of the nightingale, and finally, the crooning of a Sinatra. There is a deep meaning and strong social impact in music which no doubt emphasizes its therapeutic significance.

Sound is the principal medium by which most of the higher animals express and excite emotion. The male bird courting the female, reassures himself of his ability to procreate and thus further charges his sexual resources and generates pleasure. In many instances, the mating season alone, even in the absence of the female, offers this biological reassurance when sounds are produced. Singing in courtship makes the goal appear nearer.

The same mechanism is operative in man and is highly significant. He, too, can socialize his sexual impulses through the dance, vocal chords or self-made instruments, thus providing emotional relief for himself and safeguarding the community from aggression.

Music, the greatest outlet for man's emotions, offers ample opportunity for the sexual instincts to exercise comparative freedom of action. The animal instincts, firmly saddled by social, moral and religious imperatives, find their way out into the open, peripherally, through rhythmical movements and emotional display. Music and the primitive form of it, the dance, are nearest to the natural means of sexual gratification.

The behavior of human beings aroused by "swing" for instance, is suggestive of coitus. There is close contact, the embrace, the back and forth, the "swing" and final exaltation. So near and yet so far, that's the way of music's action. It furnishes atmosphere and excuse. The value of music to man is that it offers a "modus vivandi" to the two most bitter and irreconcilable antagonists, the brain and the spinal cord. This is the chief reason why music is welcomed and is readily accepted by the church, school and home.

Music signifies the principles of liberation in the practice of institutional psychiatry. Mental patients are in fear of and subject to restrictive treatments, often still necessary in overcrowded, understaffed institutions. The manner in which the patients are brought to the institution differs fundamentally from the customary procedures of admitting patients to other hospitals. A process of legal ostracism precedes commitment. The therapy that is offered to the mental patients still has the bad odor of the 17th, 18th and 19th century punishment and restraint. There are mechanical restraints, chemical restraints and hydriatic restraints. There is disguised punishment in the electric shock procedure. All these in addition to the over-powering force of the general mental hospital regime with its barred windows and locked doors; with its formalism and often unsympathetic attendants; with the monotony of institutional procedure where menus, the daily routine and practically all activities are regimented. The whole atmosphere tends to suppress rather than to free and expand. Traditions and the weight of organization, as well as public prejudice, make the task of healing doubly difficult.

Music, of all the dynamic arts, is capable of counteracting much of the fear and restraint inevitable in mental institutions. It disposes of therapeutic nihilism. Offering patients an opportunity to "abreact" through music is a great step toward emotional emancipation and build-up of the ego. It is amazing to watch mental patients singing and dancing in spite of the fact that their arms and legs are strapped. Obviously, under the influence of musical impact, the patients forget that they are in restraint. Listening to music, and especially singing, makes their minds feel free, just as the song throughout the dark pages of history has lessened the burden of socially, economically and politically chained people in their daily tasks.

The "Song of the Volga Boatman" provides a socialized way of overcoming life's exigencies by psychological means, even while tied to the oars. The Spirituals and Work Songs of the Southern Negroes made life endurable under very difficult circumstances. Songs like "Steal Away to Jesus" and "Swing Low Sweet Chariot" not only liberate the emotions and appease reality, but create hope for a better future. Folk music, both singing and playing, has a definite function in the practice of music therapy. It not only reacts on the collective musical consciousness of the race, but through association recalls happier memories. Its value should not be under-estimated. Boogie-woogie and jazz are certainly music of the people, and as such have definite value in mental rehabilitation of patients whose cultural level has never been raised any higher. The cultured man still retains his animal self and thus the jazz-brand of music may still affect him. To make a statement that such music is detrimental would indeed be very short-sighted. On the other hand, to expect to gain results through such media in treating patients who have been accustomed to a richer diet of Bach, Beethoven and Brahms would be equally careless.

The absence of family ties of institutionalized patients presents a problem which music helps to solve. Music provides a feeling of unity and belonging. Case after case of uncooperativeness has improved when musical activities were provided. Attendants inclined to be adverse to any procedures that might break the prescribed routine, are soon won over when they realize how music therapy lightens their own tasks. Indeed, the effect upon the attendants is as important a factor as the benefits to the patients, especially during these days of limited and overworked personnel. The public from whose ranks mental patients are bound to come, feels more reassured knowing that the hospital also provides some of the high cultural values.

Lately, the group method of treating mental patients and the servicemen suffering from combat fatigue has become the choice method, because of the time saving and the social impact which it exercises. The "coherence" of a group depends upon several factors, chief among them a leader, a goal and emotional currents. A leader is not indispensable—a group can exist on a fratriarchal basis; a goal can be minimized or become unimportant by changing events. But an emotional current always flows where there is a congregate of people. *It is precisely music that makes this emotional flow mighty.* In a mental ward music is not only valuable as a vehicle to group therapy, but as an "appeaser" of the *status quo* of the hospital atmosphere, as a morale builder, as a source for individual emotional relief and as a medium of self-expression and ego aggrandizement. In group singing such factors as inspiration, self-discipline, solidarity and friendship are cultivated.

It becomes apparent that music plays an important part in the biological, sociological and cultural departments of life and that it is linked with propagation, survival, socialization, progress and aesthetics. Possessing such unusual ingredients, it is astonishing that music's powers have not been sufficiently utilized in a practical way.

Let's hope, therefore, that in the future the physician, the psychiatrist, and the music educator will unite in this common cause and bring to mankind all the benefits that reside so plentifully in music.

THE RECOGNITION AND ACCEPTANCE OF MOOD IN MUSIC BY PSYCHOTIC PATIENTS

By BENJAMIN SIMON, M.D.,

Director Ring Sanatorium, Arlington Heights, Mass.

JULES D. HOLZBERG, Ph.D., and
SALVATORE L. ALESSI, M.S.

Conn. State Hospital, Middletown, Conn.

AND

DANIEL A. GARRITY

The idea that music has therapeutic potentialities has been accepted from time immemorial (12). Thus, music has often been used to relieve long and lonely periods of hospitalization for the physically ill. However, it is only in recent years that attempts have been made to introduce the use of music as an individually pre-scribed form of therapy in mental hospitals, the greatest impetus deriving from its use in military hospitals during the last war.

The systematic application of music as a form of psychiatric treatment is still in its infancy (12). Music in psychiatric settings has been utilized on an unscientific basis because little is actually known concerning its therapeutic significance. While there is some knowledge regarding the psychology of music in normal subjects, a real problem is to determine whether this knowledge is valid for abnormal subjects. This is crucial because music therapy is now being attempted with psychotic patients on the basis of knowledge derived from the study of normal persons.

Work in this field has been done by Altshuler (1), van de Wall

[62]

(12, 13), and Licht (4), but as Soibelman has stated, "It is symptomatic of the paucity of original material on music therapy that, although this form of treatment has been used and recommended for so long, the amount of experimental work is so meager that controlled experiments concerned primarily with the sick are practically nonexistent" (10, p. 205).

The theories of Sorantin (11) with regard to the basis for emotional experience in music are of considerable scientific interest because they readily lend themselves to experimental study. Sorantin states that certain features of a musical phrase have emotional significance and that music may be prepared to convey to the listener the feeling of joy, lamentation, longing or love by utilizing in a specified way certain musical features such as tempo, mode, melody line, harmony, and legato or staccato phrases. Rigg (6, 7, 8, 9), in his investigation of Sorantin's theories, found that he was able to substantiate Sorantin's contentions with regard to joy and lamentation. However, he was not able to demonstrate the ability of individuals to recognize love and longing on the basis of musical phrases.

Sorantin's theories and Rigg's experiments led the present investigators to the research problem at hand. Since Rigg had conducted his experiments with normal subjects, it was decided to determine whether psychotic patients would respond in the same manner as normals in their ability to recognize mood in music and to accept this mood when it was recognized. Since a research study such as this is likely to be highly complicated by the theoretical nature of music, it was explored through the collaborative efforts of psychiatrist, psychologist and musical therapist.

SUBJECTS

The subjects of this experiment consisted of four groups, i.e., normals, schizophrenics, manics and psychotic depressives.

The normal control group consisted of 51 student nurses in

[63]

their second or third year of nursing training. They were, therefore, all females with an age range of 19 to 26 and a mean of 21.7.

The schizophrenic group consisted of 53 patients of whom 24 were diagnosed paranoid, 11 hebephrenic, 4 catatonic, 7 simple and 7 other types. There were 26 males and 27 females. The age of the group ranged from 15 to 50 years with a mean of 32.9 years. The educational achievement of the group ranged from no formal education to college graduation with a mean of 9.4 grades completed.

The third group comprised 31 patients who were diagnosed manic-depressive, manic state. There were 13 males and 18 females in the group with an age range of 26 to 64 years and a mean of 42.8 years. Educational achievement ranged from no formal education to college graduation with a mean of 9.4 grades completed.

The fourth group consisted of manic-depressive psychotics in the depressed state. There were 25 patients in this group of which 9 were males and 16 females. The ages ranged from 23 to 74 years with a mean of 39.2 years. The educational accomplishments ranged from no formal education to college graduation with a mean of ten grades completed.

MATERIALS

Eight musical selections were played on a Steinway spinet and recorded by a Wilcox Gay recorder. The average length of each selection was four measures and, when played twice, which was the recording procedure, each selection took about 20 seconds. Except for two of the selections, which were devised by Rigg (9) for his experiments, all of the other selections were excerpts from well known pieces of music but not readily recognizable because of their brevity.

A questionnaire was devised consisting of eight items, one item for each selection which was played. Each item consisted of the following two questions:

(1) What kind of music was just played?

    Happy——— Sad——— Neither———

(2) Did you like this music?

    Yes——— No——— Cannot say———

Testing Procedure

The normal subjects were tested in one large group. The patients used in the study were assembled in small groups and after the recording of each selection was played, they were asked to respond to the questionnaire in writing. At a given testing, it was usual for several diagnostic groups to be represented. The order of the playing of the eight selections was the same for all subjects.[1] The first selection was one which was presumed to be a "happy" one, while the next one was "sad" and the records alternated between "happy" and "sad" for the remainder of the eight selections. There were always two examiners present so that there was no opportunity for subjects to compare responses during the experiment.

Statistical Treatment of Results

The frequency with which members of the control and clinical groups responded to the questionnaires were tabulated according to the following breakdown. The results of the questionnaire were tabulated separately for each of the two questions to every item. The results were broken down by treating the total responses to all the "happy" records and the total responses to all the "sad" records.

[1] The following constitute the eight selections arranged in the order in which they were played in the present experiment:
(a) Phrase A-1 by Rigg (9, p. 29)
(b) Phrase B-1 by Rigg (9, p. 32)
(c) Excerpt from "Don Giovanni" by Mozart (11, p. 63)
(d) Excerpt from "The Magic Flute" by Mozart (11, p. 37)
(e) Excerpt from "Sonata for Piano" by Beethoven (11, p. 70)
(f) Excerpt from "Pathetique Sonata" by Beethoven (11, p. 45-46)
(g) Excerpt from "Fifth Symphony" by Beethoven (11, p. 72-73)
(h) Excerpt from "Pagliacci" by Leoncavallo (11, p. 52)

As noted in a previous section, each item included a third possible response of "neither" for question 1, and "cannot say" for question 2. The statistical treatment of the results of these third alternative responses posed a problem. Their inclusion would be difficult to interpret since the meaning of these responses was not clear. Because of this fact, it was decided not to consider them in the statistical analysis of the data.[2] For this reason, the frequencies of responses to the two questions are unequal.

The chi-square method was used to test for the statistical significance of all relationships studied.

RESULTS

Recognition of "Happy" Records.—Table I reveals that all psychotic groups and the normal control group successfully recognize the "happy" records. These results are highly significant statistically. The normal control group, however, makes significantly fewer errors than each of the psychiatric groups (Table II). Comparisons between the psychiatric groups show no significant differences with respect to errors made (Table II).

TABLE I.—ACCURACY OF RECOGNITION OF "HAPPY" RECORDS

	FREQUENCY OF RESPONSES			
	Correct	*Incorrect*	X^2	*P*
Normals	137	4	125.46	<.001
Schizophrenics	131	19	83.62	<.001
Manics	92	12	61.54	<.001
Depressives	68	11	41.12	<.001

Recognition of "Sad" Records.—All psychotic groups and the normal control group successfully recognize the "sad" records. The correct recognition for all groups is statistically significant (Table

[2] In order to determine whether the responses to these third alternative choices occurred with sufficient frequency as to influence the significance of the findings with the first two definite choices, they were analyzed statistically. Analysis demonstrated that these responses did not occur with significant statistical frequency to invalidate the findings reported in this study.

TABLE II.—Comparison of Groups with Respect to
Accuracy of Recognition of "Happy" Records

| | FREQUENCY OF RESPONSES | | | |
	Correct	Incorrect	X^2	P
Normals	137	4		
Schizophrenics	131	19	9.65	<.01
Normals	137	4		
Manics	92	12	7.42	<.01
Normals	137	4		
Depressives	68	11	9.80	<.01
Schizophrenics	131	19		
Manics	92	12	.94	34
Schizophrenics	131	19		
Depressives	68	11	.07	79
Manics	92	12		
Depressives	68	11	.23	65

III). The normal control group and the depressive group make significantly fewer misidentifications than do the manic and schizophrenic groups (Table IV). There is no significant difference in the recognition of "sad" records between the normal and depressive groups. Similarly, no significant difference occurs between the schizophrenic and manic groups. On the other hand, the normal and depressive groups differ significantly from the manic and schizophrenic groups in their ability to recognize "sad" records (Table IV).

TABLE III.—Accuracy of Recognition of "Sad" Records

| | FREQUENCY OF RESPONSES | | | |
	Correct	Incorrect	X^2	P
Normals	155	3	146.22	<.001
Schizophrenics	100	40	25.71	<.001
Manics	65	27	15.69	<.001
Depressives	76	4	64.80	<.001

Acceptance of "Happy" Records.—All comparison groups like the "happy" records. This finding is statistically significant (Table

[67]

TABLE IV.—COMPARISON OF GROUPS WITH RESPECT TO
ACCURACY OF RECOGNITION OF "SAD" RECORDS

| | FREQUENCY OF RESPONSES | | | |
	Correct	Incorrect	X^2	P
Normals	155	3		
Schizophrenics	100	40	42.77	<.001
Normals	155	3		
Manics	65	27	41.49	<.001
Normals	155	3		
Depressives	76	4	1.80	.19
Schizophrenics	100	40		
Manics	65	27	.00	.97
Schizophrenics	100	40		
Depressives	76	4	16.36	<.001
Manics	65	27		
Depressives	76	4	17.17	<.001

V). Inter-group comparisons reveal that the manic group tends to like the "happy" records more frequently than do the normal and schizophrenic groups (Table VI). No other differences in inter-group comparisons approach statistical significance.

TABLE V.—ACCEPTANCE OF "HAPPY" RECORDS

| | FREQUENCY OF RESPONSES | | | |
	Like	Dislike	X^2	P
Normals	143	37	62.42	<.001
Schizophrenics	151	36	70.72	<.001
Manics	102	13	68.88	<.001
Depressives	74	14	40.91	<.001

Acceptance of "Sad" Records.—Although a fairly large number of normals like the "sad" records, the number disliking them is significantly greater than would have occurred by chance (Table VII). The depressive group similarly tends to dislike the "sad" records, although there are many depressives who express a liking for them.

[68]

TABLE VI.—Comparison of Groups with Respect to
Acceptance of "Happy" Records

| | FREQUENCY OF RESPONSES | | | |
	Like	Dislike	X^2	P
Normals	143	37		
Schizophrenics	151	36	.10	.76
Normals	143	37		
Manics	102	13	4.27	.04
Normals	143	37		
Depressives	74	14	.83	.38
Schizophrenics	151	36		
Manics	102	13	3.31	.07
Schizophrenics	151	36		
Depressives	74	14	.45	.50
Manics	102	13		
Depressives	74	14	.92	.35

TABLE VII.—Acceptance of "Sad" Records

| | FREQUENCY OF RESPONSES | | | |
	Like	Dislike	X^2	P
Normals	67	111	10.88	<.001
Schizophrenics	104	78	3.71	.06
Manics	76	38	12.67	<.001
Depressives	30	58	8.91	<.01

The manic group, on the other hand, likes "sad" records. Although some manics dislike them, the number of manics liking them is significantly greater than would have occurred by chance (Table VII). The schizophrenic group also tends to like the "sad" records. This trend, however, only approaches statistical significance (Table VII).

Intergroup comparisons (Table VIII) show that the normal and depressive groups are not significantly different from each other in disliking "sad" records. The manic and schizophrenic groups are not significantly different from one another with respect to liking the "sad" records. As would be expected from these findings, the

[69]

normals and depressives are both significantly different from the manics and schizophrenics in their acceptance of "sad" records.

TABLE VIII.—Comparison of Groups with Respect to Acceptance of "Sad" Records

	FREQUENCY OF RESPONSES			
	Like	Dislike	X^2	P
Normals	67	111		
Schizophrenics	104	78	11.66	<.001
Normals	67	111		
Manics	76	38	23.43	<.001
Normals	67	111		
Depressives	30	58	.32	.59
Schizophrenics	104	78		
Manics	76	38	2.67	.10
Schizophrenics	104	78		
Depressives	30	58	12.61	<.001
Manics	76	38		
Depressives	30	58	21.13	<.001

Acceptance of "Happy" Records Which Were Correctly Identified.—Because of the possibility that the individuals who misidentified the music may have confused the analysis of the results of the second question which tapped acceptance of the mood of the music, it was decided to analyze responses to this second question in terms of correct and incorrect identifications.

Table IX indicates the frequencies of liking and disliking "happy" records by those subjects who correctly identify these records as "happy." As in Table V, all groups clearly like the "happy" records, with only a few members in each group disliking them. Of all the groups, the manic group again tends to like the "happy" records most. When compared with the normal and depressive groups, this trend is statistically significant (Table X). When other intergroup comparisons are made, no significant differences are noted.

[70]

TABLE IX.—Acceptance of Correctly Recognized "Happy" Records

	FREQUENCY OF RESPONSES			
	Like	Dislike	X^2	P
Normals	119	12	87.40	<.001
Schizophrenics	118	7	98.57	<.001
Manics	85	2	79.18	<.001
Depressives	59	7	40.97	<.001

TABLE X.—Comparison of Groups with Respect to
Acceptance of Correctly Recognized "Happy" Records

	FREQUENCY OF RESPONSES			
	Like	Dislike	X^2	P
Normals	119	12		
Schizophrenics	118	7	1.18	.28
Normals	119	12		
Manics	85	2	4.10	.04
Normals	119	12		
Depressives	59	7	.11	.75
Schizophrenics	118	7		
Manics	85	2	.72	.41
Schizophrenics	118	7		
Depressives	59	7	1.59	.21
Manics	85	2		
Depressives	59	7	4.50	.04

Acceptance of "Sad" Records Which Were Correctly Identified.—Table XI shows the frequencies of liking and disliking "sad" records by those individuals who correctly identify these records as "sad." The outstanding finding is that, whereas previously (Table VII) the manic and schizophrenic groups showed a liking for "sad" records, they now indicate a very slight trend (statistically not significant) toward disliking them. The normal and depressive groups now show more of a trend toward disliking the "sad" records.

Intergroup comparisons reveal no statistically significant difference between the normal and depressive groups and between

TABLE XI.—Acceptance of Correctly Recognized "Sad" Records

| | FREQUENCY OF RESPONSES | | | |
	Like	Dislike	X^2	P
Normals	39	98	25.41	<.001
Schizophrenics	41	46	.29	.61
Manics	29	34	.39	.55
Depressives	18	51	15.78	<.001

the manic and schizophrenic groups (Table XII). The degree of disliking of "sad" records by the normal and depressive groups is significantly greater than that of manic and schizophrenic groups.

TABLE XII.—Comparison of Groups with Respect to
Acceptance of Correctly Recognized "Sad" Records

| | FREQUENCY OF RESPONSES | | | |
	Like	Dislike	X^2	P
Normals	39	98		
Schizophrenics	41	46	8.07	<.01
Normals	39	98		
Manics	29	34	5.93	.02
Normals	39	98		
Depressives	18	51	.13	.72
Schizophrenics	41	46		
Manics	29	34	.02	.90
Schizophrenics	41	46		
Depressives	18	51	7.24	<.01
Manics	29	34		
Depressives	18	51	5.71	.02

Acceptance of "Sad" Records Misidentified as "Happy."—From Table XIII, it can be seen that all the members of the schizophrenic and manic groups who misidentified the "sad" records as being "happy," also, without exception, indicated that they liked them. The normal and depressive groups did not misidentify "sad" records with sufficient frequency to justify a meaningful statistical analysis.

[72]

TABLE XIII.—ACCEPTANCE OF "SAD" RECORDS MISIDENTIFIED AS "HAPPY"

FREQUENCY OF RESPONSES

	Like	Dislike
Schizophrenics	36	0
Manics . . ., ...	27	0

DISCUSSION

This study indicates that, in general, psychotics respond as normals do with respect to the recognition of the "happy" and "sad" moods of music. While all of the groups are capable of recognizing "happy" music, the normals make significantly fewer errors. Furthermore, while all groups are capable of recognizing "sad" music, normals and depressives make significantly fewer errors than schizophrenics and manics. The accuracy of the depressive's perceptions of "sad" music may be a function of his mood disorder in which feelings of extreme unhappiness are paramount. These patients may be more responsive and more sensitive to stimuli conveying the mood of sadness. The depressive is exquisitely sensitive to the weight of reality about him and is more likely to weigh his perceptions carefully though they are shaded in the direction of his prevailing mood. His attention to reality is heightened. This observation is frequently noted on the Rorschach Test where the depressive reveals his close adherence to reality in the accuracy of his form perceptions.

It is of interest that manics, who are experiencing feelings opposite to those of the depressives, fail to show heightened perceptual accuracy with respect to "happy" records. While it is difficult to reconcile these two apparently contradictory findings in so far as recognition is concerned, nevertheless the manics show a greater liking for the "happy" records than any of the other comparison groups. While it is accepted that manics and depressives are on the same mood continuum, it does not necessarily mean that the resulting personality picture including the dynamics are at all identical.

[73]

The latter factor may account for the fact that the manic does not behave in an obverse relationship to the depressive.

Normals and depressives dislike "sad" records, whereas manics and schizophrenics like them. However, there were many manics and schizophrenics who misidentified the mood of the "sad" records. When these findings are analyzed in terms of correct recognition, the manics and schizophrenics also tend to dislike "sad" music, although not to a statistically significant degree. It is notable that *all* schizophrenics and *all* manics who misidentified the sad records as "happy" also expressed a liking for them. The degree to which schizophrenics and manics misidentify "sad" records would seem to be consistent with the psychiatric observation that the schizophrenic and the manic show impaired ego functioning, as compared to the normal and the depressive[3] (2, 3, 5). This impaired ego functioning results in inaccurate discrimination of perceptual experiences. However, the "sadness" of the music must also be considered in addition to impaired ego function in attempting to understand the extent of the misidentifications of "sad" music. This is so because the same frequencies of misidentification do not occur with "happy" music. Thus, the manic's denial of underlying guilt and depression may alter his evaluation of reality factors and perhaps it is for this reason that he has difficulty in recognizing "sad" music. For the manic, this may then be a continuation of his pattern of rejection of an overwhelming depressive reality. It may also be of importance to distinguish between euphoric manics and aggressive manics, with the former the subjects who misidentify the "sad" music. However, the present analysis did not permit such a fine breakdown of the manic group so the latter hypothesis cannot be tested. For the schizophrenic, the explanation may lie in his reorganization of his world with dissociation of his affect and in his behavioral pattern of withdrawal

---

[3] The depressive's ego is "taken over" by a rigid superego with the consequent result that the ego still continues to exercise its perceptual functions without marked disruption.

from all painful experiences. In any event, from this relationship between the manic and schizophrenic misidentifying "sad" records as "happy" and liking them, the importance of the accuracy of perceptions in the acceptance of mood in music is demonstrated.

As indicated earlier, all groups tend to dislike "sad" records when "sad" records are correctly recognized. Conversely, it is found that all of the groups show marked liking for "happy" music. This seems consistent with the known cultural pattern existing in our society, namely, that individuals tend to avoid that which is unpleasant, painful and sad.

While this study demonstrates generally consistent response patterns for each of the groups as a whole, it is nevertheless clear that not every individual responds in the same manner. This is demonstrated by the fact that there are a variable number of individuals deviating from the group trend in each group, including some in the normal control group itself. Thus, approximately 15% of schizophrenics, manics and depressives make misidentifications of "happy" records. Normals, on the other hand, make very few errors. Approximately 30% of schizophrenics and manics make misidentifications of "sad" records while very few errors are made by normals and depressives.

While all groups tend to like "happy" records, nevertheless between 10 and 20% of each group dislike the same "happy" music. When the responses are analyzed for correct recognition of "happy" records, it is found that a considerable decrease in disliking of "happy" records occurs except for the depressive group where 11% still dislike "happy" records. When the responses to "sad" music are analyzed for correct recognition, all groups are found to dislike "sad" music. However, between 25 and 45% of each group still express a liking for this music.

In attempting to explain the variations occurring within each group, it is necessary to recognize some of the uncontrolled factors operating in this experiment. Although an attempt was made to select psychiatrically homogeneous groups, psychiatric experience has demonstrated that a given diagnosis is not a pure entity. One single important personality factor, such as so-called ego strength, may vary widely within one pathologic group. This is of importance since there is reasonable evidence from this study that correct perception of mood in music is related to ego strength. In addition, while age limits were fairly well restricted for the normals, there was quite a wide range in the ages of the psychotics. Until more knowledge is obtained concerning the effect of age on emotional experiences in music, this question remains important to consider. Furthermore, no attempt was made to control the cultural patterns and musical backgrounds of the individuals in this study. It is reasonable to assume that differences in these backgrounds existed within each group. Knowledge and control of factors such as the above become crucial in attempting to understand the variations which occurred within each group.

If the ability to recognize mood in music and the liking or disliking of a given mood has meaning for the treatment of patients through musical therapy, then it will be possible to predict within reasonable limits the response of a given psychotic group to music. However, the slight but important differences between groups, and particularly the variations within groups, indicate that musical therapy, like all forms of therapy, must be based on an individualized approach to the patient. While group trends are highly significant in developing a theoretical frame of reference for interpretation of musical experience, it is equally true that the most efficacious use of music therapy will depend ultimately on its individualized application.

The present research was undertaken with a limited goal in mind—that of determining similarities and differences in the patterns of response to music of different pathologic groups. However, further questions will of necessity have to be explored before the area of musical therapy can be fully understood and applied. One of these problems is whether there is a relationship between the recognition and acceptance of mood in music and the efficacy of musical therapy. The present study did not intend to evoke a particular mood but rather asked the subjects to express intellectual judgments about brief passages of music. A necessary next step would be to determine the relationship between recognition and acceptance of mood in music and the real emotional experiences evoked by this music. Another question is concerned with the significance of the individual deviations occurring within groups, i.e., what is the effect of musical therapy on those individuals who differ in their response from the group as a whole? Further questions would be concerned with the role of associations or memories evoked by familiar music and the effect of musical therapy on those individuals who are indifferent to music or even irritated by it.

Questions such as these remain unanswered in terms of the present research, but it is felt that this study has been an attempt to explore scientifically at least one question basic to the field of musical therapy.

Summary

This study was designed to compare psychotic patients and normal subjects in their ability to recognize feelings of sadness and happiness in music. In addition, the study compared normal subjects and psychotic patients in their preferences for happy and sad music. Each abnormal group (schizophrenic, manic and psychotic depressive) was compared with every other as well as with normals. Eight recorded phrases of piano music were used. Four of these were "happy" music and four were "sad." After playing each musical phrase, the subjects were asked to designate if the music was "happy" or "sad" and if they liked or disliked it. The results of this study demonstrated considerable similarity in emotional response to music on the part of normals and abnormals but sufficient differences between groups and variations within each group occurred to suggest that the knowledge regarding the psychology of music gained from normal subjects cannot be absolutely applied to psychotics. The significance and implications of these findings for musical therapy were discussed.

REFERENCES

(1) Altshuler, I. M.: The Case of Horace F. *Proc. Music Teach. Nat. A.,* 1946, pp. 368-381.

(2) Brown, J. F.: *The Psychodynamics of Abnormal Behavior.* New York: McGraw-Hill, 1940.

(3) Fenichel, O.: *The Psychoanalytic Theory of Neurosis.* New York: W. W. Norton, 1945.

(4) Licht, S.: *Music in Medicine.* Boston: New England Conservatory of Music, 1946.

(5) Maslow, A. H., and Mittelmann, B.: *Principles of Abnormal Psychology.* New York: Harper, 1941.

(6) Rigg. M. G.: The Expression of Meanings and Emotions in Music. In *Philosophical Essays in Honor of Edgar Arthur Singer, Jr.* Philadelphia: University of Pennsylvania Press, 1942, pp. 279-294.

(7) ——: Musical Expression: an Investigation of the Theories of Erich Sorantin. *J. Exper. Psychol.,* 21:442, 1937.

(8) ——: Speed as a Determiner of Musical Mood. *J. Exper. Psychol.,* 27:566, 1940.

(9) ——: What Features of a Musical Phrase Have Emotional Suggestiveness? *Bull. Oklahoma A. & M. Coll.,* 36:1, 1939.

(10) Soibelman, O.: *Therapeutic and Industrial Uses of Music.* New York: Columbia University Press, 1948.

(11) Sorantin, E.: *The Problem of Musical Expression.* Nashville: Marshall & Bruce, 1932.

(12) van de Wall, W.: *Music in Hospitals.* New York: Russell Sage Foundation, 1946.

(13) ——: *Music in Institutions.* New York: Russell Sage Foundation, 1936.

[78]

THE ORGANIZATION OF A MUSIC PROGRAM, AS A REHABILITATION MEASURE FOR THE MENTALLY ILL

By MARY JANE PRESTON

Supervisor of Recreation, Pilgrim State Hospital, West Brentwood, N. Y.

Music is not a new activity in our mental hospitals, nor has there been a lack of appreciation through the years of the contribution of music in its entertainment and recreational value. The time has arrived, however, to investigate the greater possibilities of music for patient groups and individuals when it is carried on by highly-skilled personnel in this specialty. How shall this program be organized and how shall it function? How can it be correlated with other programs as part of the treatment effort?

The observations and suggestions in this paper are made, not by a musician but by a recreation supervisor, in the hope that some experience in the development of a music program will be helpful to others.

Since music is a vital part of the recreation program, it has seemed logical that it be further developed and extended by musicians assigned to the recreation department. The recreation supervisor has experience and knowledge of the reaction types of patients and is acquainted with many individual patients' interests and abilities. This can assist greatly in the guidance and control when integrating a more specific program. Also, the recreation supervisor has knowledge of the hospital organization, its physical facilities, its staff and administrative procedures, and he is equipped to plan and revise schedules with proper balance and consideration for the other patient-activity programs.

Music has long been an important part of the recreation program, not only for parties, dances and entertainments, but also as an integral part of scheduled classes where rhythmic exercises, musical games and folk dances are included. Formerly, the recreation supervisor has depended on other workers or on patients with musical ability to supplement selected recordings in order to have the advantages of music in the program. This arrangement has limited the potentialities of music activity, and there has been a long-felt need for personnel with a specialized musical knowledge to develop fully this part of the recreation program.

It has been stimulating to have worked at Pilgrim (New York) State Hospital with a number of qualified musicians whose emphasis in music was on "therapy" and not just on art and performance. From this experience, the writer would like to give conclusions and outline certain ideas of the organization plan in which music is used as a part of the rehabilitation program.

It is accepted that music is an aid which may strongly influence behavior by the stabilizing of emotions and the stimulating of special senses which create healthy attitudes. It should definitely be part of the treatment program, and there is increased interest in this phase of activity, as the music specialists, themselves, are becoming more aware of the scope of activity and of the contribution needed for this field.

The word "therapy" in music must be employed in its broader sense, as it would seem not proper to use the term "music therapist" unless the musically skilled had also the training and experience in the medical subjects which would enable them to apply their skills as specific therapy. Some research has been done in this field in various hospitals, and the findings have pointed to the value of this activity for certain individual patients and also for the better control of noisy patients on wards where selected compositions are played.

It is agreed that the music instructor is needed to complete the therapeutic team, to work along with the recreational instructor, the occupational therapist, the nurse, the attendant, the social worker and others, functioning under medical guidance and direction with a definite team purpose in mind—to help the patient in his mental, emotional and social adjustment. With co-ordinated activity, no one group may claim a cure-all, show a tendency to exaggerate results, or to work independently when all treatment is dovetailed, with many forces focused as therapy for the individual patient. The co-ordinator for the team must necessarily be a medical person at the administrative level whose interest it would be to correlate the activities of the various departments.

In regard to the music personnel, the writer would observe that a musician with a background and training in teaching is more adaptable for the necessary duties than is the "artist" type. To illustrate by analogy, the graduate recreational instructor, with courses in psychology, anatomy, kinesiology, etc., has a better foundation and a broader knowledge for carrying out a treatment program than has a former professional football or baseball player. The occupational therapist with arts and skills, plus professional training in the medical sciences, is more specifically prepared to carry out a treatment program than is the artist or a person skilled only in handcrafts.

The music instructor must be able to adapt knowledge, to work with others co-operatively and to organize and co-ordinate a planned music program. The instructor should be someone with an outgoing personality, with enthusiasm and a sense of humor. The program should be flexible in its application to the various types of patients, from simple and informal play activities to specific and more advanced group organizations of selected patients, requiring individual training and participation. The instructor should have the capacity to use music skills to the highest level as the needs, capacities and interests of the group become apparent.

In planning and grading the music activities of the over-all

[81]

hospital program, it is necessary to outline the types of music expression, which would be adaptable for both group and individual participation and to have some idea of to what extent participation would be active and of which patients would benefit at a passive level.

Following are some of the music activities to be discussed further in this paper. Group singing, church choirs and glee clubs are included in vocal grouping; and activities in the instrumental category are the dance orchestra, the band, the drum and bugle corps and the rhythm bands—with certain instruction and training required by all for both individual and group-activity participation. There are also special events which require full co-operative effort from other treatment departments, such as the staging of operettas, musical shows and minstrels. Marionette and puppet shows may also be added to this list, as well as special concerts and tableaux.

Music must be integrated with the recreation program not only for the daily routine class periods but also for the parties and dances which are such an important part of the socializing effort for the patients. There is also activity for the individual patient which is prescribed by the doctor as well as required co-operative effort with research projects.

Another important phase of the music therapy program is the benefit and enjoyment received by the less active groups from the efforts of vocal and instrumental performers. Also important, is the wide range of listening pleasure offered by well-selected recordings, with or without planned music-appreciation discussions. A growing library of a variety of good music albums should be the aim of every department in an effort to enrich, as much as possible, the lives of the patients in our hospitals.

To carry out a program of the foregoing variety, the music instructor, in the larger hospitals at least, needs the assistance of a bandmaster who is qualified to teach the patients time-consuming lessons in playing individual instruments and to help with the rehearsals of the band and the orchestra. The extent to which the total music advantages may be extended depends on music's integration with other therapies and on the mutual co-operative effort made to develop its potentialities.

First let us consider the group singing which may be scheduled weekly on every service or in patients' buildings for the large ward groups. It has been observed that a patient who will not talk will frequently sing when other singers in a group select familiar songs and the withdrawn one is encouraged to participate. To stimulate interest, the group singing is often varied with humming, whistling and harmonizing. Some respond well to music with action, such as singing while they march, clap hands or sway to the rhythm.

There should be a variety in the selection of tunes for singing, and repetition should be avoided in order to keep the melodies fresh and agreeable to all. Group selection of songs is very important in maintaining the interest of the group, as the younger patients enjoy the late popular pieces while the older patients often prefer the old-time melodies. A mixture is needed to keep all interested. The songs of various nationalities should be available for singing if requested. In the selection for ward groups, the interests and cultural backgrounds of the more alert patients should be considered in raising the standard and quality of the music effort.

From these ward singing groups, patients are selected with the approval of, and often at suggestion from, the doctor, for active participation in the more specialized forms of activity, such as singing in the choirs, chorus or glee club, or playing in the band or orchestra, thus adding to the possibilities of entertainment and of musical programs for all the patients in active or passive form.

The vocal program of the chorus and glee club provides a stimulating experience for those participating. These patients are individualized, and may progress to varied and advanced musical training. There are weekly practice sessions in choral and part singing. Male and female patients sing together and separately, to gain harmony as well as to establish a normal social grouping.

Interest grows, as at regular rehearsals the music practised is for coming events with a musical program planned to be given about every three months for the entertainment of the other patients.

The choirs are divided for Catholic and Protestant rehearsals; and, again, selected patients practice once weekly for the Sunday services. Singing hymns and learning Christmas and Easter holiday songs give great satisfaction to many and afford means of spiritual comfort.

In instrumental music activity, the band and orchestra are important. The band comprises from 12 to 20 patients, depending on the number who are available and who have talent or interest in playing an instrument such as the piano, violin, cello, drums, saxophones, clarinets, trumpets, and bass viol. The band gives concerts about the hospital for the entertainment of the patients. The orchestra is composed of a selected number of patients with suitable instruments who practice and play for the patients' weekly dances and keep up with the more popular airs. Both these groups receive individual training within the limitations of the personnel and are advanced as their proficiency becomes apparent.

The drum and bugle corps, a most interesting group, is composed at Pilgrim State Hospital of about 30 men and women who can play the drums, the wind instruments, the percussion instruments, the glockenspiel and triangles. They, together with the flag-bearer, the color-guards and the majorettes, practice twice weekly, plus one drill period. The march routine, formation and calls are taught by an interested attendant who is experienced in drill techniques and whose help has been invaluable. Attractive uniforms have been purchased for this group, and great pride is exhibited in the patients' attitude toward their accomplishments. In the several public appearances of the drum and bugle corps, it competed favorably with other drum and bugle groups in maneuvers and performance.

Small rhythm bands afford a simple type of instrumental music which is adaptable for the low-grade and regressed patient; and they also afford fun and stimulation to the more alert patient. The instruments are generally improvised or may be gotten with little expense. These consist of small drums, tambourines, cymbals, sticks, dry gourds, bells, wood and sand blocks. Even combs with tissue paper (to be hummed on) are used. Harmonicas and auto-harps are also simple and are good musical equipment for both group and individual music effort.

Individual music-therapy work prescribed by the doctor in charge is very important. Private instruction is given in voice, piano, and other instruments. Also, original compositions and arrangements are encouraged. Working in music with individuals has been very helpful in awakening old interests and responses, instilling self-confidence and giving encouragement.

Marionettes and puppets have not been used in the Pilgrim program, but this activity is worth considering. The construction of the puppets, the theater, scenery, manipulation of the strings and rehearsing the action necessitates the correlation of occupational therapy, recreation and music activities. Arrangements could be made for this equipment to be portable, and it could be taken from ward to ward, with performances given for patients who seldom leave their buildings. Original plays could be written and characters created which would be a great aid to the psychiatrist.

Patients who participate in the foregoing groups gain much in adjustment or satisfaction, and those who enjoy the performances are also benefited. A sportsmanlike appreciation is shown by most groups for patient performers who volunteer to play, dance or sing. The effort is applauded even if the quality of the performance is poor. However, patients are quick to recognize and duly applaud those of noticeable ability. An instructor must be on guard for those who have a tendency to attract too much attention and to monopolize time to no advantage.

In deciding the music activity for the various patient groups, it is necessary to keep in mind the reaction types of the patients with whom one is dealing—as it is in the general recreation program—

and to apply music accordingly, with a definite purpose in mind.

With regressed patients there must be an effort to develop rhythm, to awaken interest and increase initiative by means of stimulating tunes, action songs and rhythmical instruments.

Music with the disturbed groups must be highly controlled, with soft, soothing melodies designed for quieting and sedative effect and for a release of emotional tension.

For patients with trends or delusions, singing affords a means of group co-operation which has, in turn, a socializing influence on persons who are anti-social and often difficult. A well-selected program will sometimes awaken their old interests and gain their co-operation in group activity. These patients are frequently advanced to the instrumental or to the choral group, as they are often alert and are less likely to be regressed than some others.

Geriatric patients are also visited on a schedule, and it is noted that singing gives real joy to the aged group when the old familiar songs are sung. They also, child-like, enjoy the variations and the small rhythmical instruments.

For all these groups, the class period should not be too long, as interest and enthusiasm fade. Patients become restless and lose the good they have gained. Forty-five minutes make a fair class period for this activity.

With the acute treatment group, which includes the newly-admitted patients, those who are undergoing shock therapies, post-lobotomy and convalescent patients, careful thought must be given to the program in order to make it as individual as possible. The patients under this heading are treated in small groups, and all types of music activities should be tried, including individual and group efforts. Consideration should be given to the higher cultural level usually found in the admission patients and the program should cater to, and be geared to, this interest. With shock and lobotomy patients, the music should be stimulating and compelling, with action songs for small groups in order to improve attention, co-ordination and socialization. A research project has been carried on lately with this latter type of patient in an effort to prove that music can change and modify a patient's mood, change the trend of thought, soothe, and relax—so it can be applied as a definite therapy here.

The Musicians Emergency Association is sponsoring some experiments at Pilgrim State Hospital in an effort to be of service to the mentally sick and also to be in a position to recruit, select and place musicians for this humanitarian purpose. They are attempting to show that music should be prescribed and utilized on a specific therapeutic basis. Within a three-month period, a musician, assisted by two others who were musically trained, carried out several experiments under the auspices of this association. They were:

Experiment I. Music was employed in connection with electric shock treatments twice a week. There were 25 to 41 patients; and the object was to try to determine what further benefits might be obtained from the controlled use of music before and after shock therapy. The results observed led one to the belief that music was an aid, as it helped to overcome patients' fear before they were wheeled into the treatment room; and there was a calming and assuring influence when consciousness returned. It soothed and relaxed the patients, thus making it easier for them to sleep or lie quietly. The atmosphere of the entire ward was changed for the better.

Experiment II. The object of this experiment was to find out what effects constructive music periods would have on the individual patients, who responded to and appreciated them. The program ranged from folk songs to concerts and symphonies played on the recording machine. Thirty-six patients were used as subjects: nine disturbed patients; nine regressed; nine in poor contact; and nine postlobotomy patients. Twenty-three patients were retained in the experiment; and definite improvements in appearance and in behavior were observed.

Experiment III. This experiment in music as therapy consisted of a series of concerts in the day-hall for about 40 patients. Records were used for part of the program, and selections ranged from popular music to light opera and popular classics. The musician sang solos, and several numbers were sung by everyone. The program was conducted along the lines of music appreciation, with general discussion by everyone; and the type and sequence of the music was carefully controlled. This program was enthusiastically received, and the psychological effect was observed to be favorable. Further experiments are still being carried on by the musician, who now has three assistants.

SUMMARY

Music has always had a definite place in the treatment effort in our hospitals and schools, but it should be more fully developed to the limits of its potentialities by obtaining the services of persons highly skilled in music. The music instructors must be oriented as to the possibilities of their contribution to the balanced treatment effort as part of the therapeutic team. It is observed that music may be adapted for all patients at either the active or passive level and that all reaction types of patients gain by the application of music in one of its various forms.

Music offers another opportunity for a fuller and more enjoyable life in the hospital, and is another means to help the patients in their adjustment.

MUSIC AS AN ADJUNCT TO ELECTROSHOCK THERAPY[1]

By HARRY M. MURDOCK, M.D.

Medical Director, The Sheppard and Enoch Pratt Hospital, Towson, Md.

AND

MERRILL T. EATON, JR., M.D.

Dept. Psychiatry, Univ. Kansas Medical Center, Kansas City, Kansas

Music has been used in general in the occupational and recreation therapy programs of psychiatric hospitals to divert attention from abnormal preoccupations, to modify mood, and to aid in the establishment of identifications. It is believed that the use of music before, during, and after electroshock treatments can serve in these ways, and can also allay anxiety in the treatment situation and assist in reintegration and resocialization.

Shock therapy is used empirically. Adjuncts to the treatment may also be empirical. There is as yet no accepted explanation as to why shock treatment frequently helps patients. In addition to attempts at an explanation on an organic basis, there are at least fifteen theories attempting to explain its effects in influencing reactions on the basis of dynamic changes in personality orientation. If shock operates by blocking cortical impulses, creating regression, destroying inhibitions, and breaking down autism, music might be of doubtful value except as it creates a pleasant or soothing atmosphere. If, on the other hand, the benefits are considered as influencing the personality in terms of most of the latter (dynamic) theoretical formulations, the use of music as an auxiliary

[1] From The Sheppard and Enoch Pratt Hospital, Towson, Md.

measure would be expected to be quite helpful. Among such formulations would be included the idea (1) that electroshock therapy
facilitates transference by making patients helpless and dependent;
(2) the belief that the patient regards the experience as erotic;
(3) that the treatment initiates fantasies of rebirth and reorienta-
tion to external realities; (4) that the treatment serves to represent
punishment. The theory of punishment may be open to question in
that the treatments are painless and that many patients who benefit
from shock treatment do so after having failed to recover under
hospitalization, which many patients regard as punishment, and
after the use of restraint and seclusion.

In their study of music as an adjunct to hydrotherapy, Altshuler and Shebesta came to the conclusion that music prevented
patients from regarding those procedures as punitive. Perhaps, if
shock therapy is regarded as punishment, the use of music, rather
than destroying that effect, might merely serve to temper punishment with gentleness, as it might be tempered in the hands of a
kind father figure.

During the war Fong, at the Darnall General Hospital, had
units of the band play during shock therapy, and immediately after
treatment gave all patients, except the depressed, an opportunity
to dance. The depressed group was allowed to remain in bed and
listen to soft, soothing, semiclassical music. He found the response
gratifying and noted that patients previously resistive and inaccessible waited eagerly for their treatments.

At The Sheppard and Enoch Pratt Hospital, a modification of
these techniques has been in use during the past year.

Patients receiving shock have been at the hospital for observation and attempts at psychotherapy for some time prior to the
treatments; therefore, they have made the acquaintance of the
music therapists and participated in some of the hospital's musical
activities prior to this treatment situation.

The nature of shock therapy, the treatment room routine, and
the music program are explained to the patients in advance, even

in those cases who are seemingly unable to comprehend it. The word shock is not avoided, as has been sometimes suggested, since it is believed that other patients would use it and, for a similar reason, common complaints following treatment, such as memory loss and headache, are mentioned to the prospective patient.

Patients are brought to the treatment room without breakfast, at 9:30 A.M. Male and female patients are treated on separate days. The recovery beds are in the same room as the treatment table and these are screened off until the last treatment has been given, so that no patient actually sees another patient convulse. As soon as the last treatment is over, the screens are removed, so that the patients can see each other and converse. They then remain in the room usually in bed, for the next half-hour. A student nurse remains beside each bed and attempts to engage the patients in conversation as soon as they are awake. The physician circulates among the patients for the same purpose, as do the music therapists and an occupational therapist, when available. Other nurses and physicians are often present. The shock treatment is usually not given by the patient's psychotherapist, though the latter may be in the room during the recovery period. At the end of the recovery period, patients return to their wards for breakfast.

Music is provided during the entire time that the patients are in the treatment room. Recordings are used and these are chosen by music therapists who are present during treatments to note the patients' reactions to the selections and to discuss their requests with them. The actual numbers played are weighed by the therapists in terms of rhythm, melody, timbre, emotional qualities, and dissonances; final choices are left to their discretion. In general, however, music prior to treatment is soft, melodic, not highly emotional, not markedly rhythmical, slow in tempo, low or medium in pitch, and free of modern dissonances. It is meant to be calming but unobtrusive. After treatment, selections gradually become more emotional and finally more rhythmical. It is planned that the patient be aroused to activity. Both classical and popular music is used and every attempt is made to fill specific requests of the patients at appropriate times in the program. In one instance, a number not available on record was played on the violin by one of the therapists.

In a general way the "iso"-principle is followed in adjusting music to the patient's mood; that is, in the latter part of the recovery period, manic and disturbed catatonic patients are permitted rhumbas and boogie woogie, while depressed patients are given solemn, usually classical, selections. This is often modified when patients of several different types are listening at the same time.

Vocal music is avoided because of possible misinterpretation of the content of the lyrics. Histories are studied to eliminate numbers which might have unfortunate connection or association with precipitating factors in the illness. Repetitions are avoided, as are very familiar compositions, to minimize conditioning.

In addition to the music in the treatment room, patients who are interested are given special instruction in music at other times. Such instruction is geared to a slow pace and is largely on the level of music appreciation, because of the memory loss produced by the treatments.

It is impossible to evaluate our results, statistically. The patients fell within various diagnostic groups and there were many other variables, such as age and duration of illness, which could not be controlled. The patients are for the most part ones who had failed to respond to psychotherapy and who had a poor prognosis. At the same time, while receiving shock therapy, the patients have continued psychotherapy and the general milieu therapy of the hospital.

The results, however, are believed to be good. After the first treatment patients have returned to the shock room for subsequent treatments with distinctly less trepidation. Overt demonstrations of pre-treatment anxiety have been almost completely eliminated. It is less difficult to persuade the patients to co-operate in an adequate number of treatments rather than attempting to terminate the series too soon. Patients wake up more peacefully and in a more pleasant frame of mind and seem to respond to the social situation of the shock room more readily. There have been no other changes in the shock room situation, except the addition of the phonograph and the music therapist, so that the general easing of the situation would be fairly attributable to the music. Perhaps the most significant thing of all was that other members of the staff who had expressed skepticism shortly became rather enthusiastic about the use of music.

Most patients expressed appreciation of the music; a few have amnesia for it following the first treatment, but recall it after later experiences. As well as reducing the anxiety reactions of patients, the change in atmosphere has led to a reduction in the tension displayed by student nurses who assist in the treatment room, and this in turn has contributed to the well-being of the patients. In discussing their treatments with employees and other patients, they usually speak of the situation as pleasant.

It is believed that there has been some increase in the number of patients showing and maintaining improvement.

SUMMARY AND CONCLUSIONS

1. Music has been used before, during, and after electroshock treatments at the Sheppard and Enoch Pratt Hospital for the past year.

2. Before treatments, selections are soft, melodic, free of distracting features, and are meant to allay anxiety.

3. After treatment, selections become gradually more emotional and later more rhythmical, so that the patient at first awakes in a pleasant environment, has his attention directed outward, and is finally aroused to activity.

4. The reaction of patients to this routine has been encouraging.

BIBLIOGRAPHY

(1) Altshuler, I. M.: Four Years' Experience with Music as a Therapeutic Agent at Eloise Hospital. *Am. J. Psychiat., 100*:792, 1944.
(2) Altshuler, I. M.:, and Shebesta, B. H.: Music—an Aid in the Management of the Psychotic Patient. *Journal of Nervous and Mental Disease, 94*:179, 1941.
(3) Fenichel, O.: *Psychoanalytic Theory of Neurosis.* New York: W. W. Norton, 1945.
(4) Fong, T. C. C.: Neuropsychiatric Activities at Darnall General Hospital. *Mil. Surgeon, 102*:365, 1948.
(5) Gaston, E. T.: Psychological Foundations for Functional Music. *Am. J. Occup. Therapy, 2*:1, 1948.
(6) Kalinowsky, L. B., and Hoch, P. H.: *Shock Treatments.* New York: Grune and Stratton, 1946.
(7) Price, H. G., Mountney, V., and Knouss, R.: Selection of Music to Accompany Electro-shock Therapy. *Occup. Therapy, 29*:220, 1950.

SELECTION OF MUSIC TO ACCOMPANY ELECTROSHOCK THERAPY

By HENRIETTA G. PRICE, O.T.R., VIRGINIA MOUNTNEY, B.M. and RUTH KNOUSS

Occupational Therapy Department, Sheppard and Enoch Pratt Hospital, Towson, Maryland

Music has been used in the treatment program of the Sheppard and Enoch Pratt Hospital for many years, and since 1948, special attention has been given to its use before, during and after electro-shock treatments. Electro-shock has been most successful with manic-depressive and involutional patients and as an adjunct to psychotherapy in selected schizophrenics. According to Kalinowsky (1) it makes the patient more accessible to his environment, that is, to members of the hospital staff and other patients.

During the past eight months this hospital has been studying the use of recorded music in connection with electro-shock (2). Music of three types is played to correspond with the three periods of shock treatment: preparation, return of consciousness, and the after-period which includes the half hour rest in bed in the treatment room.

As the patient enters the treatment room with a nurse or attendant, recorded music of a peaceful character is played to create a reassuring atmosphere. This music is serious but not depressing, melodic but not sentimental and possesses no predominating rhythm; it is selected to meet the fearful, apathetic, depressed or anxious mood of the patient, without aggravating it. This music is not repetitious or generally familiar; dissonant music is avoided.

[95]

The effectiveness of this approach is evidenced by the increasing interest and pleasure expressed by the patients; they soon begin to listen for this music and develop a feeling of importance when they learn the music is being played especially for them. The dead silence which so often occurs when a patient is being prepared for treatment is avoided and the music helps to create a subject for conversation which diverts the patient's attention and eases the tense situation.

During the second or waking period music is used to elicit pleasure. For this period music is more melodic, sentimental, but still without strong rhythm. The music creates an interest for the patient outside himself and gradually arouses a desire for voluntary activity. As orientation returns, more lively music is used for stimulation. Finally, when the patient is ready to leave, dance rhythms are played. During the entire stay in the treatment room the different forms of music are merged unobtrusively.

Our primary concern is the degree of disturbance in each patient. Loud, lively and rhythmic recordings of the popular type match the mood of the very disturbed patient to gain his attention. During the waking period of the very depressed, selections are played which are in keeping with the sad mood of the patient. As the patient becomes more alert, gayer music is played.

The choice between classical and popular music is determined by the preference of the patient (3). Vocal recordings are usually avoided because the lyrics may be suggestive of previous experiences or associations. Our chief aim is to play music for atmosphere not concentrated listening.

We try to honor individual requests and ask the patients to name selections before or during treatment. The immediate causes of the patient's illness are studied so that music which might remind him of an unpleasant experience may be avoided. This personal attention is of great value even in cases where shock fails, for the patient becomes aware of the fact that members of the hospital staff are trying to help him.

Between shock treatments there may be varying degrees of memory loss. For this reason the patient enrolled in elementary music instruction is helped in playing simple tunes. The accompanying therapist plays the more complex part with him which relieves the strain of trying to remember and increases satisfaction and confidence. Patients with previous training are encouraged to attain previous levels of proficiency. Those with little or no training may be willing to sing to the accompaniment of the therapist. It is more important to keep the patient in contact with reality, however, than to promote musical accomplishment.

Although we have used no control groups we believe our results have been most encouraging. Many patients have been enthusiastic and expressed the desire to discuss music after their treatments terminated. If for some reason the music is omitted they call our attention to it. In a few instances, patients requested the elimination of music. One, an older agitated-depressed patient, who was a fine concert artist could not bear to have shock treatment associated with music; another, a medical secretary who loved music very much, would not allow herself the pleasure of listening to music because of feelings of guilt.

We have found the following recordings valuable in the periods indicated.

A. Entering Room or Preparation

BACH	Largo, Concerto in A	*Victor M 1017*
	Sinfonia in B flat	*Victor 7484 A*
	Suite for Orchestra	*Victor 7484 B*
	Brandenberg Concerto, No. 4	*W.G.M.* DF 500*
BEETHOVEN	Eroica Symphony	*M.A.R.***
	Moonlight Sonata	*R.C.A.-Victor 16250 A*
	Symphony No. 7, Allegretto	*Victor DM 317*
BRAHMS	Intermezzos: E flat, Opus 1; A minor, Opus 76, No. 1; E flat minor, Opus 117, No. 2; A major, Opus 118, No. 2; E flat minor, Opus 118, No. 6; C major, Opus 119, No. 3	*Victor M 893*
	First Symphony, Second Movement	*Victor DM 875*

* World's Greatest Music.
** Music Appreciation Recording.

BRUCH	Violin Concerto, Slow Movement	*Victor DM 124*
CHOPIN	First Piano Concerto, Second Movement	*Victor DM 418*
	Waltz in A minor	*Victor M 1017*
DEBUSSY	Clair de Lune	*Victor 1812*
DVORAK	Humoresque	*Victor 18222 A*
GRIEG	Morning Mood, from Peer Gynt Suite	*Victor M 404 1*
	Piano Concerto in A minor, Second Movement	*Victor DM 900*
HAYDN	Symphony 99, Second Movement	*W.G.M. 21 B*
MAILLE	Invocation	*Victor 14368 B*
MENDELSSOHN	Italian Symphony, Second Movement	*Columbia M 538*
MOZART	Symphony 40, Second Movement	*W.G.M. Sr 9*
PROVOST	Intermezzo	*Victor 4458*
RACHMANINOFF	Second Concerto, Second Movement	*R.C.A.-Victor DM 58*
SAINT-SAENS	The Aquarium (Carnival of Animals)	*R.C.A.-Victor M 785 1*
	The Swan (Carnival of Animals)	*Victor M 1017*
SCHUMANN	Arabesque	*Victor DM 1149*
	Traumerei	*Victor DM 1149*
SCHUBERT	Symphony 8, Second Movement	*W.G.M. Sr 2 A, B*
SIBELIUS	Swan of Tueonala	*Victor 7380 B*
SINDING	Rustle of Spring	*Victor 18153*
TSCHAIKOWSKY	Sixth Symphony	*Columbia MM 432 1*
WAGNER	Prelude to Parsifal	*W.G.M. Sr 12 A*
	Prize Song (Die Meistersinger)	*Victor M 1017*
	To the Evening Star (Tannhauser)	*Victor M 1017*

B. Awakening Period

ADAMSON	Time on My Hands	*Columbia C 32 1*
BARNETT	Lament for May	*Bluebird B 10743 B*
BERLIN	Eddy Duchin Album	*Columbia C 32*
	Easter Parade	*Columbia C 32 5*
BRAHMS	Rhapsody in B minor	*Victor M 893 8*
CHOPIN	Waltz in A minor	*Victor M 863 4*
	Waltz in C minor	*Victor M 863 7*
DEBUSSY	Golliwog's Cake Walk	*Victor 21945*
DOMINIQUEZ	Perfidia	*Victor 26334 A*
ENESCO	Roumanian Rhapsody No. 1	*Columbia MX 203*
FIELDS	The Way You Look Tonight	*Columbia C 43 8*
GRIEG	Anitra's Dance	*Victor M 404 3*
HAMMERSTEIN	Lover Come Back To Me	*Columbia C 32 8*
HARBURG-DUKE	April in Paris	*Columbia C 32 2*
HERBERT	Selections	*Columbia M 415*
KERN	Show Tunes	*Columbia C 34*
MOZART	Symphony 40, First, Second, Fourth Movements	
PADEREWSKI	Minuet in G	*Victor 16250 B*
ROSE	Our Waltz	*Victor 27853*
STRAUSS	Waltzes from Der Rosenkavalier	*Columbia 11542 D*
TSCHAIKOWSKY	Sleeping Beauty Waltz	*R.C.A.-Victor 11932 B*
	Waltz of the Flowers	*W.G.M. Sr 41 A, B*
	Symphony 6, Last Movement	

Introduction to Carousel	*Decca DA 400*
Famous Waltzes	*Victor P 77*
Musical Comedy Favorites	*Columbia M 430*
Wayne King Recordings	*Victor 20-1862*
Introduction to Oklahoma	*Decca DA 400*
Popular American Waltzes	*Columbia C 26*
Salon Music	*Columbia C 21, C 80*
Frenesi	*Victor 27546*
Selections from South Pacific	*Columbia MM 850*
Tangos	*Columbia C 90*

C. After Period

BARNETT	Six Lessons From Madame La Zonga	*Bluebird 10743*
BASIE	Album of Piano Rhythms	*Victor P 200*
BERLIN	Alexander's Ragtime Band	*Columbia C 662*
BRADLEY	Celery Stalks At Midnight	*Signature 15111*
GERSHWIN	I Got Rhythm	*Columbia M 430 8*
ROSE	Holiday for Strings	*Victor 27853*
RUIZ	Quanto Lagusto	*Decca 24479 A*
	Tommy Dorsey Selections	*Victor 20-1715 B*
	Woody Herman Selections	*Decca 25079 A, B*
	Hot Trumpets	*Columbia C 66*

The following selections chosen from the lists above were found valuable for use in single shock-treatment sessions.

Period A. Grieg—Morning Mood; Haydn—Symphony 99, Second Movement.
Period B. Popular American Waltzes: Holiday for Strings, Missouri Waltz, Perfidia, Beautiful Ohio.
Period C. Hot Trumpets, I Got Rhythm, Boogie-Woogie (*Victor 20-1715-B*).

For depressed patients who like classical music, the following are suggested:

Period A. Brahms—Intermezzo in E flat, Opus 117, No. 1; Saint Saens—The Swan; Wagner—To the Evening Star.
Period B. Tschaikowsky—Symphony 6, First Movement.
Period C. Tschaikowsky—Waltz of the Flowers.* (Selected from B group.)

For excited patients we recommend the following:

Period A. Alexander's Ragtime Band: Darktown Strutter's Ball. (Selected from C group.)
Period B. Victor Herbert Selections: Famous Waltzes (*Victor P 7*).
Period C. Tommy Dorsey Selections (*Victor 20-1715-B*).

In offering our observations we hope to encourage other therapists to use music in conjunction with electro-shock treatments and report their observations.

[99]

REFERENCES

1. Kalinowsky, L. B.: The function of occupational therapy as an adjunct in shock therapies and prefrontal lobotomy. *Amer. J. Occ. Ther.*, December, 1948, 2:261.
2. Murdock, H. M. and Eaton, M. T.: Music as an adjunct to electro-shock therapy. (In preparation.)
3. Licht, S.: Music in Medicine, 1946.
4. Van de Wall, W.: Music in Hospitals, 1946.

MUSIC THERAPY IN THE ANXIETY STATES

By JAMES GIRARD, M.A.

Psychologist, Boston, Mass.

All of us have our moments of anxiety; life at times is full of strange forebodings and uncomfortable feelings. Anxiety is a chronic state of internal pressures and tensions which seem to keep us on edge. For the most part anxiety is a fear of the unknown, of the unusual, of the indefinite. This fear in time leads to a state of helplessness, since no purposeful action is possible against an unknown danger.

The type of anxiety which often afflicts most of us is what is called free-floating anxiety. It brings about a general pervading sense of doom; it results in an aura of uncertainty of the future; it makes the present full of unfriendly and threatening shapes and moments.

Anxiety afflicts not only the mind but the body is also made susceptible to various disagreeable sensations. The most common of these are: fatigue, which is the result of prolonged and increased tension of the muscles; weakness, due to the expenditure of too much emotional energy; pains in the neck, due to muscular tenseness of the neck muscles; head pains and pressures, particularly constricting sensations, also due to tensions of the head muscles.

Anxiety is a universal phenomenon of our times. Today it is more widespread than ever before. Hand in hand with anxiety we find that insecurity is commonplace, and that anxiety of the future is plaguing all of us. Anxiety normally keeps us alert. It becomes both irksome and harmful when it recurs persistently in inappropriate situations.

The anxious individual is far from being a happy one. If events do not fall into their customary grooves he becomes quite upset and he begins to imagine the worst. He becomes irritable; he cannot sleep. He becomes restless and uneasy. Occasionally he has dizzy spells and palpitations of the heart. He is almost constantly under a very uncomfortable tension.

If the anxiety continues for any length of time it begins to produce ill effects on the various organs of the body: the heart, the stomach, the skin, the blood vessels. At first these changes may be of a temporary nature, but should the anxiety continue for any appreciable length of time, the changes become permanent, that is, the organs actually become diseased. It is for this reason that anxiety should be recognized as soon as it becomes established, and that measures to overcome this harmful state should be undertaken without too much delay.

There is a great deal that can be done to overcome anxiety, and music is one of the best of these. In general, what is needed is music of a pronounced rhythmic and melodic character. To name a few works, out of the vast literature of music, which are refreshing and sufficiently stimulating to keep the mind alert, and yet not demanding too much concentration, we would head the list with any of Chopin's Mazurkas and Preludes, such works as his NOCTURNE IN E FLAT, OPUS 9, NO. 2, the more cheerful songs of Schubert and Schumann and Grieg, Leybach's famous old 5TH NOCTURNE, the exhilarating yet not agitating Strauss waltzes, the melodious arias of Verdi and Bellini, which we continue to whistle and hum after the opera, and many of the standbys from the Family Music Albums, such as Nevin's NARCISSUS, MacDowell's TO A WATER LILY, Rubenstein's MELODY IN F, Dvorak's HUMORESQUE. For individuals of more strictly musical sensitivity, the pure beauty of Mozart's sonatas, his little symphony EINE KLEINE NACHTMUSIK, the first and second movements of Beethoven's 8TH SYMPHONY are highly recommended.

The library of superb phonographic recordings of good music is now so extensive that one can readily select from the classics. For the anxious individual most of the symphonic works of Brahms, Strauss and Sibelius, the later Wagner music dramas, and much of the severely modern intellectual music is to be avoided. Many of the songs of Schubert, Brahms and Wolff are too definitely expressive of particular emotions and too burdened with "thought" to be of much comfort to a person who is going through a period of anxiety and emotional tension.

There are, of course, among the works of these last-named composers many instances of sheer loveliness, free from stress and over-subjectivity, such as the SIEGFRIED WALDWEBEN, Schubert's DU BIST DIE RUH', the MEISTERSINGER PRIZE SONG, Brahms' famous LULLABY and SAPPHIC ODE, the 3rd movement of his FIRST SYMPHONY and the 3rd of his SECOND SYMPHONY which are particularly suitable for anxious moments.

Music is a natural substitute for states of fantasy, anxiety and excitement. It can be used most successfully to take you out of yourself. When you are in a state of anxiety, you are emotionally disturbed and excessively worried about matters close to you. In such times you are almost certainly self-centered, self-contemplative and preoccupied with alarming and disturbing thoughts. Music at such times helps to disrupt the preoccupation with such thoughts. For such occasions, the following have proved of great value: Tschaikowsky's MARCH MOVEMENT from the SYMPHONIE PATHETIQUE, Beethoven's EGMONT OVERTURE, Liszt's HUNGARIAN RHAPSODY, NO. 2, Ippolitov-Ivanov's MARCH OF THE SIRDARS, Godard's BERCEUSE from JOCELYN, Mascagni's Intermezzi from CAVALLERIA RUSTICANA, Beethoven's PASTORALE SYMPHONY and Mendelssohn's ON WINGS OF SONG.

For the nervous exhaustion that results from prolonged anxiety we need the serene beauty of the variations from the APPASSIONATA

SONATA of Beethoven, or the noble simplicity of the mellow German chorales like O HAUPT VOLL BLUT UND WUNDEN. For the mental fatigue of anxious moments there is the PARSIFAL GOOD FRIDAY SPELL, with its cool harmonies and promise of spiritual renewal; the largo of the SYMPHONY FROM THE NEW WORLD; the full-throated slow movement of Haydn's SYMPHONY NO. 13—like the wind through the trees of a stately park; and those deeply serene, long-phrased lyrics of Brahms' FELDEINSAMKEIT and DER TOD DAS IST DIE KUEHLE NACHT.

Anxiety is what psychiatrists call a "reality situation." We become anxious because the situation which we are up against is full of threats of an unknown origin. According to psychiatric theory, listening to music leads to fantasy and this fantasy helps us to break away from the reality situation and in this way we help free ourselves from the anxiety. Listening to music requires a minimum of effort along this direction.

Anxiety is connected with our everyday life and affairs. Music evokes feelings that are emancipated from our everyday affairs, feelings not those of daily life. When you listen to music you attain a state of consciousness free from worldly associations. You are taken out of yourself, removed from your troubled ego. This is a wholesome and most desirable experience.

George Little was constantly on edge. He was aware of a feeling of tightness almost all the time. This tightness he felt mostly in his head and around the eyes. He also had a sensation of tension around the abdomen. He stated: "When I get tightened up my energy goes. I get tired very easily, and I feel depressed and hopeless about everything. I dread facing whatever I have to do. Quite often I feel like a bump of a log." He was worried about quite a few things, about not earning as much money as he thought he should, about not being able to get along with his associates in a more amiable way, about the constant petty quarrels with his wife. Mr. Little was, as he aptly described himself, a quivering bundle of nerves. While getting him straightened out about these morbid fears we started him on musical therapy. He was asked to set aside three hours a day for listening to music, preferably at night, before bed time. The musical compositions recommended in his case were the following: Bartos, Bourgeois Gentilhomme, Suite; Berg, Lyric Suite; Bizet, Jeux d'enfants; Bliss, Miracle of the Gorbals; Boccherini, Symphony in A; Borodin, Symphony No. 2; Chabrier, Polish Dance; Delibes, Sylvia, Ballet Suite; Delius, Over the Hills and Far Away; Dukas, Sorcerer's Apprentice, and Gershwin's Cuban Overture. After a course of musical treatment which lasted three weeks, many of the acute anxiety symptoms were greatly relieved, and Mr. Little was in a much happier mood.

Doris Clemens had noticed that lately she had become quite irritable, tired easily and experienced a strange feeling of deadness in her hands and feet. She also experienced a choking sensation in her throat. There were times when she felt very tired, had frequent dizzy spells and headaches. The merest trifles set her nerves on edge and caused her to have "butterflies in her stomach." She felt that she was under a constant threat of some kind, some dark and shapeless danger seemed always to hover over her. For her music therapy was instituted with quite happy results. The musical compositions prescribed in her case were: Gillis, Alamo; Glinka, Jola, Arogonesa; Gluck, Pantomime Ballet from Don Juan; Grofe, Atlanta Crossing; Janacek, Lach Dances; Lecuona, Andalucia Suite; Moussorgsky, Pictures of an Exhibition; Ravel, Bolero; Regen, Bocklin Suite; Satie, Parade. In time her headaches disappeared, she felt less tired and the strange feelings in her hands and feet disappeared. She began to feel less apprehensive and less afraid.

Recent psychiatric studies with music in various cases of mental and emotional disturbances have brought to light the following facts:

1. Music has the property of producing various moods, and by means of appropriate music an anxious mood may be dispelled by a hopeful mood induced by music.

2. Music has the property of facilitating self-expression, and by expressing the tensions that give rise to anxieties, the latter are quite often eliminated.
3. The associative response whereby music stimulates the process of thought, and of both memory and fantasy formation, makes it evident that such stimulation may facilitate the expression of repressed or unconscious mental elements which give rise to anxiety. Thus the anxiety is eliminated.

There is no doubt that music is one of the best means of getting rid of your anxieties. It certainly requires no complicated measures to listen to good music. It is the most pleasant way to keep your emotions untroubled.

MODERATING ANGER WITH MUSIC

By JAMES GIRARD, M.A.

Psychologist, Boston, Mass.

Anger is one of the most destructive of the emotions. It is an emotional disturbance which arises from a frustration of needs, or injury where satisfaction of needs had formerly been encountered. Anger is an expression of extreme unhappiness, dissatisfaction, unfulfillment and discouragement.

In a way anger serves as an emotional safety valve; it helps to reduce our inner pressures and tensions. Excessive and frequent outbursts of anger, however, are dangerous. Emotional outburst, if carried too far, becomes a form of self-destruction. Anger is often the trigger that sets off severe headaches, palpitation of the heart and a badly upset digestion. Anger is a very unhealthy eruption for any of us to experience frequently.

How can you moderate your tendencies to anger? By replacing bad feelings with good feelings, by altering the rhythm of your emotions, you can accomplish a great deal in the way of moderating your anger. Music has been found to be an excellent means of controlling and preventing angry outbursts.

Many hundreds of years ago, Plato in his REPUBLIC said: "We do not want a nation of prize-fighters and weight-lifters. Perhaps music will solve our problem; through music the soul learns harmony and rhythm and even disposition to justice; for can he who is harmoniously constituted ever be unjust? Rhythm and harmony find their way into the secret places of the soul, bearing grace in their movements, and making the soul graceful. Music moulds character, and therefore shares in determining social and political issues."

Modern scientists have proved that music has a very definite relationship to the emotions. Dr. Hanslic asserts: "Music evokes feelings that are emancipated from worldly affairs." Anger is definitely and completely linked up with worldly affairs. Further, music has the power to modify one emotion and transform it into another. In this way anger may be modified, moderated or controlled.

Drs. Schoen and Gatewood carried out an extensive series of experiments with music in conditioning emotional effects. The following table, a summary of these experiments, is most revealing.

Emotional Quality	Relative Frequency
Rest	.39
Sadness	.45
Joy	.41
Love	.35
Longing	.30
Amusement	.12
Dignity	.20
Stirring	.28
Reverence	.14
Disgust	.02
Irritation	.08

The greatest effects of music from the emotional point of view are in inducing rest, joy and love, and the least in inducing disgust and irritation. For this very good reason it is very effective in replacing any angry mood with that of a restful one.

Psychiatric research with music in modifying the emotions has yielded the following facts. There are three categories of responses an emotionally disturbed individual makes to musical stimuli.

1. Through musical stimuli the muscular tensions which tend to bring about anger are effectively dissipated.
2. A new emotional response is awakened, by using appropriate music which replaces the state of anger with one of calmness.
3. Music stimulates thought and fantasy formation and such stimulation facilitates the expression of repressed feelings which give rise to anger.

Anger, being a violent state of emotional upheaval, requires music of a calming and sedative nature. Sedative music may be:

1. Meditative, such as SONG TO THE EVENING STAR, from Tannhauser, by Wagner.
2. Soothing, like Brahms' LULLABY.
3. Music with rhythmic flow, like LOVE'S OLD SWEET SONG.
4. Music with poetic thought, like Debussy's CLAIRE DE LUNE.
5. Reveries, such as Nevin's THE ROSARY.
6. Depressing, such as Chopin's THE FUNERAL MARCH.

In a series of experiments with music in moderating anger the following musical compositions have been found to be quite effective: Bach, Cantata No. 82; Ballantine, Variation on Mary Had a Little Lamb; Bartok, Out of Doors Suite; Beethoven, Moonlight Sonata; Bizet, Symphony No. 1 in C; Bloch, Quartet No. 2; Boccherini, Sonata No. 6; Brahms, Quartet No. 2 in A; Chausson, Symphony in B flat; Chopin, Concerto No. 2 in D Minor; Copland, Quiet City; Corelli, Suite for String Orchestra; Couperin, Concerto No. 6; Debussy, Nocturne; Dvorak, Quintet in G; Elgar, Concerto in B minor; Falla, Suite Populaire Espagnole; Fauré, La Bonne Chanson; Francaix, Serenade for 12 Instruments; Franck, Symphony in D Minor; Glinka, Trio Pathetique; Grieg, Sonata in A Minor; Grofe, Aviation Suite; Handel, Concerto in D; Haydn, Quartet in F; Ives, String Quartet No. 2; Kabalevsky, Comedians; Liszt, Sonata in B Minor; Locatelli, Trauer Symphony; Mozart, Musical Joke; Mardini, Concerto in E Minor; Prokofiev, Sonata in D; Rachmaninoff, Sonata in G minor; Ravel, Ma Mère l'Oye;

Roussel, Symphony No. 4; Saint-Saens, Carnival of Animals; Schubert, Symphony No. 6 in B flat; Schumann, Dichterliebe; Smetana, Quartet in E Minor; Tschaikowsky, Concerto in D, and Telemnan, Sonata in E Minor.

Physiological experiments on the effects of music have proved that sedative music has just the opposite effects on the body that anger has. In this rather remarkable way music has proved of very definite value in softening some of the devastating effects of anger. Anger increases the pulse rate; sedative music decreases it. Anger raises the blood pressure; music of a sedative nature has the effect of lowering it. Anger cuts down on and interrupts the flow of the gastric juices and quite seriously interferes with digestion. On the other hand, calming and soothing music restores the flow of digestive juices, often encourages it and in this way aids the digestive processes. Anger tenses up the muscles, often tying them into painful knots. Music has a relaxing effect on the muscles and cases of dark tensions.

Further psychological research has revealed the fact that tonal and rhythmic musical patterns have been found to affect the human being on all levels; on the emotional level, evidenced by emotional responses of different kinds to different kinds of music; on the rhythmic level, affecting coordination, equilibrium and bodily rhythm; on the intellectual level, stimulating thought and imagery, and on the psychic level, as evidenced by creative and aesthetic responses. These are definite responses which have been measured by various psychological tests. Particularly has music been found of value in modifying emotional responses, and as a means of moderating or dissipating anger, music is of undoubted value. This has been demonstrated time and time again in various mental hospitals and clinics.

Music has the added capacity to reconcile the most contrasted and foreign feelings. It can arouse and calm almost at the same time. It can bring us nearer to the spiritual and yet it does not separate us from the instinctual. Music, in addition to the physiological and psychological properties possesses properties which no other agents or media have; it has in it the spiritual and the aesthetic. The purity of music is even more essential than the purity of drugs and chemicals. I am thoroughly convinced that every person interested in his own emotional health can take advantage of music in a great many ways to control his undesirable and destructive emotional tendencies.

MUSIC THERAPY IN DEPRESSION

By E. P. HERMAN, M.S.

Clinical Psychologist, Brooklyn, N. Y.

Grief is not the only emotion that brings about depression. Everyone of us gets the "blues" occasionally. There are times when we feel pretty low in spirit and "down in the dumps." A feeling of depression may come as a result of feeling that we have not been able to accomplish what we should have liked to, as a result of the loss of an important position, as the result of not being able to get along with others as we should like to. There are many of these frustrations in daily life, and any or all of them are quite likely to make us feel blue.

A person suffering from the "blues" behaves in a very characteristic manner. He is sluggish in his movements, his speech and flow of thoughts. This may be mild, or in some cases rather severe. He cannot sleep, and in general feels very miserable. In some cases he withdraws from everyday interests. There is a lack of interest in his surroundings. He loses interest in his friends, in his business and in his home. He is so engrossed in his own distress, that he has no interest in any activity whatever.

In time an attitude of self-depreciation and disparagement is assumed. He believes that everyone is too good to associate with him, that he deserves no consideration or kindness. He feels that he is a useless liability. Toward the future he has an attitude of hopelessness.

The feeling of "down in the dumps" is a very unpleasant one. The victim complains of headaches, dyspepsia, a feeling of weight in the stomach, a bad taste in the mouth, constipation, blurring of vision, irritability, lassitude, general weakness and fatigue.

The pervasive feeling of depression is also productive of difficulty in doing ordinary work and in poor concentration and sustained effort. Reading and writing are difficult and whatever sleep he gets is not in the least refreshing.

There are many ways to overcome the blues and one of the best and most pleasant is by means of music. Music has been used for a great many years as a valuable and effective means of dispelling depression. The first recorded instance is that of David who cured King Saul of his black depression by playing lively tunes on his harp. Since then many thousands of instances of the value of music in overcoming depression have been recorded.

Gerald Ford had failed to win the promotion he had been so eagerly anticipating for the past three years. Following this he became morbidly depressed and anxious. He searched himself for reasons which might account for his failure to win the promotion and felt that he had been cheated. The more he thought about this the more depressed he became. He was emotionally dull, listless and apathetic. He felt fatigued and could not concentrate to do even the most ordinary tasks. He was restless and could hardly sit still for more than five minutes at a time. After about a week of being blue and utterly miserable, he consented to see if music would be of value in snapping him out of his blue funk. Accordingly, he was given musical therapy with musical compositions in the main of a stimulating mood. The compositions used in his case were: Bach, Brandenburg Concerto No. 2 in F; Bartok, Hungarian Folk Songs; Beethoven, Egmont Overture; Bizet, Carmen Suite; Brahms, Academic Festival Overture; Copland, Danzin Cubano; Debussy, Iberia; Gershwin, Second Rhapsody for Piano and Orchestra; Gilbert and Sullivan, Trial by Jury; Gillis, Songs of a Prairie School; Haydn, Creation (Oratorio); Janacek, Youth; Kabalevsky, Comedians, and Kern's Show Boat. He listened to these compositions some three hours a day. Within four days he began to snap out of his depression. He began to show a marked interest in his surroundings; he became more alive and attentive and within a week he was his normal self again.

Albert Gans had lost a considerable sum of money in a risky business transaction and he took this very much to heart. He became depressed, listless, apathetic and tense. Most of the time he brooded in silence and lost interest in his work and surroundings. He expressed a willingness to undergo a session of musical treatment to see how he would respond. He devoted three hours daily for one week listening to music. The musical compositions used in his case were: Liszt, Hungarian Rhapsody No. 2; Milhaud, Carnival; Mozart, Impresario; Offenbach, Helen of Troy; Prokofiev, Scythian Suite; Puccini, Fairy Queen; Respighi, Feste Romane; Rimsky-Korsakov, Scheherazade; Rodgers, Oklahoma; Rossini, William Tell Overture; Sibelius, Finlandia; Smetana, Wallenstein's Camp; Strauss, Music of Old Vienna; Suppe, Poet and Peasant Overture, and Wagner, Parsifal; Prelude. After two sessions he was able to relax and take an interest in his surroundings. He was able to resume his work after four sessions and at the end of the week he was entirely free of his depressive mood.

Dr. Max Schoen, who has done a great deal of research with music on the emotions, has found that there is a close connection between feeling and music. The evidence for this statement he finds in the following tendencies:

1. When people are instructed to listen to a musical composition and report what it does to them, their accounts begin often with the phrases: "It makes me feel," "I feel like," "It gave me the feeling" and similar phrases.

2. The results obtained from experimental researches on the physiological effects produced by music show that music has effects on the pulse, heart beat, blood pressure, breathing, etc.

3. Music always brings about changes which are primarily emotional in character.

Music of a lively nature is indicated in cases of the "blues." Such music has definite effects on all the processes of the body. It increases bodily metabolism, which is usually decreased in states of depression. It increases muscular energy, which is retarded when one feels "down in the dumps." It increases the blood pressure and pulse rate which are definitely slowed down in any depressive state. It helps to decrease fatigue, which is an outstanding symptom of depression. It reduces suggestibility which very often is among the prime causes of depression. It also has a tendency to reduce the extent of illusions by acting as a distracting factor.

Psychiatrists who have been using music in the treatment of emotional disorders have found that music has the additional properties.

1. It has the property of attracting attention and prolonging its span, which is very important in depression. By attracting attention away from the thoughts which produce the depression music makes an effective inroad into the consciousness of the individual and gets him out of his depressive mood.

2. Music has the property of replacing one mood with another. Thus, it replaces the feeling of being "down in the dumps" with one of pleasure and often of mild elation.

3. Music has the property of relieving the inner tensions and conflicts that give rise to the depressive mood.

4. Through the rhythmic stimuli that music brings about, muscular activity is brought about which results in physical motion, which in turn helps pull the individual out of his morbid fancies and draws his attention to things happening around him.

There is no doubt that music is one of the best antidotes against all sorts of depressive moods. It works with pleasing effectiveness, and best of all it leaves no undesirable after-effects.

RELAXING MUSIC FOR EMOTIONAL FATIGUE

By E. P. HERMAN, M.S.

Clinical Psychologist, Brooklyn, N. Y.

Emotional fatigue is a rather commonplace phenomenon in our modern, high-pressured environment. It affects all sorts of people, but particularly it affects the ambitious, the spirited and the strong-willed, who from a strong sense of duty or out of sheer enthusiasm drive their minds and emotions beyond the limit of safety. Before they are aware of it, their mental and emotional over-activity super-saturates their systems with fatigue by-products to such a degree that they must take active measures to fend off rather serious bodily damages.

When this condition has persisted for any appreciable length of time, the total physical, psychical and moral calibre of the individual may become so changed and warped that he can rarely go back to a normal, well-adjusted state without some rather drastic overhauling. In the main, emotional fatigue has the unfortunate tendency to become chronic. Quite often, in addition to other factors, emotional fatigue may be due to deep-rooted personality difficulties.

Just as undue expenditure of physical energy results in a tired feeling so will the lavishing of too much emotional energy result in a similar state of fatigue. Fear, anxiety, apprehension and worry are some of the emotions which, when uncontrolled, result in a state of emotional fatigue.

In a study conducted by a group of prominent psychiatrists as to what emotional factors commonly result in fatigue it was found that frustration, depression, induced by worry, fear and uncertainty regarding the future, anxiety resulting from the assumption of important duties, marital difficulties, financial obligations and social pressures are usually the basis of emotional fatigue.

Emotional tiredness is quite characteristic. The one so affected is quick to anger; he finds faults over trifles quite readily. He has difficulty in going to sleep, because he is usually under so great a tension that it is impossible for him to relax. Quite often he is depressed. He is quite likely to experience a great deal of anxiety, mostly over things that do not matter.

As time goes on emotional fatigue results in a loss of poise and difficulty in getting on with people. Trifles become upsetting and disturbing. Ill manners and inconsiderate acts are quite frequent when one is emotionally tired.

In the life of every person a proper balance must exist between the factors of work, rest, recreation, and special relationship with other human beings. Maladjustment to any of the above mentioned factors produces worry, which is essentially mental preoccupation with real or fancied difficulties. The effect of worry in diminishing the reserve of emotional energy and producing emotional fatigue is undisputed.

What can be done to minimize emotional fatigue? There are a few simple measures which anyone can take. At least eight hours of sleep should be obtained. Maintain a state of physical fitness. Eat the proper foods. Rest and relaxation are of the utmost value, particularly relaxation.

In this connection music is of great importance. Music is something that anyone can take. Music is easier to relax to than any other modality. It is particularly of value in all cases of emotional fatigue. This has been proven clinically and experimentally by psychological investigation.

Max Herbert was always on edge, always under unbearable pressure, ready for anger and unpleasantness. The past two months he had not spoken a civil word to any of his friends or relatives.

[117]

He was always tired, sometimes so tired that he could not sleep or relax for even a moment. In a word, Max was a victim of emotional fatigue. In addition to other hygienic measures he was exposed to musical stimuli for two hours every afternoon. This form of musical relaxation was given for a period of two weeks. These musical compositions were used in his case: Bach, Coffee Cantata; Beethoven, Creatures of Prometheus; Brahms, Mariendlieder; Britten, Peter Grimes; Chasins, Parade: Period Piece; Chopin, Nocturnes; Couperin, Concert Dan Le Gout Theatral; Debussy, La Demoiselle Bleu; Donahyi, Suite En Valse; Dvorak, Husitka Overture; Falla, Nights in the Gardens of Spain; Glinka, Sextet; Grieg, Lyric Pieces; Handel, Water Music Suite; Haydn, Trio in G; Hummel, Septet; Lamber, Horoscope, and Liszt, Mephisto Waltz. Within four days Herbert had acquired the art of relaxation to such a degree that most of his tensions were dissipated. He felt more refreshed and was less on edge, less ready to quarrel and find fault. At the end of two weeks he was back to his old self again.

Quite similar was Lena Backstrom. For the past three months she had been under a frightful tension that was insidiously being built up. She burst into tears at the least provocation. She screamed at her husband and children. She was incessantly tired; her muscles ached under the strain. She could not sleep, she could not eat properly. In short, she had all the signs and symptoms of a full-blown case of emotional fatigue. In addition to other hygienic measures that were instituted, a definite musical program to bring about relaxation was also started. She listened to and relaxed to music every mid-morning for two and a half weeks. Within the first five days she began to feel much better and had begun to acquire the ability to relax. The musical compositions used in her case were: Poulenc, Suite Française; Mozart, Adagio and Fugue in C Minor; Mendelssohn, Midsummer Night's Dream; Milhaud, Concertino de Printemps; Vivaldi, Four Seasons; Tschaikowsky, Sleeping Beauty Waltz; Respighi, Pines of Rome; Ravel, Gaspard de la

Nuite; Rameau, Les Indes Galantes; Prokofiev, Visions Fugitives; Rachmaninoff, Trio in D Minor; Schumann, Concerto in A Minor; Schubert, Divertissement à la Hongroise, and Saint-Saens, Fantasie. At the end of the musical sessions she was entirely free of all painful tensions and her emotional fatigue was a thing of the past. She was bright, cheerful and quite happy.

That music has the power to modify the condition of the individual has been demonstrated by scientific investigators. Physiological studies with music on human beings have brought to light some very interesting facts. It has been found that music tends to reduce or delay fatigue and consequently increases endurance. It has the power to speed up voluntary activities. It increases the extent of muscular reflexes.

There is no doubt that music arouses emotional responses in those who listen to it. In cases of emotional fatigue the proper kind of music also does something that transforms the inner feeling to one of peace and repose. While other stimuli arouse negative or positive moods, the mood is always positive in music. This is what raises it to the sphere of the aesthetic and makes music the universal healer.

The pleasant feeling-tone produced by music has a relaxing and soothing effect on emotional tension and fatigue. Emotional energies are moderated and evened out when the music is of a soothing nature. The physical and mental effects are quite pronounced and measurable; they become manifested in quite a short time.

In the case of emotional fatigue music of a sedative quality has the power to change the state of heightened tension and pressure to one of quiet and repose. In addition music has the power of bringing the expenditure of emotional energy from the unconscious level to that of the conscious and intellectually controlled level. In this way the unwise and unplanned expenditure of emotional outpourings is moderated and controlled.

Music has the power also of establishing and maintaining the proper emotional relationship between the individual, his work and his environment. It reduces boredom and the diffuse, aimless expenditure of energy which is used in an attempt to overcome boredom. It induces a sensation of pleasantness and contentment. It relieves inner tensions and pressures. There is no doubt that music is of value in cases of emotional fatigue.

MUSIC THERAPY FOR EMOTIONAL DISTURBANCES

By BERNARD HILLIARD, Ph.D.

Clinical Psychologist, New York, N. Y.

When an individual fails to find conditions which keep him in a constant state of well-being, he experiences an unpleasant emotion accompanied by ideas of retaliation and the use of force to gain his ends, even of the destruction of the person or things which make him uncomfortable or which thwart him. This is hatred.

Prolonged hatred can hardly produce the swift and quickly manifested tragic effects of a single shocking fear or rage reaction. But in terms of its long range destructive properties, hatred is without a doubt the most dangerous of all the emotions. Prolonged hatred means, after all, a continuous damming back of rage reactions. In time the heart, the lungs, the stomach, the blood vessels as well as the mind and spirit begin to show the corrosive effects of a long-continued smouldering hatred.

People who hate live in fear of being overwhelmed by powers they are too weak to withstand. Particularly, economically and emotionally, they are fearful of everyday events. They fear that something may happen to them which would shatter them completely. They hate because they fear and do not understand the reason for their fear. They are confused, bewildered and very unhappy.

Hatred is a poisonous, debasing and de-humanizing emotion. It is harmful in a great many ways: organically, spiritually, mentally, emotionally and socially. It gives rise to conflicts and tensions. In time it destroys.

[121]

Much can be done in the way of moderating or eliminating hatred. Music has been used for many years to replace hatred with other and more useful emotions. Music, having the faculty of conditioning moods, has been used with success by psychiatrists and psychologists in reconditioning the individual and eliminating for a while this corrosive and destructive feeling. Music, of the appropriate kind, has a soothing, calming and moderating effect. It is worthwhile for those who are easily aroused by hatred to experiment with music along this direction. In a great many instances music has proved of undoubted value in controlling hatred.

Dr. Ira Altshuler, a well known psychiatrist, who has had considerable experience with music in the treatment of mental and emotional disturbances has found that music has the power of diversion and substitution (such as distracting from morbid states and replacing them with wholesome feelings and ideas). This is applicable in cases of hatred, where the unwholesome state of hatred is replaced with a feeling of peace and security. Further he found that music has the capacity to modify the mood, that of anger in this case and replace it with a sense of peaceful satisfaction.

For moderating hatred brought on by any circumstances, music can be used with some degree of success in most cases. Here are a few suggestions:

Gounod	Soldiers' Chorus
Wagner	Sword Episode, from Die Walkurie
Wagner	Spring Song
Gounod	The Meeting, from Faust
Gounod	Love Duet, from Faust
Haydn	Water Music
Grieg	Concerto in A Minor
Ives	Largo for violin
Martucci	Symphony No. 2 in F, Op. 81
Mendelssohn	Symphony No. 4 in A, Op. 90.

Music, by acting on the increased blood pressure, the increased heart rate, the accelerated rate of breathing found in the state and condition of hatred, helps to moderate these increased physiological stresses brought about and nurtured by hatred, and in this way control the ill effects inflicted on the body. Music particularly suitable for softening these onslaughts can be found in the following compositions:

Strauss	Tales of the Vienna Woods
Herbert	Fortune Teller
Drdla	Souvenir
Chopin	Nocturne in F Flat
Kreisler	The Old Refrain
Rimsky-Korsakov	Flight of the Bumble Bee
Tschaikowsky	Waltz of the Flowers
Berniers	The Triumph of Neptune
Bartok	Quartet No. 1 in A Minor, Op. 7
Beethoven	Sonata No. 17 in D Minor, Op. 31, No. 2
Brahms	Symphony No. 2 in D, Op. 73
Bruch	Concerto No. 1 in G Minor
Corelli	Sonata in D Minor
Easdale	Red Shoes ballet music
Franck	Fantasia in C.

Since one is able to measure the effects of music on an individual's mood with fairly uniform accuracy, it is possible to select certain appropriate types of music to normalize any transient abnormal mood, such as hatred. Hatred is always accompanied by both mental and physical changes. Music has the power to modify these changes.

Various theories have been advanced to explain the relationship between music and emotion. Dr. Hanslic has said that "Music evokes feelings that are emancipated from worldly affairs . . . . feelings not those of daily life. A person attains a state of consciousness free from world association." In the case of hatred music helps to take the individual out of himself, away from the factors that are causing hatred. The stimuli causing him to hate are abolished and replaced with those of a more pleasant nature.

Dr. M. Schoen, who has done considerable experimental work with music, found that music is of the greatest value in cases of emotional disturbances. Music has the power of arousing emotion. It has the power that transforms that emotion to one of peace and repose. Dr. Schoen is of the opinion that the feeling stimulated by music is not a specific emotion, but a general feeling state, or mood. "Musical emotion is thus a state of repose in tension." While other stimuli arouse negative or positive moods, the mood is always positive in music.

Dr. Altshuler has advanced the theory that music has an effect on that part of the brain known as the thalamus. The thalamus is the main relay station of the emotions, sensations and feelings. The thalamus is situated directly below the cerebrum, or main part of the brain, and it is connected to it by nerve pathways. The stimulation of the thalamus almost invariably affects the cerebrum. Hatred is an emotion and as such is aroused in the thalamus. By close association with the cerebrum this emotion enters the higher centers of the brain, dulling judgment, reason and altering all the normal processes that go for normal interpersonal relations. Music by exerting calming and moderating effects on the thalamus directly and on the cerebrum indirectly is able to control hatred and restore normal behavior.

Music, in the case of hatred, serves as emotional catharsis. Music pieces suitable for chronic hatred, or hatred that has reached full blossom are the following:

Roussel	Symphony in G
Herbert	Italian Street Song
Sibelius	Finlandia
Burleigh	Deep River
Lalo	Symphonie Espagnole
MacDowell	Indian Suite
Haydn	Clock Symphony

Smetana	The Moldau
Bizet	Prelude from L'Arlesienne Suite
Bach	Italian Concerto
Beethoven	Sonata No. 14 in C Sharp Minor
Boccherini	Trios 1, 3, 6, Op. 35
Chausson	Poem for violin
Chopin	Ballades
Couperin	Apotheose de Lully
Debussy	En Blanc et Noir
Dvorak	Symphony in E Flat
Handel	Jephte Suite
Haydn	Symphony No. 1 in D
Ibert	Escales
Kern	Mark Twain
Kodaly	Hary Janos Suite
Lecocq	Mlle. Angol Suite
Massenet	Le Cid Ballet Suite
Milhaud	Symphony No. 1
Mozart	Fantasia in C Minor.

All of these musical compositions have definite physical and psychological effects. They ease the inner tensions and conflicts that give rise to hatred and they calm the overactive heart and brain.

Jealousy is as much a part of human nature as anger or fear or love. It belongs to us whether we like it or not. When it rises out of bounds it twists the life, not only of the jealous individual, but the loves of those he touches. Jealousy has its origin in fear or in uncertainty or in rejected tendencies which in time give rise to feelings of guilt. Jealousy arises when A loves B and A identifies B as loving C. It is a most uncomfortable feeling which takes its roots in a loss of self-esteem.

Jealousy is compounded of grief, the pain being caused by the thought of losing the one who is loved. There are feelings of enmity toward the successful rival and of a greater or lesser amount of self-criticism which tries to hold the person himself accountable for his loss.

Jealousy is not limited to any particular period in life; it appears all through life, from the cradle to the grave. Jealousy is a source of unbridled hatred in children as well as in adults. There is no doubt that jealousy of one or the other parent in children is a very real and devastating experience. There is also no doubt about the role that jealousy plays between brothers and sisters and other close relatives.

Jealousy is always a selfish emotion. It is always the fear of losing something. We hate to lose anything. There is much less pleasure in finding something than in the pain in losing something.

Jealousy is awakened and excited by wounds to self-love and to pride. Jealousy is not a matter of the sex of the individual but of temperamental constitution. Self-loving individuals are more prone to jealousy than others, irrespective of sex.

We all agree that jealousy is undesirable. Yet what can be done to moderate the pain of jealousy? Jealousy is an emotion, and as such can be, in a way, moderated and modified by appropriate musical stimuli. Under the right conditions music can be used quite successfully to dissipate some of the effects of jealousy. While music is not a panacea in this condition, it has some value.

Music replaces the devitalizing emotional effects of jealousy with a happier, more care-free mood. Listening to appropriate melodies is of definite benefit. Taking an active part in producing music is of even greater benefit. Playing a musical instrument affords a type of activity in which any inappropriate emotional conflict and pressure is effectively dissipated.

If you cannot play a musical instrument, singing is a very good substitute. The mere act of singing is a joyous experience. As a rhythmic exercise it is of undoubted benefit to both mind and body. It imparts a great sense of exhilaration, a smoothing out of emotional wrinkles and brings about a genuine recovery of good spirits. On any occasion singing is a mild but stimulating activity.

Music is a wonderful tonic to the emotions. "If I feel jealous," a friend once said to me, "I like to listen to Gershwin's RHAPSODY

IN BLUE. The scarlet of the brass in this composition lifts me out of my jealousy and makes me see things in their proper light."

Music has always had a very definite place in the scheme of things. According to Dr. Walter Cannon ". . . . music arouses emotions and releases adrenalin and perhaps other hormones." The capacity of music to arouse emotional responses can be linked with the biological evolution of music. Biologically, sounds are used to lure, to convey, to warn and to challenge. Music, which is a meaningful combination of sounds, can do all of these with greater emotional emphasis.

Dr. S. Pfeifer claims that music provides a method of escaping reality through its basic rhythm which preoccupies the consciousness to the degree that unconscious fantasies are released. Jealousy which is an emotional experience in which one is constantly preoccupied with thoughts of injury to self-esteem, is replaced by an emotionally charged mood in which these thoughts are replaced by others of a more pleasurable nature, and this is quite easily accomplished by the proper type of musical composition. In addition, music provides a feeling of unity and belonging; it serves to unite the individual with those about him on the warmest and friendliest terms. In this way it helps effectively to disrupt antisocial and ill feelings.

There are many appropriate musical compositions readily available which can be used to replace the feeling of jealousy and suspicion with a mood of emotional calm and contentment. Here are a few suggestions:

Anthiel	Piano Sonata No. 4
Auber	Overtures
Bach	Cantata No. 21
Barber	Sonata for Piano
Bartok	Quartet No. 5
Bax	Elegiac
Beethoven	Fantasia in C Minor
Bellini	Norma Overture

Bizet	Fair Maid of Perth Suite
Boccherini	Quintet in C
Borodin	Quartet No. 1 in A
Brahms	Quartet No. 3 in C Minor
Britten	Matinees Musicales
Bruch	Scottish Fantasy
Bruckner	Symphony No. 5 in B Flat
Chopin	Nocturne in D Flat
Copland	Rodeo
Cowell	Ancient Desert Drone
Debussy	La Mer
Dvorak	Quintet in A, Op. 81
Dello	New York Profiles
Elgar	Overture: Cockaigne, Op. 40
Falla	Three Cornered Hat
Fauré	Impromptu
Gillis	Men Who Invented Music
Grieg	Haughtussa
Handel	Acis and Galatea
Haydn	Octet in F
Mahler	Songs of a Wayfarer
Mendelssohn	Capricio Brillant
Milhaud	Suite Française
Mozart	Serenade No. 12 in C Minor
Prokofiev	Symphony No. 5, Op. 100
Ravel	Quartet in F
Roussel	Suite in F
Scarlatti	Cat's Fugue
Schubert	Quartet in A, Op. 114

Psychological investigation in recent years has demonstrated that music has the following properties:

1. Music can bring about different moods, conditioned by different emotional states.
2. Music has the property of stimulating different mental images and mental associations having various emotional bases.
3. Music has the property of facilitating self-expression and in

this way giving vent to disturbing emotional upheavals and dissipating them.

4. Music has the property of relieving internal emotional pressures and tensions.

Music, by exerting these various effects, is of pronounced value in moderating the devitalizing effects of jealousy and replacing them with moods that are conducive with peace of mind and inner harmony. Music, it has been ascertained, reaches the sub-cortical centers of the brain and thereby helps to integrate the personality that is being disrupted by jealousy and other unhealthy emotions.

MUSIC THERAPY FOR ACUTE GRIEF

By LOUIS M. BROWN, M.A.

Music Therapist, Brooklyn, N. Y.

Grief is an experience that all of us have to experience at one time or another. Needless to say it is a very painful experience. It entails severe emotional and mental upheavals. It disrupts the daily ordered rhythm of life and plunges us into a state of blackest misery.

Grief is an emotion that results because of the loss of a loved person by death or separation. It may appear immediately after the crisis, or it may be delayed.

The duration of grief depends upon the intensity of feeling that the bereaved had for the departed person, his ability to readjust to his new and altered surroundings, and the formation of new relationships. In general, grief is made less painful when one yields to it readily; matters are made worse when the bereaved person tenses up in an endeavor to avoid breaking down.

People react to grief in a variety of ways. One can go through a period of grief with a semblance of normal composure, or he will go through a period of grief suffering a nervous breakdown with serious after-effects. These after-effects may be temporary, or under less favorable conditions they may become quite prolonged.

A person suffering from bereavement usually exhibits the following symptoms:

1. He sighs frequently.
2. There is a considerable loss of strength. Exhaustion is quite

marked. Every little effort is very tiring. Every physical and mental task seems to be an obstacle.

3. The appetite is gone. Food has no taste.
4. The image of the departed person always occupies his thoughts.
5. All initiative is gone.
6. His behavior undergoes certain changes: restlessness, loss of zest, speaking too much, or a long depressing silence.

Music has been found to be among the best methods of allaying grief and opening the way to better emotional tone and feeling. Psychiatrists have found that music has the power of changing one mood into another; thus grief, by appropriate musical stimuli, may be moderated to a very great extent.

Indeed, there is nothing quite like music to overcome the sense of utter desolation that comes with grief. One of the most solacing compositions for the bereaved has been found to be Beethoven's SONATA PATHETIQUE. The slow movement of Brahms' 2ND CELLO SONATA has a healing in its wings. Many of the Bach chorales (which one is apt to find recorded in piano arrangements) seem to make very real that "peace that passeth all understanding."

Beethoven's EROICA SYMPHONY, Wagner's THE RIDE OF THE VALKYRIES, Chopin's WALTZ IN A MINOR, Grieg's PIANO CONCERTO IN A MINOR second movement, Haydn's SYMPHONY 99, 2nd movement, Mendelssohn's ITALIAN SYMPHONY, 2nd movement, Mozart's SYMPHONY 40, 2nd movement, Saint-Saens' THE SWAN, Schumann's ARABESQUE and Dvorak's CARNIVAL OVERTURE, which Robert Haven Schauffler described as "almost like a plunge into an electric fountain of youth," are very effective musical methods of moderating grief. Also along the same lines are Brahms' 1ST SYMPHONY, Sibelius's SWAN OF TUEONALA, Debussy's GOLLIWOG'S CAKE WALK, Paderewski's MINUET IN G, Ruiz's QUANTO LAGUSTO and Enesco's ROUMANIAN RHAPSODY, No. 1.

Allan Wentworth lost his wife in an automobile accident. Shortly thereafter he locked himself in his room, drew the blinds and would sit for hours in utter silence. He refused to take nourishment, neglected his personal appearance. He began to become aware of all sorts of strange bodily sensations, such as a choking sensation in the throat, severe pains in the stomach and a dull pressure around the heart. Musical therapy was instituted in this case. The compositions used were: Auric, Overtures; Bach, Brandenburg Concerto No. 1 in F; Berlioz, Harold in Italy; Delibes, Coppelia Ballet Suite; Elgar, Wand of Youth Suite No. 1; Falla, El Amor Brujo; Grieg, Peer Gynt Suite No. 1 and No. 2; Handel, Messiah; Hindemith, Ludus Tonalis; Kalman, Countess Maritza; Luigini, Ballet Egyptien; Marintu, Three Madrigals; Massenet, Scenes Alsaciennes; Milhaud, La Muse Mesnagere, and Monteverdi, Madrigals. After three days of these musical sessions Allan became more alert. He began to take an interest in food and in his personal appearance. After a week and a half he was free of all symptoms of acute grief.

The next case is that of Anna Fogel whose son had died of infantile paralysis. She was plunged into the deepest grief; she moaned and wrung her hands and at times burst into uncontrollable sobbing. She kept talking of her son constantly. She refused to eat and in a short time experienced severe pains all over her body. Sedatives afforded only temporary relief. Musical treatment was instituted in her case with the following musical compositions: Offenbach, Gaite Parisienne; Poulenc, Bal Masque; Prokofiev, Peter and the Wolf; Rachmaninoff, Etudes Tableux; Respighi, Fountains of Rome; Schutz, St. John Passion; Scriabin, Etude No. 11; Shostakovitch, Quartet No. 3, Op. 73; Siegmeister, Ozark Set; Smetana, Bohemian Dances; Stravinsky, Jeu de Cartes; Telemnan, Sonata Polonaise; Thomson, Louisiana Story; Vivaldi, Concerti in G Minor and E Flat; Weber, Preciosa Overture; Weill, Down in the Valley; Wieniawski, Concerto No. 2 in D Minor, and Walton, Facade.

Bringing music into the mind of one suffering with grief means bringing into it basic realities in the form of feelings, perceptions and imagery. Such material is capable of replacing states of grief, depression, hopelessness and despair. If even this is temporary, such replacements are of great value. However, after many musical sessions, this sad mood is gradually replaced by a cheerful one.

This is exactly what happened in Anna Fogel's case. She gradually became more attentive to her personal needs. She became less aware of uncomfortable bodily sensations. She began to talk less and less about her son. Her crying spells were moderated and in time ceased altogether. Within a matter of two weeks she was entirely normal.

Musical rhythm can be used to restore man to his own natural rhythm which is away from grief and depression. Moods have rhythms of their own, as has music. By utilizing the proper type of music, one mood may be changed gradually and by easy steps, into another, more desirable one.

"Music gives one a moral uplift," is the opinion of Bruno Walter, the orchestra conductor. It also helps lift you out of depressive moods. Listening to music is of value; making music, if one is capable of doing so, is even better. Singing is helpful in grief. It does not matter what you sing. You may prefer to sing a sad, slow rhythmed melody. So much the better. By singing, the unrestricted expression of self is attained and this has a healthful effect on the ego by enabling you to achieve a perfect escapist outlet.

Singing also helps you to ventilate all your pent up feelings. It helps to dissipate the emotionally-charged tensions that grief piles up. When you sing you replace the tendency to sigh and abolish one of the most distressing signs of grief. Singing also causes deeper and more regular breathing, and this also disrupts the rhythm of grief. It also improves the desire for food.

Singing or playing the piano or any other instrument will afford a very desirable form of activity which helps abolish the image of the departed person from the mind. This serves to sever the bondage to the departed and this has a tendency to moderate grief.

In general, it has been found that the major mode in music is happy, merry, graceful and playful; the minor mode is sad, dreamy and sentimental. Firm rhythms are vigorous and dignified; flowing rhythms are happy, graceful, dreamy and tender. Complex, dissonant harmonies are exciting, agitating, vigorous and inclined to sadness. Simple, consonant harmonies are happy, graceful, serene and lyrical. There are tendencies toward the expression of both exhilaration and serenity by the descending melodies, and toward dignity and solemnity by the ascending.

There is no doubt that music, of the proper tempo and rhythm, is of great value in overcoming severe grief reactions. Many psychiatrists as well as mental hospitals have had extensive experience with music as a modality in alleviating depressive states. Such findings have clinical backing. There is no doubt that music can be used by all of us to keep emotionally healthy.

MUSIC AND THE TENSION HEADACHE

By LOUIS M. BROWN, M.A.

Music Therapist, Brooklyn, N. Y.

The nervous type of headache is one that afflicts a great many of us. It is due to inner nervous tensions and to unbearable outer pressures. It has a sneaky way of coming on when a person is under tension and quite fatigued. And when it comes it stays with us for quite a long period of time.

A sick headache is precipitated in a far from calm environment. There almost always occurs an episode in which the person reacts with rage and resentment to which he is unable to give full expression. This usually follows a period of gradually accumulating tensions. The final step in this chain of events may be trivial, but it nevertheless acts as the trigger that brings on the headache.

The person who is most likely to suffer frequently with sick headaches has certain, well-defined characteristics. He is tense, driving, rigid, ambitious and inclined to be a perfectionist. He has found that doing more than and better than his associates brings many rewards. Nevertheless, this is accomplished at a great cost in energy. He strives continually to do a flawless job of whatever he attempts, disregarding his own bodily demands for relaxation.

Such a person, full of drive, always striving to be perfectionistic in his work, and yet unable to attain the perfect results he demands, the ordinary, commonplace events of daily living, produce gradually accumulating tensions which in time result in a rather severe type of nervous headache.

Even the most efficient machine cannot be going day after day at high speed, without a let-up, and continue to function at a high level of efficiency. A human being certainly cannot do so without paying a price. Your nerves can be stretched just so far before they snap. Relaxation is the first rule of living under such circumstances.

That time is of the essense is quite true. This, however, does not certainly mean that you have to do everything at once and at the greatest possible speed. It may be true that you have a great deal of work to do, but it can be done more effectively without being under great pressure to do it. It does not have to be done at a steady pace. You should relax once in a while.

What should be done to prevent sick headaches? First, do not repress emotions, drives and desires. Let them seek their expressions through the normal avenues of discharge. Second: relax, relax, relax.

One of the best and easiest ways to relax is by means of music. Milo E. Benedict has said: "Rhythms are for conducting our train of thought away from all unhappy things that beset us. They convert our thought impulses into mere motion. It is motion with no particular thought purpose. During a performance of rhythms one's intellectual processes are probably the nearest to being nil that one can arrive at outside of sleep itself. Hence the rest we derive from the pursuit of rhythms."

What rhythm shall we pursue in quest of relaxation and freedom from nervous headaches? Fortunately, there are a great many of such rhythms. I have found that certain types of classical music are of value in moderating headaches due to accumulating tensions. This has been proved in quite a few instances. The pieces of music that have stood the test admirably are: Hindemith, Mathis Der Maler; Khachaturian, Masquerade Suite; Lalo, Symphonie Espagnole; Lambert, Rio Grande; Lehar, Der Zarewitsch; Liszt, Hungarian Rhapsody No. 1; Mendelssohn, Elijah; Mozart, Don Giovanni; Nicolai, Merry Wives of Windsor; Offenbach, Tales of Hoffmann; Ponchielli, La Gioconda; Prokofiev, Alexander Nevsky;

Adam, Giselle—Ballet Music; Albeniz, Iberia; Anderson, Irish Suite; Bach, Goldberg Variations; Bartok, Hungarian Peasant Songs; Beethoven, Fidelio; Berlioz, Romeo and Juliet; Bernstein, Age of Anxiety; Bizet, Arlesienne Suite; Borodin, Prince Igor: Polovstian Dances; Brahms, Hungarian Dances; Carissimi, Jepthe; Casadesus, Danses Mediterranines; Chabrier, Danse Slave; Chopin, Polonaise Fantasie; Copland, Lincoln Portrait; Debussy, Estampes; Donizetti, Il Campanello; Dvorak, Slavonic Dances; Franck, Symphonic Variations; Gershwin, American in Paris; Gilbert and Sullivan, Pinafore; Gillis, Portrait of a Frontier Town; Glinka, Ludmilla Overture; Gluck, Orpheus and Eurydice; Gordon, Rake's Progress; Gounod, Faust Ballet; Grofe, Mississippi Suite and Haydn, Dances for the Redoutensaal.

In a study of the effects of music on the mood Dr. Max Schoen found that music was productive of rest and relaxation in a great many instances. Listening to music brings about a sense of inner peace and contentment with a subsequent relaxation of tensed up muscles. This feeling of contentment abolishes any tendency of overloading the nervous system with noxious stimuli which invariably brings on a nervous headache.

While listening to music feelings are evoked which emancipate us from the immediate, tension-producing affairs that occupy our daily lives. Feelings, far removed from the humdrum world of activity are induced and a feeling of rest and relaxation is brought about. Further, the individual listening to music is removed from his conflicts and tensions and a peace with self is the result.

Dr. W. Bingham in an experiment based on data obtained from 20,000 persons, reported the effects produced upon their moods by a variety of 290 phonograph records. The feeling most frequently induced by music was that of rest and relaxation.

Within recent years a new instrument, called the electroencephalograph has given us a great deal of information concerning brain activity. This instrument records brain waves and these give us precise information about brain activity and function. It has been

[137]

found that music can affect these brain waves. A great deal of interesting research is now under way, using the electroencephalograph to record how music affects brain activity and function. When these results are published we will know how nervous people are affected by listening to the proper music. At this date, we know from experience that music relaxes us and is for this reason of great value in controlling any moderately nervous headaches.

MUSIC THERAPY AND THE PSYCHOPATHIC PERSONALITY

By HAROLD BRADLEY, B.M.

Music Therapist, Newark, N. J.

The subject of personality has long been an interesting one. A great many environmental and accidental factors go into the makeup of the personality, and as many may be responsible for its warping. Personality is, however, to a great extent dependent upon many physical qualities and external conditions. It is related to the integrity of the internal glands of secretion, to the structure and chemic well-being of the brain, and to various physical and mental habits which enter into the daily lives of every one of us.

Music has a definite influence on many of these factors. This is now being realized more than ever before. According to a report of the Federal Music Project in New York City, which has for several years been conducting classes in seven city hospitals and two women's prisons, music can be utilized as a means of treating the maladjusted. More than sixty-five hundred persons are treated monthly with music, either as listeners or through active participation.

Children of low intelligence-quotient and disturbed personality who cannot be approached in any other way are susceptible to musical influence. It has been found that such youngsters often have a strong sense of rhythm, and can be taught to follow a conductor's beat. Utilizing music as an initial means of arousing interest and attention to further mental and emotional development in such retarded children can be accomplished by slow and patient stages.

Interest in opera and operettas has been aroused by means of music in maladjusted adolescents. When induced to take an active part in music-making the results have sometimes been remarkable. This method has been found to be of great value in dealing with reformatory inmates.

As the musical treatment is continued a perceptible improvement occurs. Miss Ruth E. Collins, Superintendent of the House of Detention for Women in New York City, where piano instruction and courses in musical appreciation are given, said: "We definitely observe that as a better taste in music is developed, a general improvement in personal appearance, courtesy and morale takes place. Time after time a complete change in both manner of conduct and purpose in life is evinced, proving beyond a doubt the therapeutic value of music in adult personality and adjustment."

Some time ago a serious insurrection was in progress in a New York women's hospital. Dr. Willem van de Wall, who has been investigating the beneficial effects of music for a great many years, happened to be visiting the prison at this time. He thought that music might prove helpful in calming the inmates. He was told that the women were in no mood for singing, but he insisted upon being given a chance to see what he could do. After he had succeeded in getting their attention Dr. van de Wall began the singing with THE BATTLE HYMN OF THE REPUBLIC, a song of quick movement, lively melody and in harmony with the excited state of the inmates. Gradually he worked down into a group of less belligerent songs and ended up with SHE SLEEPS, MY LADY SLEEPS. By this time he had succeeded in calming the rebellious women.

Maladjusted children are very susceptible to music. A violent ten-year-old child, mentally deteriorating, a menace to other children, was a young bull in a china-closet until he was taken into a music class. There he was able to enjoy himself, to sing with his fellows and even came to express concern as to whether the other children were having a good time.

An eight-year-old boy who had driven his parents frantic—

they had been forced to lock doors and windows and disconnect the gas when he was home—became the music teacher's darling for his exemplary behavior—after he had learned to listen to and like music, and later to join in the active participation of musical programs.

A nine-year-old emotionally disturbed girl, whose mother had threatened to kill any one who tried to put her in school, and who spent her four days in the ward crying, shed all signs of emotional instability when she was permitted to play in the rhythm band which had just been organized.

Personality disorders are particularly amenable to musical therapy. Arthur Futz of Boston University, studying the application of music to cases of personality disorders, is of the opinion that music is of great value in personality reconstitution, and foresees wider use of this medium for the treatment of warped personalities.

In the treatment of hopelessly maladjusted children, music has proved very helpful. Dr. Lauretta S. Bender, head of the Children's Psychiatric Ward at Bellevue Hospital, believes that music therapy reaches the child's brain closed to other group-therapy treatments such as plastic and visual arts, dramatics and play activities. She has published several case histories which indicate that music may divert potential criminals into normal pathways.

Many correctional institutions now provide a complete program of musical activities. One such institution has gone to the extent of including the following in its regimen:

1. Instrumental and vocal group practice and performance with orchestra, band and chorus.
2. Individual music study, supervised by the leader. This instruction may comprise sight-reading, instrumental and vocal work, music appreciation and history and theory.
3. Creative work in composing songs and elementary types of instrumental works.
4. The making and repairing of various musical instruments.
5. Participation in performance for purposes of institutional

service, such as band or choral work at religious services, sports events, assemblies and stage shows.

While many persons can not play any instrument or may find it impossible to make much progress when given the opportunity, everyone can sing in some fashion. Even this type of participation in making music goes farther in correcting personality defects than does merely listening to music. Singing has proved a fascinating activity for thousands of inmates of correctional institutions who can not read notes and who have no aptitude for performances on instruments. Those who have good, sonorous voices will usually take considerable trouble to memorize songs. Once the interest in singing is aroused, a very important step has been taken for further personality improvement.

There are many simple songs that inmates can learn to sing together in an acceptable fashion. The everyday, well-known songs are best. Dr. van de Wall found that the following program of twelve songs is not beyond the ability of the average person. They can be learned easily in a short time.

Patriotic	America
Plantation	Old Folks At Home
Negro	Swing Low, Sweet Chariot
Italian	Santa Lucia
Comical	Old Zip Coon
Popular	The Old Spinning Wheel
Operatic	Anvil Chorus from Il Trovatore
Lyrical	Ah, 'Tis a Dream
Regional	Cowboy Song
Popular	Peggy O'Neill
Round	Lovely Evening
English	Sally in Our Alley.

A session of song singing at frequent intervals will make life more tolerable during confinement. It will give the inmate a feeling of freedom and pleasure. Certainly it will not permit the harboring, at least temporarily, of antisocial thoughts.

Within the past few years rhythm-bands have become popular in correctional institutions for maladjusted children who are incapable of learning to play the regular musical instruments. These rhythm-orchestras are made up of drums, cymbals, triangles, tambourines, double castanets, bells, clogs, sand-blocks and rhythm sticks. All are percussion instruments and are capable of making pleasing music.

Dr. van de Wall has found that rhythm orchestras are capable of exerting much good in helping emotionally unstable and disturbed children and even young adults to find themselves and to shed their tensional problems. These simple rhythm-bands have now been employed in many correctional institutions with exceedingly good results.

It is quite an easy matter to organize a simple rhythm-band. Such equipment as rhythm-sticks, jingle clogs, sleighbells, cymbals, triangles, wood blocks, are all that is required and can obviously be adapted in number and variety to the size of the band, as there is no limit to the number of members in a rhythm-band. A 45 piece band can be arranged with little effort. A number of rhythm orchestra scores have been published, and can be used to develop a sense of rhythm in even the most backward.

Of course, after sufficient progress has been made attempts may be made to learn the standard musical instruments. A well organized orchestra in a prison is now considered a vital necessity. It plays a very important part in rehabilitation.

The psychopathic personality is one who is a problem to the community and to himself. The psychopath is an individual who was a problem child who follows that course through life. Emotional problems began to confront him early in life and all his life to follow he will find himself in emotional tangles of various kinds. The psychopath is self-centered and lacks the capacity to feel for others. He is unable to give up personal desire in the interest of others. He is severely maladjusted to his environment and is in need of help in order to become a useful, effective human being.

[143]

Music has, in many cases, proved to be of great value in helping the psychopathic personality to face his environment in a realistic manner.

Such an individual was Walter Rich. His parents died when he was six, following which he went to live with an uncle. He completed high school when he was nineteen, after which he was left to shift for himself. For five years he was a hobo, living by his wits. He learned how to drink quite heavily at an early age. He never held any job for any length of time. He was arrested a dozen times for various crimes such as theft, trespassing, passing bad checks, vagrancy and drunkenness, for which he served several short jail sentences. He stole an automobile and was sentenced to serve five years. When he entered the penitentiary he stated: "Life never meant anything to me, and now life means absolutely nothing."

For the next three months Rich was sullen, depressed and spoke very little. He was increasingly nervous and irritable and was very little interested in his surroundings. He felt neglected, unwanted and utterly alone. Various forms of occupational therapy gave little results. It was learned that he liked to listen to music. He could not play any musical instrument but he evinced a desire to learn. He was given lessons on the banjo, and for the first time in his life he began to feel free of tensions and he was able to relax. In time he became a rather competent musician, joined the prison band. His adjustment to his environment and to his various difficulties thereafter became easier and more effective. Upon release from prison he continued his musical activities with increased application and with notable improvement in his personality difficulties. He drank less, all nervous tensions were gone, his social activities were more acceptable and he was able to function as an effective social unit in his community.

Another psychopathic personality was Richard Lang. As a child he had very indifferent parental supervision. His mother died when he was ten years old. He barely finished the fifth grade, but he was of normal intelligence. He had always been impulsive, moody and emotionally unstable with a history of anti-social behavior and alcoholism dating back to youth.

At the age of eighteen he embarked on a criminal career which consisted of petty thefts, vagrancy, assault and battery and finally armed robbery for which he was given a long sentence. He arrived in prison full of resentment, self-pity and with a sense of complete rejection. For several weeks he was very depressed, irritable, suffering from insomnia and severe stomach upsets.

For the first year Lang remained withdrawn, spoke very little and preferred to be left alone. One day a cousin who was his only visitor left him an harmonica. At first he showed little interest in it, but as time went on he began to experiment and in time learned to play it rather well. He felt happiest and most at ease when he was playing the harmonica. He was given lessons on the clarinet which he learned to play rather expertly. He became a member of the prison band and this led to the first real step in his rehabilitation. After serving his sentence Lang returned to the outside world with many of his antisocial tendencies abated. He was able to effect further adjustment and to lead a normal life.

These are but two of many cases of warped personalities which have come to my attention in which music has served as a very valuable means of enabling the individual to effect a satisfactory adjustment within himself and to assume a place in the community as a socially acceptable individual.

The use of music in the rehabilitation of emotionally disturbed and warped personalities is now widespread in quite a few areas. In England, Drs. S. D. Mitchell and A. Zanker combined music therapy with group therapy in the treatment of various personality disorders with very good results. They found that the use of music had definite therapeutic value as manifested by increased group cooperation and interpersonal relationships. These were accomplished by emotional release and facilitation of better integration of the personality.

Music for the maladjusted is as good a medicine as can be

obtained. There are a great many musical compositions currently available. Here are a few out of many which have been found particularly applicable:

Military Polonaise	Chopin
Song of the Flea	Moussorgsky
Appasionata Sonata (1st movement)	Beethoven
Til Eulenspiegel	Strauss
Lenore No. 3 Overture	Beethoven
Credo from Othello	Verdi
Overture to the Marriage of Figaro	Mozart
March from Le Coq d'Or	Rimsky-Korsakov
Toreador Song from Carmen	Bizet
Marche Joyeuse	Chabrier
La Valse	Ravel
Carnival Romain	Berlioz
G Minor Symphony (No. 40)	Mozart
Fire Dance	de Falla
Hora Staccato	Dinici
Polka from the Golden Age	Shostakovitch
La Mer	Debussy
Dance of the Blessed Spirits	Glick
The Moldau	Smetana
Scherzo and March from Love of Three Oranges	Prokofiev

MUSIC THERAPY IN PSYCHOSOMATIC GASTRIC DISORDERS

By PAUL SUGARMAN, Mus.M.

Music Therapist, Chicago, Illinois

The stomach is one of the most sensitive organs in the body; it responds only too readily to all sorts of stimuli and irritations from the outside world. Any slight unpleasantness can cause the stomach to act up. Why? The stomach is richly supplied with nerves which connect one part with another, and with the brain. This connection with the brain once served a useful purpose. It helped our primitive ancestors to make a quick get away from danger. Now it is a nuisance.

Today man quite frequently undergoes intense emotional upheavals, not only in the face of physical danger as he did a great many years ago, but also in the very competitive world in which we must live. The connections between the brain and the stomach are still there. The powerful chemicals still pour into his blood, but since he does not use them up in muscular action, they remain to irritate his stomach and upset it and cause pain.

For the sufferer with nervous stomach upsets the art of relaxation is a necessity. It must be acquired and put into daily practice. At the dinner table all matters that tend to cause emotional upsets should be avoided. A pleasant environment is a great help. Music is one of the most effective ways of bringing this about.

Music while dining is not a recent innovation. From earliest times music has brought an aesthetic calm and dignity to the art of dining. It was for this very reason that Epictetus called a table without music a manger. Musicians were rarely absent from the feasts and banquets of the early Egyptians, Greeks and Romans. Plutarch was strongly of the opinion that the flute could not be spared from the dining room. "Its rich and full tones spread peace and tranquility throughout the soul." They also spread peace and tranquility throughout the digestive tract. Centuries later, Sir Thomas More, in his COMMONWEALTH, made the proposal that music should be played at the meals of every class of society in his model community.

Dr. Ivan Pavlov, the famous Russian experimental physiologist, offered a concise and illuminating explanation as to why music has such a favorable effect on the digestion. Stated briefly, music by arousing pleasurable emotions promotes the flow of digestive juices. This increased flow quite naturally brings about a more thorough digestion of the food. Still another important fact is that the principal nerve of the tympanum (middle ear) ends on the center of the tongue and connects with the brain, reacting alike to the sensations of taste and sound. For this reason, good food and good music is a most ideal combination.

The stomach is a very special kind of organ with a personality of its own; it reacts very quickly and quite often rather decidedly to emotional changes. Unpleasant emotions bring about certain changes which give rise to distress. When the stomach is upset the pylorus (a muscular structure at the base of the stomach) closes up, almost in a knot. The contents are banked up in the stomach, the organ remains awash and sensations of heaviness, distension and acid risings result.

If the unpleasant emotions continue to plague the stomach, matters become much worse. The person who is thus upset shows drowsiness, mental inefficiency and a tendency to abstraction and day-dreaming. His temper begins to wear thin. He becomes irritable, boorish and unreasonable.

There are so many things to worry each one of us that it does not take a great deal to make the stomach squirm and twist in

[148]

agony. What is needed in cases of this kind is something that will fight off the unpleasant feelings and replace them with a pleasure-arousing element. Music is the best antidote for unpleasantness at the dinner table.

Music may serve either as a strong emotional catharsis or as a mild stimulant or sedative. Each has its proper place, but for dining, an emotional upheaval is entirely out of place. We must have soothing music. After much experimentation, and trial and error, I have arrived at a treasury of music compositions which I have found eminently satisfactory for the dining table. These are the musical pieces I recommend:

Brahms	Trio for Piano in C
Bartok	Sonata for Violin
Boccherini	Concerto in D for Flute and Strings
Bach	Concerto in D Minor for Two Violins
Beethoven	Sonata No. 7 in C Minor
Mozart	Sonata in A Minor
Prokofiev	Summer Day Suite
Rameau	Pieces En Concert
Ravel	La Valse
Satie	Three Pieces in the Shape of a Pear
Schubert	Sonata in A, Op. 162
Schumann	Sonata in A Minor, Op. 105
Tschaikowsky	Trio in A Minor, Op. 50
Chopin	Sonata No. 2 in B Flat Minor
Debussy	Children's Corner Suite
Dvorak	Serenade for Strings, Op. 22
Hindemith	Sonata in D for Violin and Piano
Ives	Sonata No. 2 for Violin and Piano
Liszt	Concerto No. 2 in A
Mendelssohn	Octet in E Flat

Curiously enough the stomach acts in rhythms, much in the same way as music. The stomach is a muscular organ, the activity of which consists of rhythmic waves of contraction which pass along it similar to the waves which pass over the heart and which are known as heart beats. In the stomach, these waves of contraction are called peristalsis, and their rate is much slower than the rate of the heart. But, unlike the rhythm of the heart, the rhythm of the stomach may be considerably influenced by the rhythm of the music.

Digestion is influenced by two factors: glands and nerves. Music acts upon both. Dr. George W. Crile, who was famous for his important researches on the relationship between emotions and glands, believed that music has a marked effect on the glands, causing either an increased or decreased secretion of their important substances into the blood.

Upon the nervous system music exerts either a stimulating or calming effect. As far as the nerve mechanism of the stomach is concerned, only calming music is desirable. Overstimulation causes spasm of the stomach and of the pylorus, and indigestion is the natural result.

Shrill, sudden noises, strident and discordant tones interfere quite markedly with the normal rhythm of the stomach and upset it. This leads us to the observation that an overdose of Wagner is just as disastrous for the stomach as a powerful drug. TRISTAN UND ISOLDE is quite out of place at the dinner table. Its powerful cascade of sound is far too overwhelming for the natural rhythm of the digestive tract. Swing and be-bop, while good for dancing and jitterbugging, is entirely out of place in dinner music.

Even classical music must be chosen with care as far as the dining room is concerned. Modern, atonal music, such as that of Schoenberg and Stravinsky is best avoided. The spirited overtures of Donizetti are too stimulating as are the Brahms' Hungarian Dances. These are fine tonics for the blues, but they are far too distracting and disturbing for the ordered rhythmic waves of the stomach. Calm, soft, soothing music is what we want for dining.

A MUSICAL PROGRAM FOR EMOTIONAL HIGH BLOOD PRESSURE

By PAUL SUGARMAN, Mus.M.

Music Therapist, Chicago, Illinois

One of the commonest ailments of modern, high-pressure living is increased blood pressure. There are many factors which shoot the blood pressure up, but one of the most frequent is emotional upset, such as worry, tension, anxiety and fear. These not only elevate the pressure but help to keep it up day after day, week after week and sometimes year after year.

The high blood pressure personality tends to walk and work faster than the average person. He is often more sensitive and more easily embarrassed than the person with normal blood pressure. Whereas the blood pressure of the normal person may rise from 10 to 30 mm. of mercury during excitement, the person suffering from emotional high blood pressure will suffer a rise from 30 to 100 mm. Similarly, when mentally at ease, the blood pressure of the emotional high blood pressure individual will fall more than that of the person with normal pressure.

While quite a few other causes may bring on symptoms of high blood pressure excessive emotionalism helps to maintain and keep the pressure at a high level. Most often these symptoms become worse following emotional difficulties. There is no doubt that in modern life infections have diminished and nervous strains have increased.

There is little doubt that this increased tension in modern life is responsible for increased arterial tension or high blood pressure.

If an emotional reaction is intense, bodily disturbances may occur which involve the entire body. The movements of the gastro-intestinal tract are stopped, the digestive secretions are inhibited, the heart is made to beat more rapidly and the blood pressure goes up.

How can you learn to keep your blood pressure down to within normal limits if it is due to emotional causes? One of the best ways is to learn to relax with music.

That music has definite effects on the heart and blood pressure has been known for many years. In 1918 Drs. I. H. Hyde and W. Scalapino had all the modern blood pressure machines at their disposal when they conducted a series of experiments in the physiological laboratories at the University of Kansas in an effort to determine the influence of music on the heart action and blood pressure. They found that soothing music as provided by melodies in the minor mood caused a fall in blood pressure.

Dr. N. W. Treves conducted a series of experiments with music on patients in a hospital ward and he also found that sedative music had a definite tendency to lower the blood pressure. He states: that from a purely psychological and possibly from a psychotherapeutic standpoint, these patients were benefited.

A little later three Canadian physiologists undertook a most interesting study of the effects of music on the blood pressure of a number of persons classified as musical, moderately musical and non-musical. Tones, scales, arpeggios were played to them, and they listened to piano pieces, songs and orchestral works. It was found that quiet, uneventful music produced a fall of pressure. Vocal music was judged to be less effective, and an orchestral work had the same effect as a piano piece.

In 1929, Drs. Swale Vincent and J. H. Thompson conducted a very interesting series of experiments on the effects of music on blood pressure. They used a concealed phonograph in their experiments. They found that soft, soothing music invariably lowered the blood pressure.

Several years later Dr. A. Wascho conducted a series of experiments with music on men and women and ascertained that there was a definite fall in blood pressure. He came to the conclusion that music properly prescribed can assist in lowering the blood pressure and that music has therapeutic uses in clinical medicine.

From these experiments and observations there is no doubt that music of the right kind has very definite effects in lowering the blood pressure. It is also a pleasant and painless way to do so. In a series of cases of emotional high blood pressure I have used the following musical compositions with very gratifying results: Bach, Concerto in D Minor for Violin; Bartok, Sonata for Piano; Beethoven, Sonata No. 8 in C minor; Boccherini, Concerto in D for Flute and Strings; Borodin, Quartet No. 2 in D; Brahms, Quartet No. 1 in G Minor; Bruckner, Mass in E Minor; Chopin, Sonata in G Minor for Cello and Piano; Debussy, Pour le Piano; Dvorak, Sonata in F; Franck, Quintet in F Minor for Piano; Gould, Spirituals for Orchestra; Handel, Sonatas Da Camera, 5 and 6; Haydn, Sonata No. 1 in E Flat; Hindemith, Noblissima Visione; Ives, Symphony No. 3; Liszt, Les Preludes; Marcello, Concerto in C Minor; Mendelssohn, Sonata No. 6 in D Minor; Messiaen, Visions de l'Amen; Mozart, Mass in C Minor; Prokoficv, Sonata No. 6; Rachmaninoff, Isle of the Dead; Ravel, Sonatine for Piano; Scarlatti, Motetto Da Requiem; Schubert, Mass in E Flat; Schumann, Fantasia in C; Tschaikowsky, Swan Lake Ballet and Vivaldi, Concerto in A Minor.

Experimental and clinical work on the blood pressure lowering effects of music are still going on. In 1935 Drs. J. R. Miles and C. R. Tilly used a special apparatus to take the blood pressure over long periods of time. This tended definitely to confirm the fact that music of a soothing nature has a tendency to lower the blood pressure.

In 1946 Dr. Lloyd F. Sunderman conducted a series of experiments with music and its effects on the blood pressure. From 594 women who had done considerable work in music, 248 were chosen for this study. Another 247 who had not studied music were chosen from 12,000 to serve as controls. He found that musicians, on the whole, tended to have lower blood pressure readings. He concluded that the lower pressures of musicians were due to the more relaxed conditions in their lives. There is no doubt that music has quite a great deal to do with this.

EFFECTS OF MUSIC IN THE HEART

By EDWARD PODOLSKY, M.D.

Department of Psychiatry, Kings County Hospital, Brooklyn, N. Y.

Every observant doctor from the earliest times has known that the emotions exert a definite influence on the heart. It has been known that emotions can speed up the heart, can bring about palpitations and even cause severe pains and spasms.

It has been found that in time the heart may actually become damaged by emotional stress. At first the emotional disorder causes functional heart trouble. If the disturbance continues for any length of time structural changes take place and the heart is actually damaged. When the physiological effects of emotion, under certain circumstances, become habitual, they quite often result in structural changes in the heart.

Civilization as we know it in Western Europe and America, the ambition, effort and community state of mind in these areas, the increasing prevalence of functional heart disease is coincident with mounting tensions. The inner adjustment to life, the real spiritual control of life, whose outer evidence is poise and tranquility of mind is not very inviting to this disabling disease.

What should be done to avoid functional heart ailments caused by emotional stress and strain? Good results are achieved by learning how to keep calm inwardly, by learning to relax and let go of inner tensions. Among the methods recommended for this purpose music is among the best.

For many years psychologists have been evaluating the effects of music on the heart and circulation. The first really scientific experiments on the influence of music on the heart were performed by Drs. Binet and Courtier in 1895. They found that the pulse was markedly affected by the type of music played. Lively music acted as a stimulant to the heart while soft music acted as a sedative.

In 1918 Drs. Hyde and Scalapino conducted a more exhaustive study of the effects of music on the heart and circulation. They found that the proper kind of music exerted a calming and sedative effect on the heart.

Drs. Vincent and Thompson also conducted a series of experiments with music on the heart rate and circulation. They ascertained that soothing music decreased the heart rate and brought about a more ordered rhythm in cases where the emotions caused the heart to act up.

Dr. Treves in 1927 conducted a series of experiments with music to determine its effects upon the heart and pulse rate on a group of ward patients in the New York Memorial Hospital. The experiments were carried out under nearly constant conditions and by the same persons. Some 280 observations were recorded. Dr. Treves found that programs of sedative music had a pronounced tendency to reduce the heart rate.

In 1933 Dr. Washco conducted a study with music on a group of students. From his data Dr. Washco concluded that music properly prescribed assists in lowering or raising the pulse rate, that music is of definite value as a therapeutic agent in certain abnormal conditions of the mind and body.

Dr. Schonauer in 1935 reported the results of a series of experiments which were designed to test the effects of music. He found that "music is capable of producing several kinds of reaction, sphygmographic, pneumographic, and psychic, all of which can be individualized, distinguished and reproduced, each one varying in relation to the musical, individual and surrounding factors."

In a series of cases of high blood pressure due to emotional causes, good results were obtained by using music as a relaxing agent. Urgent tensions were moderated, muscular relaxation was obtained after several sessions with recorded music, and a general feeling of inner calm was brought about. The compositions used in these cases were: Mahler, Youth's Magic Horn; Mendelssohn, Concerto in E Minor for Violin; Milhaud, Le Boeuf Sur Le Toit; Mozart, Ode Funebre; Prokofiev, Quartet No. 2 in F; Rachmaninoff, Symphony No. 2 in E Minor; Ravel, L'Enfant et Les Sortileges; Reger, Serenade for Orchestra; Saint-Saens, Symphony No. 3 in C Minor; Britten, Ceremony of Carrots; Bruckner, Quintet in F; Buxrehude, Four Cantatas; Chopin, Sonata in B Minor for Piano; Debussy, Jeux, Poeme Danse; Donahyi, Suite in F Sharp Minor; Dvorak, Concerto in A Minor for Violin; Falla, Concerto for Harpsichord; Fauré, Ballade for Piano and Orchestra; Bach, Art of th Fugue; Bartok, Microskosmos; Beethoven, Sonata No. 5 in F Berg, Concerto for Violin; Berlioz, Requiem; Bliss, Checkmat Ballet; Bloch, Baal Shem; Boccherini, Trios 2, 4, 5; Brahms Concerto in D for Violin; Francaix, Concertino for Piano and Or chestra; Franck, Trio No. 1 in F Sharp Minor; Gould, Interplay for Piano and Orchestra; Handel, Trio Sonata Op. 5 No. 6; Haydn, Sonata No. 43 in A Flat; Hindemith, Das Marienleben; Kodaly, Te Deum, and Liszt, Concerto No. 2 in A.

Experimental work still going on in the clinic and laboratory confirms the fact that music has very definite effects on the emo tional components of the heart and circulatory system. First, it ha been found that music influences the electrical conductivity of the human body as manifested by increased fluctuations in the psycho galvanic reflex. This is a very good indication that music exerts measurable effects on those emotions which control bodily func- tions. Second, musical stimuli have very definite effects on the pulse rate, pulse pressure and circulation of the blood. As these are all intimately associated with the blood pressure, music has thus a very definite effect on blood pressure elevations. Finally, clinically it has been confirmed that music is a very pleasant as well as effective means of moderating high blood pressures due to emotional causes.

EFFECTS OF
MUSIC ON RESPIRATION-AND
HEART-RATE

By DOUGLAS S. ELLIS

Iowa State College, Ames, Iowa

AND

GILBERT BRIGHOUSE

Occidental College, Los Angeles, California

The increasing use of music as a therapeutic agent directs attention to experimental investigations of the effects of music on behavior.[1] Although there are many aspects of human behavior that might be investigated, it would seem particularly valuable to have information concerning the effects of music on behaviors which play an important rôle in disease conditions. Respiratory and cardiac activity are examples of such behavior. Minimizing respiratory activity is an important aspect of the treatment of the tuberculous patient, while control of cardiac activity is frequently desirable in the treatment of various heart conditions. The present research was undertaken to investigate the influence of music on these two aspects of behavior.

Early experiments dealing with the effects of music on the respiration- and heart-rate have been summarized by Schoen[2] and

[1] S. D. Mitchell and A. Zanker, The use of music in group therapy, *J. Ment. Sci.*, 94, 1948, 737-748; E. Podolsky, *The Doctor Prescribes Music*, 1939, 1-134; D. M. Schullian and Max Schoen, *Music and Medicine*, 1948, 1-499; Doris Soibelman, *Therapeutic and Industrial Uses of Music: A Review of the Literature*, 1948, 103-203; Willem van de Wall, *Music in Hospitals*, 1946, 1-86.

[2] M. Schoen, *The Psychology of Music*, 1940, 103-108.

[158]

Soibelman.[3] These pioneer researches tend to indicate that music may influence respiration- and heart-rate, although the lack of adequate statistical treatment and the small number of cases used makes interpretation difficult.

In a study of the effects of repetition of recorded musical selections, Gilliland and Moore obtained heart-rates after the first and twenty-fifth playings of both popular and classical records.[4] They found that jazz music tended to increase the rate to a greater extent than classical music, and that this relationship held under repetitive conditions. Hyde investigated the effects of music on electrocardiograms, pulse rate, and systolic and diastolic blood pressure.[5] She concluded that cardiovascular functions can be modified by music, but that the effects varied widely with the individual. The effects of music on blood pressure, pulse rate, and mental imagery were investigated by Washco, who found differences in these aspects of behavior according to the kind of music employed.[6]

It is not our purpose here to elaborate the weaknesses and virtues of each of these experiments, but a review of these studies indicates that further experimentation is needed.[7] Specifically, the present study was designed to meet the following requirements: (1) Individual rather than group treatment of Ss. (2) Careful control and adequate specification of the conditions under which Ss are exposed to music. (3) Use of several musical selections. (4) Experimental design allowing for adequate statistical treatment of results. (5) Provisions for obtaining adequate measures of behavior before, during, and after music.

METHOD

Subjects. The Ss, 36 college students (18 men and 18 women), were selected at random from volunteers in undergraduate psychol-

[3] Soibelman, *op. cit.*, 21-63.

[4] A. R. Gilliland and H. T. Moore, Immediate and long-time effects of classical and popular phonograph selections, *J. Appl. Psychol.*, 8, 1924, 309-323.

[5] I. M. Hyde, Effects of music upon electrocardiograms and blood pressure, in M. Schoen (Ed.), *The Effects of Music: A Series of Essays*, 1927, 184-197.

[6] A. Washco, *Effects of Music upon Pulse Rate, Blood Pressure, and Mental Imagery*, 1933, 226-229.

[7] D. S. Ellis, The effects of music on the respiration-rate and the pulse-rate, M.A. Thesis, Occidental College, 1948, 5-9.

ogy courses at Occidental College. The experiment was conducted during the spring of 1947.

Music. Three recorded selections were employed. (1) Hall's *Blue Interval* (Blue Note #31); (2) Debussy's *Prelude to the Afternoon of a Faun* (Victor Red Seal 17700-A); (3) Liszt's *Hungarian Rhapsody No. 2* (Victor Red Seal 14433-B). These records might be characterized, respectively, as a subdued jazz selection in the blues idiom, a soothing classical selection, and a vivid and dynamic classical selection. All of the selections were recorded on 12 in. records and were orchestral numbers which do not involve vocal performance.

The music was reproduced by a phonograph operating in conjunction with an amplifier and a 12-in. Jensen high fidelity speaker. The volume and tone control settings used were determined by averaging the judgments of three graduate students as to the best setting for optimal reproduction of each selection.

Apparatus. Cardiac activity was measured by an electrocardiograph, using the conventional arrangement in which electrodes are attached to *S*'s left wrist and right leg. Respiratory activity was measured by a pneumograph, adjusted to the region of *S*'s diaphragm. Both instruments recorded by capillary pens on a continuous speed, electrically driven polygraph, which was equipped with a 1-sec. interval-timer driven by a synchronous motor. Since the use of an electrocardiograph requires adequate shielding of leads, it was necessary to place *S* in a shielded cage for the course of the experiment. This cage was equipped with a mattress so that *S* could assume a comfortable prone position.

The equipment was arranged in two adjoining rooms, hence it was possible for *S* to be in isolation during the course of an experimental session. *S*'s room was kept in a constant state of dim illumination, and contained the shielded cage, loudspeaker for record reproduction, and the speaker of an inter-office communicator which was used for presenting reading materials (see below). The polygraph, phonograph turntable and amplifier, and inter-office communicator were placed in *E*'s room. One-way vision glass between the two rooms allowed *E* to observe any overt movements by *S*.

Experimental design and procedure. A completely counterbalanced experimental design which permitted exposing each of the

[160]

36 Ss to the three musical selections was used. Since three experimental conditions involve six possible orders of presentation, three men and three women received each order of presentation. All the Ss served in three 30-min. experimental sessions which were at least 24 hr. apart. Each session was devoted to the presentation of one of the musical selections.

A procedure which permitted determination of respiration- and heart-rates before, during, and after music was followed during the course of any experimental session. The session was initiated by S's reading instructions designed to give the impression that the experiment was one in reading in which the music was only an incidental factor. The following excerpts from these instructions show how an attempt was made to camouflage the true nature of the study.

> You are about to take part in a test to see what effect reading has on you, and if music influences this effect. If you just make yourself comfortable and act as you naturally would, you will have done all that the test requires and you will have helped us a great deal.
>
> You can see that the procedure requires nothing of you but listening to the reading and the music. We are not going to ask any questions about the reading material because we are not interested in whether you remember it or not. We just want to see if the reading will have any effect on you, and if music will influence this effect.[8]

Following completion of the instructions, S was made comfortable in the shielded cage while the cardiograph electrodes and pneumograph were adjusted. A woman assistant applied the electrodes and pneumograph to the women who served as Ss. E and his assistant then left S's room and did not return until the end of the

---

[8] The reading materials were condensations of six articles from the *Reader's Digest*. The articles, which consumed approximately 2 min., were read to S by E over the inter-office communicator. Two articles were used for each session, one being presented at the start and the other being presented at the finish of the session. The order of presentation of the articles was so counterbalanced that no pair of articles was consistently presented with a given musical selection. At the conclusion of the third experimental session, S was questioned concerning the purpose of the experiment. Since only 2 of the 36 Ss gave responses indicating awareness of music as the independent variable, it may be concluded that the instructions were successful in concealing the true purpose of the experiment.

[161]

experimental session. The appropriate article was read to S, and this in turn was followed by the pre-music period.

The purpose of the pre-music period was to establish stable values of respiration- and heart-rate. The pre-music period was terminated when three conditions had been fulfilled: (1) at least 9 min. had elapsed since presentation of the initial article; (2) three successive 1-min. intervals had occurred in which the respiration-rate did not vary more than two cycles per minute; (3) three successive 1-min. intervals had occurred in which the heart-rate did not vary more than two cycles per minute. Once these conditions had been fulfilled, the music period was initiated in which S was exposed to the appropriate musical selection. A 5-min. post-music period followed the end of the music, and was in turn followed by the reading of the second article.

Results

(1) *Respiration-rate.* The respiration-rates before, during, and after music for the three musical selections are plotted in Fig. 1. Each point is based on 36 Ss. Examination of Fig. 1 indicates that the onset of music is accompanied by general increases in respiration-rate. With cessation of music, the rate tends to return to its pre-music level, although there is a slight but consistent rise in the rate during the second minute of the post-music period.

The statistical significance of these data may be analyzed by means of the statistic *t*. This procedure involves comparing respiration rates during and after music with pre-music rates. Such an analysis is presented in Table I. It can be seen that the rates during music are significantly greater than before it, with the single exception of the first minute of *Afternoon of a Faun.*

Table I also indicates that none of the post-music rates are significantly different from those of the pre-music period. Although the increased rate of Minute 2 of the post-music period is not significantly greater than the pre-music rate, it is worthwhile to compare it with the rate of Minute 1 of that period. The *t*s obtained from such a comparison were 2.61, 2.04, and 2.04 for *Blue*

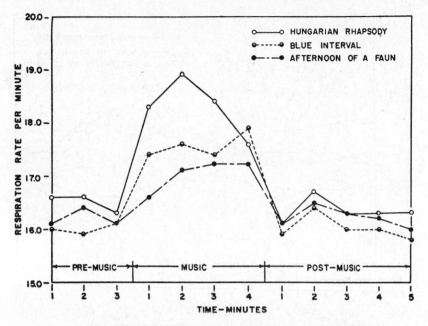

FIG. 1. MEAN RESPIRATION-RATE BEFORE, DURING, AND AFTER MUSIC
(Every point based on the results of 36 Ss.)

Interval, Afternoon of a Faun, and *Hungarian Rhapsody,* respectively. All of these *t*s are significant at the 5-% level of confidence, and indicate that the increased rate during Minute 2 of the postmusic period is significantly greater than the rate during Minute 1 of that period.

(2) *Heart-rate.* Fig. 2 presents the variation of heart-rate with the various experimental conditions. It can be seen that the curves are fairly flat, although there appears to be a tendency for the heart-rate to increase during the music.

The results of the statistical analysis of the heart-rate are arrayed in Table II, where it can be seen that the rates during and after music are generally not significantly different than the premusic rate. A single exception is Minute 2 of *Hungarian Rhapsody,* where the rate is significantly greater than the pre-music rate.

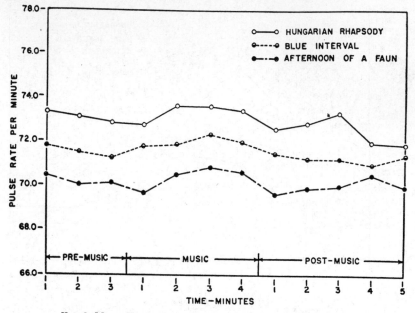

Fig. 2. Mean Heart-Rate Before, During and After Music
(Every point based on the results of 36 Ss.)

(3) *Inter-comparisons*. The fact that three musical selections were used permits comparisons to be made regarding their relative influence on respiration- and heart-rate. Fig. 1 shows the relative effects of the three selections on respiration-rate, and Fig 2, on heart-rate.

An inspection of Fig. 1 shows that the effectiveness of the musical selections, from most to least effective, is *Hungarian Rhapsody, Blue Interval, Afternoon of a Faun*. A more precise comparison could be made by the use of *t* if it were known that the pre-music respiration-rates of the selections were the same or about the same, *i.e.* that they did not differ significantly. Table III indicates that the pre-music rates do not differ significantly and Table IV presents the *t*-values of the comparisons among the three selections.

Examination of Table IV indicates that the *Hungarian Rhapsody* was accompanied by significantly faster breathing than the

[164]

EFFECTS OF MUSIC ON RESPIRATION- AND HEART-RATE

TABLE I

RESPIRATION; COMPARISON OF PRE-MUSIC RATE WITH RATES DURING AND AFTER MUSIC

The *t*-values reported here are based on Minute 3 of the pre-music period
as the standard of comparison.

	Musical selection		
Minute 3 of pre-music *vs.*	*Blue Interval*	*Afternoon of a Faun*	*Hungarian Rhapsody*
Minute 1 of music	4.34*	1.32	4.40*
Minute 2 of music	4.70*	2.93*	7.15*
Minute 3 of music	3.05*	3.23*	5.00*
Minute 4 of music	4.89*	2.76*	2.78*
Minute 1 of post-music	——	——	——
Minute 2 of post-music	0.89	——	1.18
Minute 3 of post-music	——	——	——
Minute 4 of post-music	——	——	——
Minute 5 of post-music	——	——	——

* Significant at the 1-% level of confidence. Blank spaces indicate *t* not calculated because of negligible change in the respiration-rate.

TABLE II

HEART BEAT: COMPARISON OF PRE-MUSIC RATE WITH RATES DURING AND AFTER MUSIC

The *t*-values reported here are based on Minute 3 of the pre-music period
as the standard of comparison.

Minute 3 of pre-music *vs.*	*Blue Interval*	*Afternoon of a Faun*	*Hungarian Rhapsody*
Minute 1 of music	1.06	1.06	——
Minute 2 of music	——	——	2.31*
Minute 3 of music	1.77	1.50	1.88
Minute 4 of music	1.10	——	1.43
Minute 1 of post-music	——	——	0.63
Minute 2 of post-music	——	——	——
Minute 3 of post-music	——	——	——
Minute 4 of post-music	——	——	1.33
Minute 5 of post-music	——	——	1.70

* Significant at the 5-% level of confidence. Blank spaces indicate *t* not calculated because of negligible change in the heart-rate.

TABLE III

RESPIRATION: COMPARISON OF THE PRE-MUSIC RATES PRECEDING THE DIFFERENT MUSICAL SELECTIONS

The *t*-values reported here are based on Minute 3 of the pre-music period.
None approaches significance at the 5-% level of confidence.

	Hungarian Rhapsody vs. *Afternoon of a Faun*	*Hungarian Rhapsody* vs. *Blue Interval*	*Blue Interval* vs. *Afternoon of a Faun*
t-values	0.43	0.48	0.00

TABLE IV

COMPARISON BY THE USE OF t OF THE EFFECTS OF THE THREE MUSICAL SELECTIONS ON RESPIRATION-RATE

Period	Hungarian Rhapsody vs. Afternoon of a Faun	Hungarian Rhapsody vs. Blue Interval	Blue Interval vs. Afternoon of a Faun
Minute 1 of music	2.93*	1.81	1.52
Minute 2 of music	4.06*	2.54†	0.80
Minute 3 of music	2.03†	1.63	——
Minute 4 of music	——	——	——
Minute 1 of post-music	——	——	——
Minute 2 of post-music	——	——	——
Minute 3 of post-music	——	——	——
Minute 4 of post-music	——	——	——
Minute 5 of post-music	——	——	——

* Significant at the 1-% level of confidence. Blank spaces indicate t not calculated because of negligible difference in respiration rate.
† Significant at the 5-% level of confidence.

TABLE V

NUMBER OF Ss SHOWING INCREASES AND DECREASES IN RESPIRATION- AND HEART-RATES DURING MUSIC

Changes in rate were determined by comparing S's average rate during music with his rate during Minute 3 of the pre-music period.

Music	Repiration-rate		Heart-rate	
	increase	decrease	increase	decrease
Hungarian Rhapsody	31	5	22	14
Blue Interval	33	3	22	14
Afternoon of a Faun	27	9	19	17

Afternoon of a Faun throughout most of the recording. During Minute 2 of music, the *Hungarian Rhapsody* was also accompanied by significantly faster respiration than the *Blue Interval*. There were no statistically significant differences between respiration associated with the *Blue Interval* and the *Afternoon of a Faun*. In no instance is there a significant difference between the rates following the three selections.

A similar analysis was made for the heart-rate. Since no significant differences among the selections were found, the results are not presented in detail.

(4) *Individual differences.* Table V presents data bearing on

the problem of how consistently the three selections affected respiration- and heart-rate. While the results previously discussed deal primarily with group-trends, these data are significant from the stand-point of predicting individual reactions. Inspection of Table V indicates that only a small number of Ss showed decreases in the rate of respiration during the music. The data also indicate that as far as the rate of the heart-beat is concerned, the group is fairly evenly split between those showing increases and those showing decreases. This result would be expected if it is recalled that none of the musical selections cause significant changes in heart-rate.

Table VI deals with the relationship between changes in res-

TABLE VI

INTERCORRELATIONS OF CHANGES IN RESPIRATION-RATE DURING THE THREE MUSICAL SELECTIONS

Rank-difference correlations. None is significant at the 5-% level of confidence. Changes were determined by comparing S's average rate during music with his rate during Minute 3 of the pre-music period.

Hungarian Rhapsody vs. Afternoon of a Faun —0.30	Hungarian Rhapsody vs. Blue Interval +0.19	Blue Interval vs. Afternoon of a Faun —0.08

piration rate during the three selections for each S. Since none of the correlations reported are significantly different from zero, it appears that an individual's reaction to music is fairly specific to the music used.

Discussion

The major results concerning the effects of music on respiration- and heart-rate may be briefly summarized as follows.

(1) All of the statistically significant increases were in respiration-rate.

(2) One of the three selections (*Hungarian Rhapsody*) caused significantly greater increases in respiration than either of the other two.

(3) Two of the selections (*Hungarian Rhapsody* and *Blue Interval*) caused increases in respiration in almost all of the Ss.

[167]

(4) There was no correlation among the Ss' changes in respiration during the three musical selections.

(5) None of the musical selections was accompanied by statistically significant changes in heart-rate.

Results summarized in (1), (2), and (3) are generally consistent with the view that music may be used as a therapeutic agent, provided that one is interested in increasing the respiration-rate of an individual who is in a fairly relaxed state.

On the other hand, results summarized in (4) and (5) clearly indicate limitations in the use of music for therapeutic purposes. In the first place, the evidence indicates that the magnitude of an individual's reaction to music is fairly specific to the music employed. Evidently, there is no general trait of reactivity to music, and thus it would be hazardous to predict an individual's reaction to different musical selections on the basis of his reaction to one or two. Of course, not much can be said concerning the degree of specificity of reactions to music on the basis of only three musical selections. One might suspect from the general findings concerning the organization of human abilities that reactivity to music would consist of rather narrow group factors in the sense that a small number of closely related musical selections would have a similar effect on behavior.[9]

Secondly, the results on heart-rate emphasize the complexity of the problem of the effects of music. The consistently negative findings concerning this bit of behavior indicates the importance of considering all relevant aspects of behavior in the therapeutic use of music.

The problem of the after-effects of music on the respiration-rate also merits some consideration. No significant changes in respiration-rate relative to the pre-music respiration were found for 5 min. following the music. It was found, however, that respiration during Minute 2 of the post-music period was significantly

[9] R. H. Seashore, Work methods: An often neglected factor underlying individual differences, *Psychol. Rev.*, 48, 1939, 123-141.

greater than that for Minute 1 of that period. This result warrants emphasis, since it might be interpreted as evidence for the 'cathartic' effects of music. A more parsimonious explanation in terms of compensatory mechanisms governing respiration is favored. Workers with the electroencephalograph have noted that after hyperventilation the respiration tends to oscillate with successively decreasing magnitude about the normal rate. In other words, following artificially increased respiration, there is a regular cycle of over-compensation, under-compensation, etc. It may well be that such a mechanism was operating to produce our results, since in all cases the respiration-rate was significantly increased during music.

In general, the experimental results indicate that the effects of music are highly complex. Accurate prediction of the effects of music awaits further investigation. Future research in this field might well be concerned with a broader sampling of the various types of music, the use of longer musical scores and longer post-music periods, and the investigation of other aspects of behavior besides respiration- and heart-rate.

THE USE AND THERAPEUTIC VALUE OF MUSIC IN THE HOSPITAL AND OPERATING ROOM

By KENNETH L. PICKRELL, M.D., JAMES T. METZGER, M.D., N. JOHN WILDE, D.D.S., M.D., T. RAY BROADBENT,* M.D., and BENJAMIN F. EDWARDS, M.D.

From the Division of Plastic Surgery, Duke University School of Medicine and Duke Hospital, Durham, North Carolina

Music is now recognized and appreciated universally as a source of pleasure, relaxation, and diversion. Even though the therapeutic value of music has long been known, its possibilities and potentialities as a specific or supplementary form of therapy have been essentially unexplored.

For ages warriors have been led to battle to the sounds of martial strains. The influence of the war-chant upon the warrior is known even to savage tribes. David charmed away Saul's evil spirit with his harp. The use of music to lighten the burden of work is centuries old. The pyramids of Egypt and the great walls of China were built to the accompaniment of songs and chants of the masses. In our own country, the boats on the Mississippi have been laden and unloaded to the crooning of negro spirituals and melodies. Our transcontinental railroads were built to the tune of "Drill, Ye Tarriers, Drill." Many large industrial and manufacturing plants use music as a subtle stimulus for greater production. This is said to be especially effective when the task is a monotonous one. The inspiration offered by music is well-known. It

* Trainee, National Cancer Institute.

The Instruments and Records for the Present Study Were Supplied by the RCA Victor Division of Radio Corporation of America, Camden, New Jersey.

may be a stimulus to intellectual work as well as to labor. Bacon, Milton, Alfieri, and Warburton needed music to stimulate them in their work, and it is said that Bourdaloue always played an air on his violin before preparing to write.

Homer, Plutarch, Galen, and Theophrastus were of the opinion that music helped to cure the pests and the stings of reptiles. Bonet, Baglivi, Diemerbroeck, Kercher, and Desault mention the efficacy of music in phthisis, gout, hydrophobia, and the bites of venomous snakes. Frequent case reports are found in which convulsive seizures are said to have been "terminated" upon hearing music. Patients with "violent fevers" and "conditions of delirium" are said to have recovered their senses and health upon hearing melodious music.

While it is true there is little basis in fact of the foregoing tales, nevertheless, it is well-known that music exerts an influence simply as a psychic stimulus which, in turn, produces physiologic effects.

From the more practical point of view we should not ignore the possible value of music in health and disease. In melancholia and hysteria it is probably of benefit, and sufferers of insomnia relate its beneficial effects in inducing sleep. Classical scholars will not forget that the singing of birds was tried as a remedy to overcome the insomnia of Malcenas. It is well-known that music is a good antidote to the pernicious habit of introspection and self-analysis, which is often a curse both to the highly cultured as well as to the hysteric.

The specific and rational effects of music have been widely accepted by both the laity and the medical profession at large. But only a few surgeons (1, 2, 3, 4, 10) have applied the principles to be here outlined, to their practice. The distinctive feature of music is its beneficial effect upon emotional disturbances. Perhaps the largest single cause of deep emotional upset of the hospitalized patient is the apprehension and anxiety of the surgical patient. Most people have psychologic weak spots, and most surgical patients are apprehensive, anxious, reacting emotionally rather than rationally.

The ideal response to a projected surgical operation would be a calm acceptance of the procedure as the means of overcoming a disfigurement or a disease process, with the expectation that while it will be an unpleasant experience, it will be tolerable. The patient should be expected to cooperate willingly and to bear with fortitude a certain amount of discomfort. Most patients, however, respond with fear and anxiety. These abnormal responses stem from several causes: The fear of death, the fear that a malignant condition may be found, the fear of loss of function, or of residual or resultant deformity or disfigurement. Despite adequate premedication and encouragement from friends and medical personnel, the surgical patient's normal reaction is one of anxiety and apprehension.

The art of surgery implies not only skillful execution of an operative procedure, but in addition, the expert handling of the patient as a sensitive, living human being. The experiences of our predecessors show that the success of professional medical effort depends greatly on developing and maintaining a close personal relationship between the physician and his patient. The intimate knowledge which a plastic surgeon acquires about each of his patients as a result of this relationship offers an advantage in extending the range of surgical and psychological service. Consequently the effects of our patients' mental experiences prior to operation, during its execution, and throughout the postoperative course have been a matter of concern and study for more than six years. The problem has taken on increased significance in the past decade as a result of the marked increase in the use of local, regional, and spinal anesthesia. These patients have presented an added opportunity to study their more complex experiences and reactions since they were conscious during the operation.

In days gone by, the surgeon's first concern was the preservation of life and function. But as surgery developed, greater security and more favorable results were envisaged, and with these advancements, other aspects, previously neglected or regarded as secondary now demand closer consideration. The use and value of music is among these.

THE USE AND VALUE OF MUSIC IN THE OPERATING ROOM

It is now well recognized that the emotions have a definite bearing on the patient's postoperative course and that an emotional or psychic state is a potent factor in the production of undesirable physiologic reactions. It has been shown (5, 6) that emotional states, such as fright or anxiety, stimulate the sympathetic nervous system and exhaust the vasomotor centers to a degree sufficient to initiate shock.

Types of Adult Patients

No patient looking forward to an operation is free from some degree of apprehension, regardless of whether or not the fact is betrayed in his demeanor. There are: (A) Those patients possessed of a placidly cheerful state of mind, making few inquiries, and meeting all circumstances cheerfully with apparent mental composure. (B) Others are nervous, loquacious, haunted by exaggerated forebodings, and who approach the operation with fear and trepidation. (C) The gloomy fatalistic type are characterized by a morbid indifference or a hopeless resignation. Finney (7) related that Halsted refused to operate upon patients with this fatalistic attitude or "I shall surely die if operated upon" complex.

A calm, confident state of mind manifested by the tranquility which comes from hopefulness rather than that of hopeless resignation undoubtedly will go far to increase the patient's fortitude and resistance to the operation, its sequelae, and promote a more pleasant convalescence.

Even at the beginning of our study about six years ago, it was apparent that music, although not alone, will help to eliminate fear, establish confidence and by producing a congenial environment will help to allay apprehension.

[173]

The introduction of music in the patient's room, the anesthesia room, the operating room, and the recovery room simplifies the task for the surgeon, the house officers, the nurses, and perhaps of even greater importance, the patient.

Few, if any, of the foregoing concepts or those which are to follow are new, for music was used in the anesthesia room as early as 1914 by Kane (1), who used a phonograph as a "means of calming and distracting the patients from the horror of the situation when undergoing the introduction." In 1929 Farr (2) advocated the use of music during surgical procedures under local anesthesia. He reported that time seemed to pass more quickly for the patients and they were less fearful of being hurt when their minds were otherwise occupied. In 1930 McGlinn (3) reported the use of a radio to divert patients' attention. Erdmann (8) used recordings. Straith (10) has used a radio in his Plastic Surgical Clinic for almost a decade. His patients have been grateful for this diversion when being operated upon under local anesthesia. The radio is located in an instrument cabinet and is controlled by one of the nurses. More recently Brown, Livingston and Williard (4) utilized a double, self-winding tape recorder to supply continuous music. They developed a duo-channel magnetic tape recorder which utilized a 4800 foot reel of standard one-quarter inch magnetic recording tape which when played at a speed of 7.5 inches per second will play for a total of four hours. This was achieved by using half of the width of the tape for each recording channel. In the forward direction, the top channel is used for a two-hour recording, at the end of which a solenoid is automatically activated, which reverses the direction of the tape and places the bottom channel in operation. Thus, the top channel rewinds while the bottom channel is playing. Even though these instruments are rather large and expensive, having been especially constructed by a recording engineer, the authors are sufficiently enthusiastic so that additional recorders are being constructed to provide a selection of classical, popular, and music suitable for children.

The Use of Music at Duke Hospital

In 1929 when the hospital was built, radio reception speakers and outlets were installed into each room on the private and semi-private floors, also individual "tap-ins" for each patient's bed on the wards. The only difference was in the type of instrumentation —private and semi-private patients could receive a selection of radio programs either through a wall speaker adjacent to the bed or through sponge rubber cushioned reception units or earphones. The program selector and volume are controlled by each patient. To avoid conflicts and the consequent jargon of multiple programs being delivered simultaneously, open ward patients have only "tap-ins" for cushioned earphones and hearing pieces.

Wall speakers are provided on the children's and infants' floors. Program selection and volume is controlled by the nurses in charge. Similar speakers are located in the ward utility and preparation rooms as a background subtle stimulus when tasks are monotonous. "Tap-ins" and speakers are strategically located in the recovery rooms.

Music in the Operating Room

Because of the effectiveness of music to the preoperative as well as to the post-operative patient, it occurred to us that it might be even more beneficial to those patients who are operated upon under local, regional, or spinal anesthesia. Thereupon, a portable radio was first installed into the plastic surgical operating and dressing room in March 1944. The comfort and composure of our patients was apparent immediately, their fears were allayed for their minds were diverted and occupied by the music rather than the thought of the operation.

A "push-button" type of radio is preferable to the hand turned dial in order to facilitate change of station and selection of program. However, there are several disadvantages in the use of the radio. An important one was our inability to obtain the type of

[175]

music or reading most suitable to the patient at hand. Another annoyance was the static interference from the electro-surgical units or X-ray apparatus on the operating room floor. However, the task of our nurses, the anesthetists, and orderlies has been lightened considerably by playing either the radio or record player between cases and at the end of the day. Because our radio-record players (figs. 1, 2, 3) are small and portable, they can be moved readily within our operating rooms or to an adjacent room. It has given pleasure and broken the monotony for our night shift and weekend-on-call nurses, supply and preparation room attendants, etc., whose task, in addition to emergency operations, is to thread needles, prepare packs, etc., for the next day. All in all, the use of music has made our operating rooms a more pleasant place in which to work.

Because of our interest in the therapeutic value of music, RCA Victor Division of the Radio Corporation of America made available to us several combination radio-phonograph instruments and a supply of records of various types of music and selected readings for children. The introduction of slow playing, unbreakable, vinyl plastic records has simplified the use of the record player. Because of their small size, their various colors and essential indestructibility, the problem of storage, cataloging, and selection of the various types of music (by the color of the records) is simplified. The unbreakable feature of the records is of especial importance for the instrument on the children's floor, where the instrument is operated by them (fig. 1).

Cushioned earphones are used primarily for those patients operated upon under local, regional, or block anesthesia. Aviator type of headphones* (fig. 2, 3) are readily available from most radio supply houses or stores handling war surplus materials.* This cushioned type of headpiece is preferable to the stethoscope variety, for cleansing is not necessary, irritation and pressure is

---

* Head set HS-33, manufactured by Radio Speakers, Inc., Chicago, Illinois.

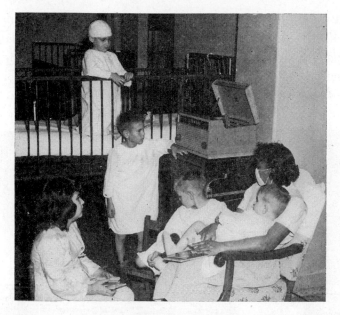

FIG. 1. The pleasures which children derive from a radio-phonograph simplifies markedly their custodial care. Unless preoccupied and distracted during hospitalization, many children become morose, despondent, and homesick, for they are unable to comprehend the necessity of elective procedures. The transfer of a child's emotion of abject fear and terror, to one of reassurance, sympathy, and understanding consideration is enhanced by the use of music, stories, and readings.

Childhood experiences may condition the response of the adult. Unfortunate memories in infancy may have irreparable fears, for a child is vulnerable and fragile, both physically and psychically.

avoided, and of greater importance, all extraneous noises and conversation are excluded.

The earphone attachment or headpiece is readily installed using a telephone type or radio jack on the secondary circuit of the speaker (fig. 2). When radio or phonograph music or readings are to be played via the earphones for the patient's exclusive hearing pleasure, the plug is inserted into the instrument. At the end of the procedure, the plug may be withdrawn to play music for the occupants of the room. The radio or record player can be used alternately as desired by turning a switch.

A sustaining program of infinite length and variety can be arranged without difficulty or inconvenience for the entire day. With 33 or 45 R.P.M. records and automatic changer, it is not necessary to change records oftener than once each hour. The use of electrical coagulation-desiccation units, X-ray equipment, etc. do not interfere with the reproduction of recorded music as they do with the

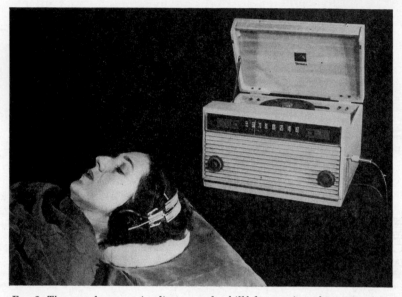

FIG. 2. The art of surgery implies not only skillful execution of an operative procedure but in addition, expert handling of the patient from a psychic standpoint. Music helps immeasurably in this task for it helps to prevent psychic trauma.

As shown, the instrument for a continuous program of the patient's choice is small, portable, and inexpensive. It is readily adaptable for induction of general anesthesia or when the operation is performed under local anesthesia. Music or readings will help to carry the patient's thoughts, mood, and emotions along pleasingly distractful avenues.

radio reception. The instrument is grounded constantly to avoid static spark and hazard when explosive gases are used.

Psychic Control of the Patient With Music

It is not sufficient to have mastered the technique of local, regional, or spinal anesthesia and to be expert in one's special field of surgery, for these factors are unquestioned prerequisites. Of equal importance is one's ability to prepare psychologically the patient for operation. To that end, we outline to the patient the preoperative routine and what is to be expected prior to, and during the operation if it is to be performed under local anesthesia. Another friendly call from the house officer or the anesthetist, the night prior to operation, is extremely comforting to the patient and helpful to the surgeon. An undetailed enumeration of what will take place is made, outlining the benefits of the sedative given at bedtime and the hypodermic to be given in the morning. To those patients who have had operations in the days when induction of anesthesia was a frightening, strangulating experience, is stressed the ease of induction with sodium pentothal, or the advantages of local anesthesia.

If the operation is to be performed under local or spinal anesthesia, it is explained that music will be played exclusively for their pleasure. It is too late to try and explain this immediately before or during the operation. For this only helps to arouse suspicion, apprehension, and anxiety. Every effort is made to minimize the patient's mental and physical discomfort. To maintain the same position for an hour or longer, taxes the patience of the calmest and most obedient individual.

Music will direct the attention of the patient from himself to the music. With the cushioned earphones, the "silence" of the operating room is not disturbed. The operator's discussion of the findings, the assistants' questions, the explanation of the procedure to be executed may be discussed. Since the cushioned head-set excludes almost all sounds, it is essentially impossible for the patient to hear any conversation or sound of operative procedure, and hence, there is no chance of erroneous interpretation or the development of harmful suspicions in a mind already tortured by doubt.

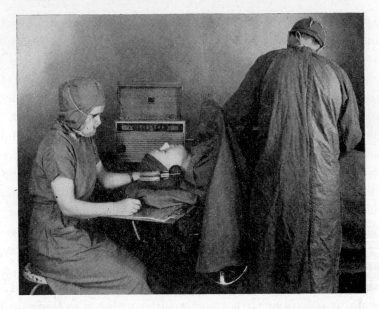

FIG. 3. Too often, patients under local, spinal, or regional anesthesia are permitted to hear details of the operation, of their pathology, or to hear the teaching of the surgeon or instruction of the assistants and nurses. The patient hearing this, may fear that he is being handled by incompetent personnel, or he may interpret his condition or the findings as unfavorable. The request for or the noise of instruments is in itself suggestive of pain. All of these unpleasantries are unnecessary and can be avoided by the use of music or readings played directly to the conscious patient via the earphones. The cushioned headset excludes all sounds, there is no chance of erroneous interpretation or the development of harmful suspicions in a mind already tortured by doubt.

The photo shows the rear view of the Barnes Hospital gown, the original pattern of which was supplied by Dr. F. R. Bradley. The gown is sterile front and back, and is tied in front by the wearer.

Psychic Control of the Child With Music or Selected Readings

Childhood experiences will, in many instances, condition the response of the adult. Unfortunate experiences with surgery in childhood may leave irreparable fears, for a child is vulnerable and fragile, both psychically and physically. It is not uncommon to see a child screaming with terror taken from his bed to the operating room, where this fear is accentuated by strangers with green caps, masks, gowns, and gloves. This abject fear is accentuated as he is forcibly restrained with the induction of the anesthetic agent. These experiences may leave psychic scars with the child, who is usually unable to comprehend the necessity of the procedure.

Children are prepared psychically for operation by being told as much as they can understand about the procedure. It is very important to emphasize that the operation will not be performed until the child is asleep. If the child is old enough, the difference between unconsciousness and sleep is explained. This will avoid the postoperative fear of going to sleep. During the afternoon story-telling period (fig. 1), the nurses and aides act out the operative procedure using dolls, followed by mimicked dressings, feedings, use of a bedpan, etc. The need for reassurance, sympathy, and understanding consideration at this period is greater than at any other single time in the life of a child. Children so conditioned will, in many instances, welcome the operation, for they are then the center of attraction and can command unusual attention.

"Early to Bed and Early to Rise" Makes———?

Following admission and routine workup and preparation for operation not infrequently the patient is left entirely alone, without food or water, and without any source of comfort except music, while he waits with apprehension, anxiety, and fear throughout the night for his summons to the operating room. While the selection of music, readings, or radio programs may not be of his first choice, nevertheless, it comforts, soothes, and distracts him sufficiently to transfer his personal preoccupation to that of the music or program. This transfer of attention along avenues other than his own, has lessened the anxiety of the preoperative patient and has made his convalescence so much more pleasant.

The day of operation. Having been given a "light" supper twelve or more hours previously, the patient awakes or is awakened very early to check his temperature, pulse, and respiration, following which he is left entirely alone to await, perhaps for many hours, his fate.

[181]

Since it may not be possible to schedule operations as to exact time, the patient is sometimes moved to the anesthesia room adjacent to the operating room prematurely. There he remains in fear, suspense, and apprehension for many long minutes. Music or readings at this time are especially comforting and most welcome. This, in contrast to the distressing noise of a patient's groan, a child's cry, the noise of clanging basins, glassware, and instruments, the misinterpreted conversation of the operating floor personnel. Patients do appreciate deeply a short visit from their surgeon immediately prior to the operation.

The Operation. Too often, patients under local, spinal, or regional anesthesia are permitted to hear details of the operation, of their pathology, or to hear the teaching of the surgeon or instruction of the assistants. The patient hearing this may fear that he is being handled by an incompetent surgeon, or he may interpret his condition or the findings as unfavorable. The request for or the noise of instruments is in itself suggestive of pain. All of these unpleasantries are unnecessary and are avoided by the use of music or readings played directly to the conscious patient via the earphones (figs. 2, 3).

Types of Music Conducive for the Patient

Literally all types of music and many selected readings are available on slow revolving plastic records. Appropriate musical selections and readings are also available for children of various age groups. Soft, soothing, melodious orchestrations and vocals were found to be appreciated by most of our patients. The music of Wayne King, Sammy Kaye, and the singing of Vaughn Monroe exemplify favorites. The music of these artists is slow, restful, and suggestive of sleep and calm. Bass and baritone solos and quartet arrangements, exemplified by the music of the Mills Brothers was especially pleasing to many patients. Soprano vocals were pleasing to only a small group of our patients, who were musical artists themselves. Piano, violin, and string quartets were very welcome providing the tempo was slow and melodious. After-dinner types of music carried well the patient's thoughts, mood, and emotions along pleasingly distractful avenues.

Hymns, spirituals, and martial music in some patients increased the emotional tension and were the least acceptable.

Types of recorded music used in our study included the following: Symphonies, classics, opera, piano, piano and violin, string quartets, martial and band music, hymns, spirituals, jazz, swing, scores from musicals, westerns, hillbilly, theme songs, old time favorites, and the current classics and popular music.

Stories, selected readings, and music for children preoccupied their minds in a most gratifying way thereby facilitating the change of painful dressings or the induction of anesthesia. Soft music was restful and suggestive of sleep at naptime (fig. 1).

The radio may provide diversion for the personnel between operative cases and at the end of the day, and while it is helpful to break the monotony for the nurses and attendants on night duty, its scope for use in the operating room is limited because of the inability to obtain the type of program most conducive for each patient. The use of other electrical equipment—the electro-cautery, shavers, X-ray apparatus, etc. may interfere with reception. When these interfering factors were not present, variety and musical programs were acceptable. News broadcasts were to some patients informative and pleasing, while to others they were quite distressing, depending upon the content.

The patients tested prior to, during, and following operations came from all walks of life; were of both sexes and all age groups. Those tested during operation were predominantly adults on whom local, regional, or spinal anesthesia was used.

While women may have less physical resistance and are more susceptible to nervous disturbances than men, they are as a group more tolerant and adapt themselves more readily to hospital routine.

[183]

Postoperative Use of Music

There are many devices which can be used to occupy the patient's interest following operation. Of extreme importance is the daily visit from the physician or surgeon to assure the patient that all is well. Confidence must be displayed to inspire the patient. Unless distracted in some way, the patient may, and often does, focus his attention upon himself or his experiences. Pain, discomfort, insomnia, sadness, apathy, and dissatisfaction often stem from periods of "cerebral inoccupation." These "symptoms," at least in some instances, may be exaggerated by over-sedation and make him feel that he is still an ill patient. We have found that in some patients, especially where self-preoccupation was pronounced, that music diverted their attention to a degree sufficient so that the need for medication was reduced, and the clarity of mind, absence of confusion, with their attentions directed along avenues other than their own, has made our patients' convalescence easier and more pleasant.

DISCUSSION

The significance of the mental outlook upon patients was recognized as early as the thirteenth century when Henri de Mondville wrote: "Encourage the patient with music of the sweet-stringed psaltery and with forged messages describing the death and confusion of his enemies or his elevation to a bishopric if he be a churchman." Hunt (9) stated, "It is the mind which bears the burden of every illness and directs the adjustment of the individual to pain, deformity and invalidism in all its various forms, so that any clinical method which ignores this master function of the body is greatly defective and may lead to serious error in interpretation and treatment."

The success of our professional medical and surgical efforts depends greatly on developing and maintaining a closer personal relationship between the physician and patient. The intimate knowledge which we acquire about our patients as a result of this relationship offers a peculiar advantage in extending the range of our surgical and psychological service. As specialists, we must be ever mindful to consider the patient as a very sensitive human being, and not to be prejudiced in our view of the patient by our natural preoccupation with our specialty. This approach not only to tissue pathology and the primary surgical or medical, but to the needs and desires of the patient, takes but little extra time, patience, and energy. This is not a specialty, but part of the art of medicine and surgery.

The patient who is emotionally prepared and intellectually occupied during the pre and postoperative phases of his hospitalization will suffer less from psychic trauma, and will have a shorter and more comfortable convalescence. Music helps to accomplish this result.

Conclusions

Music for our patients has done much to eliminate fear, anxiety, and apprehension by establishing first a congenial mood and environment in their rooms.

Music augments the advantages of local, regional, and spinal anesthesia, for it relieves the psychic strain of the patient. It will divert the attention of the patient from himself to music. Cushioned earphones exclude all sounds from the operating room, thereby placing the patient, surgeon and assistants at comparative ease since the possibility of erroneous interpretation of conversation or the development of harmful suspicions is eliminated.

A radio-phonograph with automatic record changer supplies an almost continuous source of music or readings most conducive to the patient, adult or child. The instrument is versatile, small, readily portable, and inexpensive. Slow revolving unbreakable records are available with essentially unlimited selection of type of music. Reproduction is excellent and no mechanical knowledge is necessary for its operation.

[185]

Soft, soothing, melodious, sweet orchestrations were most acceptable to all patients. Hymns, spirituals, and martial music were the least acceptable.

The inherent value of music to our patients, our associates, assistants, nurses, anesthetists and operating room personnel has made us enthusiastic advocates of its use. A better atmosphere is created for all by the alleviation of tension. It is self-evident that any agent which will do this is worthwhile. Music accomplishes this and has made our operating room a more pleasant place in which to work.

The art of surgery implies not only skillful execution of an operative procedure, but in addition, expert handling of the patient from a psychic standpoint. Music helps immeasurably in this task for it helps to prevent psychic trauma.

BIBLIOGRAPHY

1. Kane, E.: The Phonograph in the Operating Room. *J. Am. Med. Assoc. 62*:1829 (June 6), 1914.
2. Farr, R. E.: Practical Local Anesthesia. 2nd Edition. Phil'a., Lee and Febiger, 1929, Chapter V.
3. McGlinn, J. A.: Music in the Operating Room. *Am. J. Obst. and Gynec. 20*:678, 727 (Nov.) 1930.
4. Brown, R. E., Livingston, H. M., and Williard, J.: Silent Music Soothes the Surgical Patient. *Modern Hospital, 72*:51 (Apr.) 1949.
5. Cannon, W. B.: Traumatic Shock. New York, D. O. Appleton Company, 1923.
6. Crile, G. W. and Lower, W. E.: Surgical Shock. Phil'a., W. B. Saunders Company, 1920.
7. Finney, J. M. T.: The Role of the Imponderables in Surgery. *J. Florida M. A., 25*:11, 1938.
8. Erdmann, A. F.: The Silent Gramophone in Local Anesthesia and Therapy. *Anesthesia and Analgesia, 13*:570 (Nov.-Dec.) 1934.
9. Hunt, J. R.: Nature and Treatment of Psychic and Emotional Factors in Disease. *J. Am. Med. Assoc. 89*:1014, 1927.
10. Straith, Claire L.: Personal Communication and Observation at the Straith Plastic Surgical Clinic, Detroit, Mich.

CONTROL OF ATHETOTIC TREMORS BY
SOUND CONTROL

By MARTIN F. PALMER* and LOUIS E. ZERBE

There are apparently few references in the literature to the objective study of the use or effects of music in relation to cerebral palsy, and the available references are difficult to review because as a rule the authors have not reported specific symptomatology. Moreover, references are usually to "spastics," and are therefore either limited in scope or ambiguous.

In 1937, Lord (*10*, 13-14) stated: "Massage or rhythmic exercises done to favorite tunes are usually considered pleasurable and relaxing. . . . If the rhythm is sufficiently slow so that the child is not under the strain of 'keeping up' to the time, the rigid limbs relax and the athetoid motions noticeably decrease. As the child's whole body swings into rhythm, the bells, clappers, or cymbals selected according to the capacity of the child sound more and more accurately in time and give convincing evidence of increased efficiency of motion." It is not clear whether or not Lord meant that the children were attempting to play musical instruments. Donaldson (*5*, 8) claimed that "spastics" were usually monotones but could make improvement.

The possible uses of music in treating cerebral palsy are illustrated by Carlson's (*2*, 324) case of a spastic girl who was so muscle conscious during meals that she could not feed herself, but

* Martin F. Palmer (Sc.D., Michigan, 1937) is Director of the Institute of Logopedics and Head of the Department of Logopedics of the Municipal University of Wichita. Louis E. Zerbe (M.M., Arthur Jordan Conservatory of Music, 1938) was formerly Professor of Violin, Municipal University of Wichita, and has done graduate work in musicology at Yale University. He is at present a member of the New Haven Symphony.

[187]

nevertheless was able to forget herself at music to the extent that she played the piano most satisfactorily. Also Myers (*11*), in 1938, advised muting rhythmic musical instruments so as to render them less distracting or shocking to the already over-stimulated brain. "Often in the enthusiasm and interest in playing an instrument with a group of others, you will find a child able to use both hands quite readily and his exultation when he finds he can is great" (*11*, 84). It will be noted that this statement by Myers concerning the muting of instruments is not confirmed in the present experimental series.

In 1934, Carlson (*3*, 3) advised having the patient concentrate on something else besides the exercises and stated: "Low, rhythmic music will obviate this difficulty, or anything which will tend to reduce the sensorial input to a minimum will be helpful." Later (1939), he said: "Rhythmic movements of the limbs accompanied by soothing music, heat . . . are among the factors that are conducive to relaxation" (*4*, 7).

The remainder of the literature concerned with music and cerebral palsy is similar in scope and description.

The following pertinent statement by Altshuler (*1*, 792) is in order: "It is amazing that with such a large body of information and observation regarding the various properties of music, little has been translated into practice. One would expect that a medium which affects emotion, the endocrines, the circulation, the respiration, the blood pressure, the mood, association and imagery, would be worthy of further investigation." According to Altshuler (*1*, 793), mental patients difficult to reach through the spoken word are still accessible rhythmically and tonally via the thalamus. Musical sounds apparently make themselves known on the cortex through the thalamus. A logical supposition follows that musical training would have definite effects on all malfunctions caused by brain lesions because of this tendency to produce cortical function and voluntary movements in time with the music.

Turning to athetosis itself, the literature is surprisingly scanty from the standpoint of objective study. Herz (*6*, 320) gives a good discussion of the symptomatology and his excellent description applies in some part to the subject studied in the present experiment.

Klingman and Carlson (*9*, 212-216) have published some

kymographic tracings in athetosis.[1] Actually there appears to be no long-time consecutive study of athetotic tremors by means of the kymograph, and while detailed material cannot be presented in this article, this particular series of experiments represents the first long series of kymographic tracings in such a case.

According to Hoefer and Putnam (8, 11), the tremor in athetosis occurs as a result of irregular simultaneous motor unit discharges to antagonist muscles. Vermiform movement in athetosis is the result of this irregular discharge. The antagonists are in almost constant simultaneous innervation.

THE SUBJECT

The subject was examined at the Institute of Logopedics of the Municipal University of Wichita in February, 1938. He had cerebral palsy, no intelligible speech, poor locomotion and, at the age of twenty-one years, was unable to dress himself.

The symptoms were a combination of spastic paralysis and tension athetosis. There were no overt vermiform movements. He was an honor graduate of high school and has since graduated from the University of Wichita. He now has intelligible speech, adequate locomotion, writes crude longhand and earns his own living.

In September, 1943, his right hand assumed suddenly some degree of relaxation. Upon disappearance of the tension athetosis, a true vermiform movement of the fingers of the right hand began, which was particularly marked in the index finger. The kymographic curves obtained by recording this movement changed constantly throughout the experiments, a finding which is in itself of interest. Most typically, the finger went into a slight extensor contraction, was held there temporarily, then moved downward, each joint moving in turn proximodistally until the finger was depressed with considerable force upon the tambour. There was then a slight pause, which was not a true pause but a more or less sinusoidal

---

[1] During the present series of experiments, the subject at one time or another demonstrated all of the curves illustrated in the article cited, plus many others.

curve. In the tracings (see Figures 1, 2 and 3), lateral movements as well as vertical movements are represented, since these could not be distinguished by means of the apparatus. Nevertheless all of the muscles involved acted in a similar fashion.

This phenomenon was called to the attention of Professor Zerbe, of the Department of Music, and it was agreed that a study should be made of the effect of musical tones and rhythms, primarily those of the violin, on this tremor. The findings made for the first time in these experiments are therefore to be considered joint findings.

PROCEDURE

The subject was seated in a school desk chair where he could not see the recording styli or the experimenters. Into the inkwell hole of the desk a large tambour from the Lombard radial pulse apparatus was inserted. The subject's forearm was strapped to the desk to avoid involuntary movements of his arm. His finger was placed directly upon the tambour.

The finger movements were recorded on a Miller kymograph with the usual apparatus. A 1/5 second timer was used. The paper records ran about twelve minutes each, and it was possible to make two records each experimental day. The violin used in most of the experiments was an original Pressanda made in 1827 in Turin, Italy, and came from the Dykes collection in London. The room was sound-proofed, but some noise did come through the door. In all except one experimental day the only persons present were Professor Zerbe, Professor Palmer and the subject.[2]

For each experiment the authors prepared an outline in advance. When the outlined procedure had been completed, innovations were tried on the basis of the day's results. These improvisations are reported as part of the regular series of experiments.

[2] The subject was highly intelligent and not naive to experimental procedures. He quickly grasped the purpose of each experiment in spite of the utmost precautions. He could observe to some extent changes in the method of procedure. It may also be of some significance that he was extremely fond of music and reacted quite emotionally to music in general.

The records were carefully analyzed by the usual techniques. The mass of detail, all of it important, was so great that the authors were forced to select only certain phases to report at this time. The records, complete analysis and all the data are on file at the Institute of Logopedics. A graph of the rate of the tremor was made for all experiments except 74, 98, 99, 110, 111, 112, 113, 119, 120, 121, and 125. These experiments could not be graphed. Most of the conclusions reached are based upon changes in rate and actual cessation of the tremor, rather than on the extent and vigor of the movements. The experiments which could not be graphed will be reported separately as the martele series.

FINDINGS

Two very distinct groups of sound stimuli are represented in this series of experiments: (1) a more or less heterogeneous group and (2) a homogeneous group consisting of very sharp explosive isolated sound surges, which will be described later under the general title "Martele Series." It should be remembered that during the latter part of the series, the experiments comprising the martele series have been arbitrarily excluded for separate discussion, although actually they were part of the learning series of the experiment.

Tables 1 and 2 should be read as follows: *X* under *Experimental* means a stable vigorous pattern of tremor movement, *X* under *Control* means complete or nearly complete remission of tremor; *X?* under *Experimental* means a vigorous but somewhat irregular pattern of tremor movement, *X?* under *Control* means some reduction in rate of tremor; *O?* under *Experimental* means that the rate was not stable or vigorous but that there seemed to have been some effect upon it, *O?* under *Control* means a very slight reduction in rate which could not be considered mathematically certain; *O* under *Experimental* means that no effect could be observed, under *Control* it means that no reduction in rate occurred.

Full descriptions of the stimuli used in this experimental series are as follows:

[191]

Scale G to G without vibrato. Sustained notes of approximately 15 seconds duration on the violin, low G to G one octave above (experiments 1, 3, 4 and 122).

Scale G to G with vibrato. Sustained notes on the violin of approximately 15 seconds duration with vibrato, low G to G above, vibrato on low G "faked" (experiments 2, 5 and 123).

Scale C3 to C4 harmonics with and without vibrato. Sustained tones of approximately 15 seconds duration (experiments 6 and 7).

Open G on stylus downbeat. Open G arco on downbeat of stylus mezzo forté, on extension phase of tremor (experiments 8, 16, 94, 96 and 108).

Open G on stylus upbeat. Open G arco on upbeat of stylus mezzo forté, on flexion phase of tremor (experiment 9).

Low A vibrato on stylus downbeat and upbeat. Same as for open G (experiments 10, 11 and 11a).

C3 and C4 with and without vibrato on stylus upbeat and downbeat. Similar to open G and open A stimuli (experiments 12, 13, 14, 15 and 15a).

Scale G to G and return to low G. Sustained notes without vibrato from low G to G above, then reversing the scale to low G again with approximately 10 seconds on each note of the upward scale and 15 seconds on each note of the downward scale (experiment 17).

Pizzicato chords on downbeat. Theme from Sevcik, Opus 2, Part 6, played in pizzicato on downbeat of stylus (experiments 18, 20, 22, 31, 41, 82 and 105).

Pizzicato single notes on downbeat. The notes used were the fundamentals from the Sevcik theme (experiments 19 and 32).

Spiccato à ricochet. The Sevcik theme played in spiccato à ricochet with a strong beat on the fundamental of each chord, each beat being on the downbeat of the stylus, four notes to each chord. In all such experiments the stylus indicated volume as well as tempo (experiments 21, 23, 24, 25, 26, 27, 30, 33, 34, 36, 38, 40, 42, 44, 67, 72, 75, 77, 86, 95, 97, 100 and 104).

"Rigaudon" in beat. "Rigaudon" from "Siciliano and Rigaudon" by Fritz Kreisler played allegro using the stylus as a tempo indicator (experiments 27, 29 and 35, experiment 43 at concert rate).

"Siciliano" not in beat. "Siciliano" from "Siciliano and Rigaudon" by Fritz Kreisler played at the usual concert rate without using the stylus as a tempo indicator (experiments 28 and 29).

"My Old Kentucky Home." Arranged by Louis E. Zerbe in double, triple and quadruple stops for violin alone played at usual concert rate without attention to stylus tempo (experiments 37, 39 and 45).

Tschaikowsky slow movement. "Concerto for Violin and Orchestra," by Tschaikowsky, slow movement, played at usual concert rate without attention to the stylus tempo (experiments 46, 48, 50, 52, 70, 71, 88 and 126, violin muted during experiment 71).

"Danse Tzigane." "Danse Tzigane" by Tividar Nachez, the friska or presto movement played at the usual concert rate without attention to stylus tempo (experiments 47 and 51).

Low G and high C orchestra bells. Repeated lowest and highest notes respectively on the orchestra bells, one note on each downward beat of the stylus (experiments 53 and 54).

Thirds, orchestra bells. Repeated thirds on the orchestra bells, middle C and E above, one chord on each downward beat of the stylus (experiments 55 and 56).

Arpeggios, orchestra bells. Simple harmonic triads in arpeggio formation throughout a simple harmonic progression with four notes to each downward beat of the stylus (experiments 57 and 58).

"Swanee River," orchestra bells. Melody of "Swanee River" by Stephen Foster played at usual concert rate, without attention to the stylus tempo (experiments 59 and 61).

Minor tune, orchestra bells. Free extemporization of a folk-like melody similar in tempo and length to "Old Black Joe" by Stephen Foster (experiment 60).

Cigar box on downbeat. Bell hammer tapping lid of closed cigar box using the stylus as volume and tempo indicator, one tap per beat (experiments 62 and 87).

Cigar box, various rhythms. Bell hammer tapping lid of closed cigar box with two to four taps per stylus beat, chosen haphazardly (experiment 63).

Tapping various items. Tripod stand, table, cigar box, etc. tapped haphazardly, one tap per stylus beat (experiment 64).

Clapping hands on downbeat. Hands clapped very loudly, one clap per stylus downbeat (experiment 65).

Alternate bell and cigar box. Lowest G on the orchestra bells tapped alternately with lid of cigar box, one tap per stylus down-beat (experiment 66).

Max Bruch Adagio. Second movement, "Adagio," from the "Concerto in G Minor for Violin" by Max Bruch played at the usual concert rate without attention to the stylus tempo (experiments 68 and 69).

TABLE 1. Specific experimental effect of each sound stimulus.

Day	Run*	Exp. No.	Stimulus	Experi- mental	Time in Seconds	Con- trol	Time in Seconds
1st	1st	1.	Scale G to G without vibrato	0	ca.120	0	ca. 120
1st	2nd	2.	Scale G to G with vibrato	0	ca.120	0	115.2
1st	2nd	3.	Scale G to G without vibrato	X?	99.6	0	39.6
2nd	1st	4.	Scale G to G without vibrato	0	113.8	0	62.8
2nd	1st	5.	Scale G to G with vibrato	0	106.0	0	28.2
2nd	2nd	6.	C3 to C4 harmonics without vibrato	0	119.5	X?	48.3
2nd	2nd	7.	C3 to C4 harmonics with vibrato	0	120.0	0	76.6
3rd	1st	8.	Open G on stylus downbeat	0	29.6	0	70.8
3rd	1st	9.	Open G on stylus upbeat	0	45.3	X	34.9
3rd	1st	10.	Low A vibrato on stylus downbeat (Curve pattern of tremor changes)	X?	62.2	0	27.8
3rd	1st	11.	Low A vibrato on stylus downbeat	0	28.6		
		11a.	followed by low A vibrato on upbeat		154.2		
3rd	2nd	12.	C4 on stylus downbeat	0	59.0	0	30.6
3rd	2nd	13.	C4 on stylus upbeat	0	32.4	0	27.4
3rd	2nd	14.	C3 vibrato on downbeat	0	31.2	0	30.4
3rd	2nd	15.	C3 vibrato on upbeat	0	31.8	0	24.2
3rd	2nd	15a.	C4 on downbeat	X	196.7		
4th	1st	16.	Open G on downbeat	X	60.0		
4th	1st	17.	Scale G to G and return to low G	0	228.9	0	66.2
4th	1st	18.	Pizzicato chords on downbeat	(1) X	18.0	X?	12.8
				(2) X	14.6	X?	22.4
4th	1st	19.	Pizzicato single notes on downbeat	X		X	
4th	2nd	20.	Pizzicato chords on downbeat	(1) X	21.6	0	20.4
				(2) X	21.4	0	21.4
				(3) X	22.4	0	21.2
4th	2nd	21.	Spiccato à ricochet	(1) X	26.4	0	20.0
				(2) X	34.4	X	19.5
				(3) X	27.2	X	19.4
4th	2nd	22.	Pizzicato chords on downbeat	(1) X	18.4	X?	24.6
				(2) X	18.6	X?	26.0
4th	2nd	23.	Spiccato à ricochet	(1) X	19.8	X	32.6
				(2) X	23.6	X?	21.6
				(3) X	20.0	X	ca. 7.0
5th	1st	24.	Spiccato à ricochet	(1) X	18.8	X	19.4
				(2) X	21.6	X?	30.0
				(3) X	21.0	X	23.2
				(4) X?	18.4	0	34.0
				(5) X	19.6	X	59.8
5th	1st	25.	Spiccato à ricochet	(1) X	19.0	X	26.0
				(2) X	16.2	X?	22.0
				(3) X	21.0	X	41.8
		(Subject coughed)		(4) X	26.0	0	22.2
		(Arm and shoulder tremor)		(5) X	22.6	0	ca. 20.0

Table I. *(Continued)*

Day	Run*	Exp. No.	Stimulus		Experi-mental	Time in Seconds	Con-trol	Time in Seconds
5th	2nd	26.	Spiccato à ricochet		(1) X	16.2	X?	18.8
					(2) X	17.0	X	19.8
5th	2nd	27.	Spiccato à ricochet and Rigaudon in beat		(1) X?	8.6		
					(2) X	38.2	X	32.2
					(3) X	18.6	X	13.2
5th	2nd	28.	Siciliano not in beat		(1) X	27.8	X	14.8
					(2) X	22.6	X	20.2
					(3) X?	30.0	X?	18.2
5th	2nd	29.	Rigaudon vs. Siciliano	Rig.	(1) X	18.4	X	48.2
				Sic.	(2) X	20.4	X	39.6
				Rig.	(3) X	17.0	X?	32.4
6th	1st	30.	Spiccato à ricochet (Eblen assisting)†		(1) X?	21.0	0?	17.6
					(2) 0?	25.0	0	24.2
					(3) X	25.2	0?	27.6
6th	1st	31.	Pizzicato chords on downbeat (Eblen assisting)		(1) X?	26.8	X?	16.6
					(2) X	18.4	X?	20.6
					(3) X	17.8	X?	32.0
6th	1st	32.	Pizzicato single notes on downbeat (Eblen assisting)		X?	23.0	X?	41.0
6th	1st	33.	Spiccato à ricochet (Eblen assisting)		(1) 0?	58.2	X?	35.8
					(2) X?	22.4	X?	35.2
					(3) X	21.6	X	24.2
6th	2nd	34.	Spiccato à ricochet (Eblen assisting)		(1) X	22.2	X?	23.2
					(2) 0	23.6	0	18.8
6th	2nd	35.	Rigaudon on downbeat (Eblen assisting)		(1) X?	26.8	0	13.6
					(2) X?	36.6	0	35.8
					(3) X	36.2	0	18.6
6th	2nd	36.	Spiccato à ricochet (Eblen assisting)		X	19.2	X	19.8
6th	2nd	37.	My Old Kentucky Home (Eblen assisting)		X	43.8	0?	23.0
6th	2nd	38.	Spiccato à ricochet (Eblen assisting)		(1) X?	19.4	X?	23.8
					(2) X?	19.0	X?	25.4
6th	2nd	39.	My Old Kentucky Home (Eblen assisting)		(1) X?	18.0	X	20.2
					(2) X	17.0	X	17.4
					(3) X	5.4	X	13.6
7th	1st	40.	Spiccato à ricochet		X	19.0	0	27.2
7th	1st	41.	Spiccato and pizzicato chords		X	31.4	0?	38.8
7th	1st	42.	Spiccato a ricochet		X	25.6	0?	35.6
7th	1st	43.	Rigaudon not in beat		X	25.8	X?	33.6
7th	1st	44.	Spiccato à ricochet		X	19.8	X?	32.8
7th	1st	45.	My Old Kentucky Home		(1) X	20.6	X	24.4
					(2) X	11.0	X	16.6
					(3) X	10.4	X	16.2
					(4) X	7.6	X	13.8
					(5) X	11.0	X	22.6
					(6) X	4.4	X	19.4
					(7) X	3.6	0?	20.0
7th	2nd	46.	Tschaikowsky slow movement		X?	23.4	X	22.4
7th	2nd	47.	Danse Tzigane		X	17.6	X?	14.2
7th	2nd	48.	Tschaikowsky slow movement		X	23.0	X	39.8
7th	2nd	49.	My Country Tis of Thee		X	9.0	X	38.0
7th	2nd	50.	Tschaikowsky slow movement		(1) X	36.0	X	36.8
					(2) X	42.4	X	56.2
7th	2nd	51.	Danse Tzigane		X	31.4	X	13.2
7th	2nd	52.	Tschaikowsky slow movement		(1) X	10.6	X	46.6
					(2) X	40.8	X	17.2
8th	1st	53.	Low G orchestra bells		(1) X	18.0	X?	17.4
					(2) X	19.2	0?	22.6

TABLE I. *(Continued)*

Day	Run*	Exp. No.	Stimulus	Experimental	Time in Seconds	Control	Time in Seconds
8th	1st	54.	High C orchestra bells	(1) X	20.8	0?	24.4
				(2) X	17.4	X	24.2
8th	1st	55.	Thirds orchestra bells	(1) X	22.2	X	37.6
				(2) X	20.6	X	21.2
8th	1st	56.	Thirds orchestra bells	(1) X	3.4	X	3.6
				(2) X	2.6	X	6.6
				(3) X	3.4	X	24.2
8th	1st	57.	Arpeggios orchestra bells	(1) X	22.8	X?	23.0
				(2) X	18.2	X	24.8
				(3) X	13.4	X	14.4
8th	1st	58.	Arpeggios orchestra bells	(1) X	2.2	X	10.2
				(2) X	2.0	X	13.4
				(3) X	5.8	X	10.4
				(4) X	5.0	X	5.0
8th	2nd	59.	Swanee River orchestra bells	(1) X	17.2	X?	23.2
				(2) X?	16.4	X?	40.4
				(3) X	17.6	X	28.4
8th	2nd	60.	Minor tune orchestra bells		X?	33.6	X?	68.4
8th	2nd	61.	Swanee River orchestra bells	(1) X	3.6	X	18.8
				(2) X	4.0	X	11.4
				(3) X	6.8	X	14.0
				(4) X	2.0	X	12.2
8th	2nd	62.	Cigar box on downbeat	X	17.2	X	17.2
8th	2nd	63.	Cigar box, various rhythms	X	25.8	X	18.6
8th	2nd	64.	Tapping various items	X?	37.4	0?	33.6
8th	2nd	65.	Clapping hands on downbeat	X	21.0	X	27.8
8th	2nd	66.	Alternate bell and cigar box	X	20.4	X	10.0
9th	1st	67.	Spiccato à ricochet	(1) X?	20.8	0?	23.6
				(2) X	18.4	0	23.2
				(3) X	18.6	0?	34.0
8th	1st	68.	Max Bruch Adagio	(1) X	30.0	0	24.8
				(2) X	30.0	X?	28.6
9th	1st	69.	Max Bruch Adagio	(1) X	99.0	X	22.2
				(2) X?	56.8	X?	43.2
9th	2nd	70.	Tschaikowsky slow movement	X	70.2	X?	14.6
9th	2nd	71.	Tschaikowsky slow movement muted	X?	70.4	X?	15.4
9th	2nd	72.	Spiccato à ricochet (muted)	(1) X	10.2	X?	10.4
				(2) X	1.0	X?	3.4
				(3) X	1.4	X	3.4
				(4) X	2.4	X	7.8
9th	2nd	73.	Rapid C scale	X	3.0	X	3.0
9th	2nd	74.	Martele series				
9th	2nd	75.	Russian Soldier's Song and spiccato a ricochet	X?	27.4, 6.4	X?	18.0
9th	2nd	76.	Russian Soldier's Song	X	43.8	X?	12.8
9th	2nd	77.	Spiccato à ricochet	(1) X	14.4	X?	15.0
				(2) X	19.8	X	23.0
9th	2nd	78.	Rondino—Kreisler	X	59.8	X?	14.8
10th	1st	79.	Octave glissandi in beat	0	78.4	0	17.4
10th	1st	80.	Octave glissandi not in beat	X?	36.6	X?	11.6
10th	1st	81.	Improvised non-legato tune in rhythm	0	35.0	0?	36.2
10th	1st	82.	Pizzicato chords in beat	(1) X	39.6	X	20.2
				(2) X	16.6	X	19.4
				(3) X	17.0	X	24.8
10th	1st	83.	Octave glissandi in beat	X	26.6	X?	17.8
10th	1st .	84.	Octave glissandi not in beat	X	35.4	0?	20.6
10th	1st	85.	Simple glissandic melody not in beat	X	23.0	X	24.4
10th	2nd	86.	Spiccato à ricochet	X?	41.8	0?	23.6
10th	2nd	87.	Tapping cigar box in beat	X	24.4	X?	33.4

[196]

TABLE 1. *(Continued)*

Day	Run*	Exp. No.	Stimulus	Experi- mental	Time in Seconds	Con- trol	Time in Seconds
10th	2nd	88.	Tschaikowsky slow movement	X	58.4	X?	24.6
10th	2nd	89.	Russian Soldier's Song	X	30.0	X?	27.2
10th	2nd	90.	Old Black Joe	X	41.4	X?	11.2
10th	2nd	91.	Cradle Song—Hauser	(1) X	40.2	X?	17.8
				(2) X	39.6	X	12.8
10th	2nd	92.	Traumerei—Schumann	(1) X	37.6	X	16.8
				(2) X	37.4	X?	12.6
10th	2nd	93.	Mazurka—Wieniawski	X	42.6	X?	9.4
11th	1st	94.	Open G on downbeat	(1) X?	23.8	X?	14.4
				(2) X	18.4	X?	23.8
				(3) X	15.0	X	26.4
11th	1st	95.	Spiccato a ricochet	(1) X	19.4	X?	17.2
				(2) X	19.2	X	19.4
11th	1st	96.	Open G on downbeat	(1) X	20.0	X?	19.6
				(2) X	17.6	X	24.4
				(3) X	19.6	X?	18.2
11th	1st	97.	Spiccato à ricochet	X	25.6	X	21.8
11th	1st	98.	Martele series				
11th	1st	99.	Martele series				
11th	2nd	100.	Spiccato à ricochet (Subject cooperating)	(1) X	15.6	X	16.0
				(2) X	18.6	X	20.0
				(3) X	23.8	X	32.4
11th	2nd	101.	Russian Soldier's Song (Subject cooperating)	(1) X	30.6	X?	16.8
				(2) X	19.4	X?	23.6
11th	2nd	102.	To a Wild Rose (Subject cooperating)	(1) X?	18.0	0?	20.4
				(2) X	18.0	X	12.6
11th	2nd	103.	Russian Soldier's Song (Subject cooperating)	X	14.2	0	15.2
11th	2nd	104.	Spiccato à ricochet (Subject cooperating	X	14.6	X	21.2
11th	2nd	105.	Pizzicato chords in beat (Subject cooperating)	(1) X	21.0	0	20.2
				(2) X	10.0	X	15.8
11th	2nd	106.	To a Wild Rose (Subject cooperating)	X	16.2	X	19.6
11th	2nd	107.	Cradle Song—Hauser (Subject cooperating)	(1) X?	15.6	X	26.0
				(2) X?	28.4	X?	13.2
12th	1st	108.	Open G on downbeat	(1) X?	19.0	X	24.2
				(2) X	21.6	X	34.0
				(3) X	20.0	X	50.2
12th	1st	109.	Martele scale on downbeat	(1) X	24.8	X	14.4
				(2) X	24.4	0?	21.0
12th	1st	110.	Martele series				
12th	1st	111.	Martele series				
12th	2nd	112.	Martele series				
12th	2nd	113.	Martele series				
12th	2nd	114.	Strongly accented tune	X?	19.4	X	9.2
12th	2nd	115.	Strongly accented tune and Cradle Song—Hauser	X	22.0, 30.6	X	15.8
12th	2nd	116.	Cradle Song—Hauser, and strongly accented tune on downbeat	X?	16.0		
			Strongly accented tune not in beat	X	15.2		
			Cradle Song—Hauser, and strongly accented tune	X	2.2, 2.2	X?	8.8
			Cradle Song—Hauser	X	14.4	X	2.0
			Glissandi in beat	X	6.2	X	3.2
			Arpeggios in beat	X	7.0	X	9.6
12th	2nd	117.	Slow piano minor improvisation	X	23.0	0?	15.8
13th	1st	118.	Slow piano major improvisation	X	88.0	X?	27.6

[197]

TABLE 1. *(Continued)*

Day	Run*	Exp. No.	Stimulus	Experi- mental	Time in Seconds	Con- trol	Time in Seconds
13th	1st	119.	Martele series				
13th	2nd	120	Martele series				
13th	2nd	121.	Martele series				
14th	1st	122.	Scale G to G without vibrato	X	117.0	X	60.4
14th	1st	123.	Scale G to G with vibrato	X	117.0	X	160.8
14th	1st	124.	Visual experiment	(1) 0?	37.0		
				(2) X	20.2		
14th	2nd	125.	Martele series				
14th	2nd	126.	Slow movement, Tschaikowsky	X	22.8	X	54.0
14th	2nd	127.	Confirmation-martele series				

* Two runs of the apparatus were made each experimental day. Except for Experiment 118, from one to two minutes of silence were allowed to elapse as an initial control period before any stimuli were given.

† On January 22, 1944, Mr. Roy E. Eblen, Jr., Director of the Winfield Unit of the Institute of Logopedics, assisted by palpating all of the muscles of the right arm during the experimental periods and controls in order to rule out the possibility that the subject might be assisting the effect of the experiments by going into a tension athetosis. The results of the extra sensory stimuli were that the experimental periods were more irregular in rate, and in the first part of the series of that particular day remissions from tremor were rare. In every control period, however, Mr. Eblen reported that the normally "tense" muscles of the subject appeared to be perfectly relaxed.

TABLE 2. Effect of the various specific types of stimuli without regard to seriatim position.*

Stimulus	Exp. X	Exp. O	Cont. X	Cont. O
Scale G to G without vibrato	2	2	1	3
Scale G to B with vibrato	1	2	1	2
C3 to C4 harmonics without vibrato	—	1	1	—
C3 to C4 harmonics with vibrato	—	1	—	1
Open G on downbeat	10	1	9	1
Open G on upbeat	—	1	—	1
Low A vibrato on downbeat	1	—	—	1
Low A vibrato on downbeat and upbeat	—	1	—	1
C4 on downbeat	—	1	—	1
C4 on upbeat	—	1	—	1
C3 vibrato on downbeat	—	1	—	1
C3 vibrato on upbeat	—	1	—	1
Scale G to G and return to G	—	1	—	1
Pizzicato chords on downbeat	12	—	10	4
Pizzicato single notes on downbeat	2	—	2	
Spiccato à ricochet	38	3	27	14
Spiccato à ricochet and Rigaudon	3	—	2	1
Siciliano not in beat	3	—	3	—
Rigaudon on downbeat	5	—	2	3

[198]

Stimulus	Exp. X	Exp. O	Cont. X	Cont. O
My Old Kentucky Home	8	—	6	2
Spiccato and pizzicato	1	—	—	1
Rigaudon, not in beat	1	—	1	—
Tschaikowsky slow movement	7	—	7	—
Danse Tzigane, not in beat	1	—	1	—
My Country 'Tis of Thee	1	—	1	—
Low G orchestra bells	2	—	1	1
High C orchestra bells	2	—	1	1
Thirds orchestra bells	5	—	5	—
Arpeggios orchestra bells	7	—	7	—
Swanee River orchestra bells	7	—	7	—
Minor tune orchestra bells	1	—	1	—
Cigar box on downbeat	2	—	2	—
Cigar box, various rhythms	1	—	1	—
Tapping various items	1	—	—	1
Clapping hands on downbeat	1	—	1	—
Alternate bell and cigar box	1	—	1	—
Max Bruch Adagio	4	—	3	1
Tschaikowsky (muted)	1	—	1	—
C scale rapidly	1	—	1	—
Russian Soldier's Song	5	—	4	1
Rondino	1	—	1	—
Octave glissandi in beat	2	1	2	1
Octave glissandi not in beat	1	—	—	1
Simple glissandic melody	1	—	1	—
Old Black Joe	1	—	1	—
Cradle Song—Hauser	5	—	5	—
Traumerei—Schumann	2	—	2	—
Mazurka—Wieniawski	1	—	1	—
To a Wild Rose	3	—	2	1
Martele scale on downbeat	2	—	1	1
Strongly accented tune, downbeat	1	—	1	—
Strongly accented tune, downbeat and Cradle Song	1	—	1	—
Strongly accented tune, not on downbeat and Cradle Song	1	—	1	—
Arpeggios in beat	1	—	1	—
Minor pianissimo improvisation	1	—	—	1
Major pianissimo improvisation	1	—	1	—
Vision	1	1	—	—

* For simplicity in calculation, all X?'s in Table 1 were called X, all O?'s were called O. The fallacy probably does not vitiate the result.

Rapid C scale. C scale on the violin, played legato and rapidly from low G upward (experiment 73).

Russian Soldier's Song. "Russian Soldier's Song" by Dubensky using the beat of the stylus as tempo indicator (experiments 75, 76, 89, 101 and 103).

Kreisler Rondino. "Rondino on a theme by Beethoven" by Kreisler played at the usual concert rate without attention to the stylus tempo (experiment 78).

Octave glissandi in beat and not in beat. Four ascending alternating glissandi with four descending glissandi on each string with the first finger. The order of strings was: D string, A string, E string, then G string; e.g., on the D string—E to E, then down to E again, F sharp to F sharp and down to F sharp again, etc. (experiments 79, 80, 83, 84 and 116).

Improvised non-legato tune in rhythm. A series of improvised tones related in a definite time scheme to the stylus tempo, one, two or three notes being played for each beat but with no legato or glissandi between notes (experiment 81).

Simple glissandic melody not in beat. Simple melodic improvisation with every note joined by a glissando to the next in an attempt to produce continuous sound. No attention was paid to stylus tempo (experiment 85).

"Old Black Joe." Melody of "Old Black Joe" by Stephen Foster played forté and largo without attention to the stylus tempo (experiment 90).

"Cradle Song." The "Cradle Song" by Hauser played at the usual concert rate without attention to the stylus (experiments 91, 107, 115 and 116).

"Traumerei." "Traumerei" by Schumann played at the usual concert rate without attention to stylus (experiment 92).

"Mazurka." "Obertass Mazurka" by Wieniawski played forté fortissimo at the usual concert rate without attention to the stylus tempo (experiment 93).

"To a Wild Rose." "To a Wild Rose" by Edward MacDowell played at the usual concert rate without attention to stylus tempo (experiments 102 and 106).

Martele scale on downbeat. Martele scale from low A to second A above and return, one note of the scale for each downbeat of the stylus (experiment 109).

Strongly accented tune. Improvised strongly accented tune in a major key played marcato, forté, allegro (experiments 114, 115 and 116—in tempo only in experiment 116).

Arpeggios in beat. Arpeggios on a major triadic progression with the stylus serving as tempo indicator (experiment 116).

Slow piano minor improvisation. Minor adagio improvisation played pianissimo without attention to stylus tempo (experiment 117).

Slow piano major improvisation. Before the subject was brought into the experimental room a major adagio improvisation was begun and played pianissimo throughout the experimental period, no attention being paid to stylus tempo (experiments 118 and 121).

Visual experiment. The operator suddenly rose and in full view of the subject deliberately manipulated the apparatus in an apparently meaningful but actually purposeless manner, then waved his arms, making a vigorous downward conducting movement for each downbeat of the stylus (experiment 124).

Martele series.

1. Part A, four isolated martele type major triads at about 3.0 seconds; Part B, the same on the downbeat of the stylus; Part C, eight chords as in Part A at intervals from 1.0 to 3.0 seconds (experiment 74).

2. Two octaves upward from low A to second A above with brief martele bow strokes played forté, and the same notes played downward. In both cases no note was played so long as the tremor was in remission; as soon as a free tremor movement occurred a group of notes was played at about one to two second intervals (experiments 98, 99, 110, 120 and 121).

3. Bowed chords played similarly to the martele technique from the theme by Sevcik, Opus 2, Part 6, again using the teaching techniques described above (experiments 111 and 112).

4. Shouting isolated "da" (about 100 dvs.) sounds, using a tone pattern similar to the Sevcik theme (experiment 113).

5. Open G martele using the same general techniques (experiment 119).

The tabulation of the series shows that it was possible to obtain remissions of tremors in varied ways.

Disregarding the conditioning and learning effect it is possible to study the effect of the stimuli by grouping them as shown in Table 2.

From the complete analysis it would seem that pizzicato chords or single notes in harmonic progression, and in beat with the tremor would have been more effective than spiccato à ricochet. Since a detailed analysis was not made until the close of the series, the spiccato was used mainly because it was obviously effective. However, use of the pizzicato alone might have produced the same results.

Statistical evaluations of the kind here employed are to be considered with due reference to the possible effects of any learning or conditioning factors involved in the experiments. It is, however, possible to rank the general types of sound stimuli used, on the basis of the average of their effectiveness in the experimental periods, and in the control periods. The ranking in Table 3 on a basis of 1 to 10 gives some information.

Too much reliance should not be placed on the tabulation in Table 3 because of the data from the martele series. The validity of the ranking is also doubtful for the following reasons:

A. Each day there were approximately 16 experiments. The sound stimuli occurring early in the daily series would be expected to be less effective than those occurring later.

B. The same consideration is pertinent when the series as a whole is reviewed. The temporal distribution of the various types of sound stimuli with reference to the sequences of the experimental series was not systematically varied or controlled, and for this reason the ranking of the different stimuli as to their effectiveness may not be taken as of unquestioned validity.

C. Position in the experimental series is important in determining experimental success. The average number of experiments per run of the apparatus was approximately 8 (7.7). Table 4 indicates: (1) That rhythmic sound stimuli related to the tremor beat, sound stimuli without intellectual and emotional components, and

TABLE 3. Comparative effect of general types of sound stimuli on the athetotic tremor.

Stimulus	Rank
1. Sound stimuli with intellectual and emotional components (e.g., composed music)	1.5
2. Sound stimuli of a rhythmic nature, not related to the tremor rhythm	2.0
3. Sound stimuli of a "noise" character	2.0
4. Sound stimuli of a rhythmic nature, with the rhythm related definitely to the tremor rhythm	5.0
5. Sounds of a more or less continuant nature	5.0
6. Sounds having a surge character, with a definite accentual and isolated beat	5.5
7. Sound stimuli of a more or less arbitrary structure with probably little emotional and intellectual configuration	6.5
8. Sound stimuli of relatively low pitch	8.0
9. Sound stimuli of an arrhythmic nature	9.0
10. Sound stimuli of relatively high pitch	10.0

sound stimuli of more or less continuant nature, all occurred on the average at least one experiment earlier than their converses. (2) That the experimental and control failures of these converses occurred on the average 1.42 experiments earlier than the successful experimental and control periods.

This internal evidence shows that sound stimuli with emotional and intellectual components, not related to the beat of the tremor, and of a continuate character are at least no more effective in increasing and remitting the tremor than the converses, and probably also shows merely that the experimental order was at fault. Further, it shows that successes and failures with all types of sound stimuli may occur anywhere throughout such a series of experiments. Table 5 gives similar evidence.

The first three groups in Table 5 occur approximately one experiment earlier in the series than the last two groups. The failures of the first three groups occur 1.65 experiments earlier than the successes. This is true also for the only failures that occurred in the last two groups, and is confirmed by the fact that the music with emotional and intellectual components also failed

[203]

TABLE 4. A tabulation by seriatim and success.

Stimulus	Ave. daily positional rank in series	Success X-X	Failure O-O	Exp. per.		Cont. per.	
				X	O	X	O
Rhythmic related	4.19	4.98	2.93	4.31	3.13	4.93	3.64
Rhythmic not related	5.03	5.41	...	5.09	...	4.96	6.09
Arrhythmic	2.51	xxx*	xxx	xxx	xxx	xxx	xxx
Intellectual and emotional	4.93	5.35	...	4.93	...	4.95	4.46
Not intellectual and emotional	4.06	4.85	2.76	4.29	2.81	4.53	3.11
High pitch	2.92	xxx	xxx	xxx	xxx	xxx	xxx
Low pitch	3.00	xxx	xxx	xxx	xxx	xxx	xxx
Noise	6.13	xxx	xxx	xxx	xxx	xxx	xxx
Surge character	3.93	4.74	3.62	5.03	3.51	4.13	3.51
Continuant	4.53	5.16	2.25	4.71	2.52	4.98	3.49

* Too few cases for accurate analysis.

TABLE 5. A selection of certain types of stimuli occurring most frequently.

Stimulus	Ave. daily positional rank in series	Success X-X	Failure O-O	Exp. per.		Cont. per.	
				X	O	X	O
Open G on downbeat	2.69	2.87	1.00	2.79	1.00	2.97	1.00
Pizzicato chords on downbeat	4.11	4.88	...	4.11	...	4.88	2.58
Spiccato	4.00	4.36	1.70	3.99	4.20	4.36	3.22
Composed music related to tremor	4.75	5.97	...	4.75	...	5.97	2.93
Composed music not related to tremor	5.16	5.15	...	5.29	...	5.05	4.80

when placed early in any series. Thus this type of music probably has no greater effect than the non-intellectual type.

So far as the subject of this experiment is concerned, the authors feel justified in the assumption, particularly when the martele series is reviewed, that sound stimuli of a rhythmic character related definitely to the athetotic tremor rhythm must be used to produce an increase in the vigor, rate and stability of the tremor and consequent remission of it during periods of silence immediately following the stimuli.

The distribution of the successes and failures of the experimental and control periods shows a learning effect. Control periods with little or no effect on the remission of the tremor occur as a mean at sequence 68, while control periods reducing or eliminating the tremor occur as a mean at sequence 111. There remissions from tremor are skewed even more towards the end of the series than successful experimental periods. It should be noted that failures in both the experimental periods and controls can occur at any time during such a series, but that they become less and less frequent. Successes in both the experimental periods and controls

TABLE 6. Arbitrary ratings of success and failure for the first fourteen days.*

Day	Experimental Period	Control Period
1st	— 60	—100
2nd	—100	— 70
3rd	— 75	— 76
4th	84	5
5th	100	40
6th	51	12
7th	100	72
8th	100	86
9th	100	50
10th	90	68
11th	100	72
12th	100	**74**
13th	100	100
14th	77	100

* On any one day successful experimental periods were counted as plus two, questionably successful experimental periods were counted as plus 1, questionable failures of the experimental periods as minus 1, and experimental failures as minus 2. The addition was expanded into plus or minus 100 due to the difference in numbers of experiments on any one day. Days were from one week to six weeks apart.

can occur early in the series (18th experiment) and become more and more frequent.

There was a significant difference found in regard to the proportionate amounts of success and failure when the results for single days were tabulated. This is illustrated in Table 6. On the fourth day of the series, the experimental period was classified for the first time as "successful." This was probably due in some part to the change in techniques, but it is also further evidence that remissions from tremor in the control period do not begin to occur until the tremor in the experimental periods has been increased in rate, severity and stability.

SUMMARY OF FINDINGS

A study of the experimental and control periods shows that the remissions from tremor were causally related to the techniques used. A study of the *successful* experimental periods and controls demonstrates further that in order to obtain remissions from athetotic tremors at will by means of sound stimuli, it is necessary to be able to produce an increase in the severity, vigor, stability and rate of the tremor during the sound stimuli and follow it immediately with a period of silence.

Other observations made during this study which appear to be significant are as follows:

1. Sound stimuli of the patterns used in this experiment tended to produce a tremor of almost predictable rate.

2. Any sound stimuli (or visual stimuli) in any pattern usually had a stabilizing effect on the tremor rate.

3. Control periods (periods of silence) were usually less stable in rate than experimental periods.

4. Control periods on experimental days prior to any experimental periods were more irregular in rate than subsequent control periods.

5. Sudden onsets of sound stimuli after periods of silence usually produced gains in the tremor rate. When the sound stimuli did not produce this gain in rate, the tremor rate in the preced-

ing control period had been above the lower rate predicted as 84 per minute minus 21.6.

6. Cessation of sound stimuli at the close of experimental periods was usually followed by a decrease in tremor rate.

7. The onset of sound stimuli at the beginning of experimental periods, and the cessation of sound stimuli at the beginning of control periods in every instance produced changes in the tremor rate.

8. An effect tentatively called an "innovation effect" was sometimes noticed in these experiments. The result of introducing new material, or abruptly changing the experimental or control conditions in some cases, was to decrease the tremor rate. This effect was not predictable. Apparently it depended upon the endogenous psycho-physical organization of the subject at the time of innovation. Or perhaps what was considered by the authors to be an innovation was not actually received as such by the subject, or vice versa.

9. In this series, timing the rhythm of the sound stimuli to the extensor portion of the tremor produced better results than timing it to the flexor portion.

During the tenth and eighteenth experiments, the character of the curve pattern changed suddenly and continued to change throughout the series. Prior to the tenth experiment, the curve was irregular in extent, duration and length of time on any phase. At the tenth experiment there was a definite change to a curve more stable in rate, with the greatest amount of time spent on the phases of greatest flexion. By the eighteenth experiment, the curve had changed again, becoming very vigorous, large in extent and higher in rate, and the extension portion was rounded, while the flexion portion of the curve tended to run to a peak. This characteristic increased throughout the records. Both the experimental and control period curves changed at about the same time, with the experimental periods changing slightly ahead of the controls.

[207]

The Martele Series

The martele technique on the violin produces a sound of great volume with very little crescendo effect, an instantly loud sound, giving a very definite auditory shock. This series was suggested because of previous success obtained by using orchestra bells. The martele experiments fell haphazardly throughout the rest of the experiments. The conclusions here developed are contingent upon the total experimental sequence described since there is no way of judging whether the martele series would have been successful in producing remissions of tremor as an independent series. It is the opinion of the authors that the conditioning effect of the other experiments was necessary.

It was generally concluded that isolated sounds of an instantly loud character as used in the martele series produced an experimental situation entirely different from the regular series of experiments. Production of tremor movement was positive and certain. Remissions from tremor were definitely under the control of the experimenters. Although this portion of the series was not controlled adequately, it seemed to be possible to follow the flexion curve of the subject during remission, strike a note as this tension began to increase, and by several repetitions produce as long a remission as was desired under the conditions of the apparatus. An analysis of the martele experiments, in contradistinction to the remainder of the series, showed little or no significant difference with respect to time of occurrence in the series, type of stimuli, or other changes in the situation. These conclusions are presented only to clarify the study as a whole and must be accepted as tentative.

DISCUSSION

A number of significant questions are raised by the foregoing data and conclusions.

1. Occasionally during the series when a familiar sound

sequence returned suddenly, the rate of the tremor increased. Since it was shown that increase in rate, i.e., control of the tremor by sound stimuli, was requisite for tremor remission, would deliberate experimental sequences of this sort increase the rapidity of control?

2. The success of the martele experiments, with their instantaneously loud sounds, and the apparent fact that the time interval between them is unimportant, leads to the question: What would happen if a loud bell were simply to be rung at regular intervals for a long period of time? Or were the intervals of time more significant than supposed?

3. The series is inconclusive on the effect of pitch. Does a lower pitch produce a greater effect? Does the tremor pattern change with change in pitch? On the experiments in which steady tones were played at relatively long durations in scale, there appeared to be changes in the curve pattern of the tremor at points near the changes in pitch.

4. The fact that pauses in the tremor usually occurred at a point of extension of the finger, and that resumptions of tremor usually occurred after some flexor tension had developed, leads to the question of developing new techniques specifically aimed at producing the requisite extension or flexion.

5. From experiment 18 on, with the exception of the martele series, the sound stimuli were related primarily to the extensor portion of the tremor. In the martele series, the stimuli were related to the flexor portion. Since the martele series only produced results on flexion, and the results were better than in the other series, would rhythmic music related to the tremor be more effective if related to the flexor portion of the tremor?

6. One whole segment of the data has been omitted from the report—that concerned with the pattern of movement. It has been noted that the entire character of the tremor changed at experiment 11a, and it was only at experiment 18 that the series began to be successful. Is such a pattern change necessary for successful

results, and what is the significance of the pattern changes? What do the sinusoidal waves, the fibrilations, the respiratory-like curves, etc., mean relative to this problem?

7. After the tremor pattern had become vigorous and stable, the most vigorous movement in the tremor was the flexor portion. Any delay between tremor movements usually occurred during extension, not during flexion. Could this be used as a teaching device?

8. After the tremor had become conditioned, any stimuli with the exception of the martele technique on the violin produced about the same kind of a tremor, although slow soft music was not so effective as vigorous music. What predetermines this effect?

9. In these records it was impossible to determine with any exactness the point on the tremor at which the stimuli was stopped. Perhaps the small variations in the results may be due to differences in the places where the music was stopped. The authors feel that their records show that the music must cease at extension, or shortly before.

10. The introduction of another observer in experiments 100 to 107 caused obvious changes in the results. Statistically, the results paralleled other experiments. On a practical basis, some provision should be made for this additional stimulus.

11. When the subject was uncomfortable (*vide* 79), when there was coughing, etc., the results were never as good. Any further experimental series should investigate more deeply the question of endogenous stimuli.

12. Pauses infrequently occurred during experimental periods. If the stimuli had been stopped at these places, would longer remission have occurred?

13. Why should there have been a predictable rate, and what were the determinants of this rate?

14. In the control periods it was noticed that return of tremor tended to occur at the same places where it had occurred in pre-

vious experiments. Would the techniques have been more or less effective if the control periods had been equal in time?

15. It is obvious that the reports in the literature of the effect of music on cerebral palsy have not been based on objective study. Nearly every commonly held theory has been controverted in the study of this one subject. The question is (and this question refers to the whole study), will this type of research produce similar results in more severe cases, or even in similar cases?

16. While it is an over-extension of application, it is probable that the effects of music on normals working in highly skilled trades have been misunderstood. Should not the music used in industrial workshops be re-evaluated in terms of its effect upon skilled habitual muscle action?

17. The relationship of this series to the study of normal individuals is a very broad question with many ramifications. The vibrato used by the violinist, the normal human tremor, and mus-

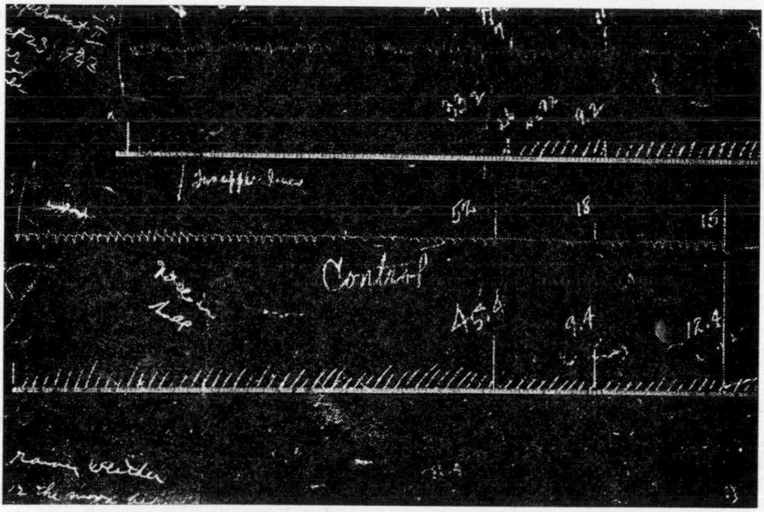

FIGURE 1. Upper line, control period prior to experiment No. 4 and beginning of experiment No. 4. Second line, time at 1/5th second. Third line, control period prior to experiment No. 6 (note change in pattern). Beginning of experiment No. 6. Fourth line, time at 1/5th second.

[211]

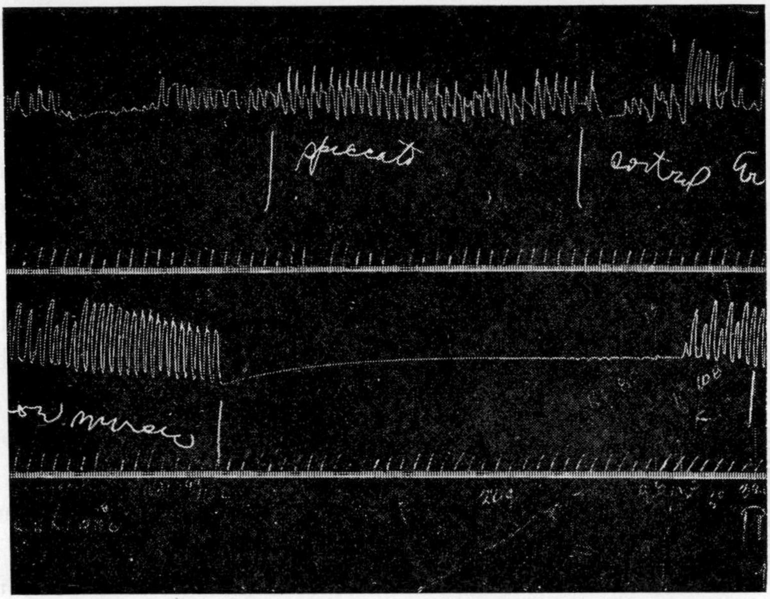

FIGURE 2. Upper line, control preceding fifth repetition of spiccato à ricochet in experiment No. 25—spiccato à ricochet, failure of control period following the spiccato (arm and shoulder tremor). Second line, time at 1/5th second. Third line, second experimental period of experiment No. 29 ("Siciliano," by Kreisler). Control period following showing characteristics of remission curve. Note change of pattern in this successful experimental period. Fourth line, time at 1/5th second.

cular repetitive action in general need to be studied in relation to these findings.

18. Finally, would similar techniques be of benefit in the treatment of paralysis agitans and similar conditions?

SUMMARY AND CONCLUSIONS

A young adult male, with cerebral palsy, presenting a typical athetotic tremor of the right index finger, was subjected to a series of 126 mainly auditory stimuli of varying lengths under controlled conditions. It was possible to increase and control the severity, rate and stability of this tremor by means of sound (and visual) stimuli. When such an increase in the tremor had occurred, it was

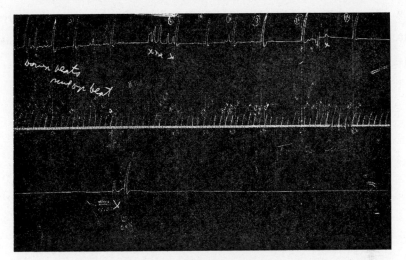

FIGURE 3. Upper line, notes 1 to 10 in experiment No. 119. Note single tremor movement at every note of violin; "x" below the line refers to tremor movements not accompanied by sound. Second line, time at 1/5th second. Lower line, remission preceding and following note 15 in experiment No. 120.

discovered that sudden cessation of the stimuli (rhythmic, arrhythmic, musical, not musical, etc.) produced remissions of the tremor for considerable lengths of time. Instantaneously loud sounds, produced as described above, gave the best results. Remission following the experimental series lasted for six weeks.

REFERENCES

1. Altshuler, Ira M. Four years experience with music as a therapeutic agent at Eloise Hospital. *Amer. J. Psychiat.*, 1944, *100*, 792-794.
2. Carlson, Earl R. Infantile cerebral palsy: its treatment by selective inhibition of sensory stimuli. *Ann. intern. Med.*, 1937, *11*, 324-334.
3. ——. Neurological aspects and treatment of birth injuries. *New York St. J. Med.*, 1934, *34*, 1-6.
4. ——. Understanding and guiding the spastic. *Amer. J. Nurs.*, 1938, *39*, 356-366.
5. Donaldson, Alice A. *Research study in the field of individual differences.* Elyria, Ohio: Nat'l Soc. Crip. Child.
6. Herz, Ernst. Dystonia. *Arch. Neurol. Psychiat.*, 1944, *51*, 305-355.
7. ——. ibid., *52*, 20-26.
8. Hoefer, Paul F. A. and Putnam, Trace J. Action potentials of muscles in athetosis and Sydenham's chorea. *Arch. Neurol. Psychiat.*, 1940, *44*, 517-531.

[213]

9. Klingman, W. O. and Carlson, Earl R. Observations on factors inhibiting choreo-athetosis. *Bull. Neurol. Inst., New York,* 1936, *5,* 212-216.
10. Lord, Elizabeth Evans. *Children handicapped by cerebral palsy.* New York: Commonwealth Fund, Oxford Univ. Press, 1937.
11. Myers, Jane. Occupational therapy as a treatment for spastics. *Occup. Ther. Rehab.,* 1938, *17,* 81-87.

THE USE OF MUSIC AS A THERAPY

HERMINA EISELE BROWNE

Director, Music Therapy Department, New Jersey State Hospital at Marlboro

Down through the years, from the beginning of time, man has used music as a therapy, to heal the sick heart and the wounded spirit. When King Saul was restless from the many cares of state, David would be called to play his harp until Saul relaxed and was well again. Hippocrates, the great physician, took his patients to the temple, where there was music, when he could not cure them with medicines. Europe has used music regularly in the rehabilitation of mental patients.

In this country well-known artists presented music in hospitals during World War I, just as they did during World War II, and a few of them made copies and accurate records of the types of program presented and the particular wards or types of patient to whom they were presented, and noted the responses. As a therapy, music is used for the greatest benefit of the patient—to give him not only what he wants, but also what he needs to help him get well, to direct antisocial habits toward socially acceptable behavior, to alter destructive moods, and to guide overactive patients to constructive thinking and activity. The artist's identity is lost, except as the medium through which music is made available. It is, therefore, essential that the therapist know and understand music thoroughly, in order to be able to select suitable music numbers for particular purposes. Rhythmic patterns, tempo, dynamics, harmonies, and melody are most important considerations

[215]

in selecting music for altering moods and getting active participation responses.

Mrs. Harriet Ayer Seymour, for many years piano teacher at the Henry Street Settlement, New York City, and Willem van de Wall, music educator, were among the first to pioneer in the uses of music in hospitals and institutions in the United States. Having noted the response to it during World War I, they continued their studies and observations after the war was over. Mrs. Seymour, who died in 1944, was organizer of the Foundation for Music Therapy. Dr. van de Wall was selected by the Committee for the Study of Music in Institutions—headed by Dr. Charles W. Tremaine, and Dr. Samuel W. Hamilton, psychiatrist—to make a thorough study of the uses of music in institutions, including mental hospitals.

In 1927, Dr. van de Wall, with the coöperation of Dr. Ira Klopp and Dr. Hamilton, organized a formal program of music therapy at Allentown (Pennsylvania) State Hospital. A year later he brought in Miss Lois Hannaford, a music educator, to take charge of this department, which is still functioning very effectively.

Since then, other hospitals have added music as a departmental activity, but very slowly. The decision to set up a music program was invariably dependent upon finances and upon the medical director's belief in the efficacy of such a program. Music has been used on a hit-or-miss basis in many institutions for some time, being fostered either by volunteers or by the recreational or the occupational-therapy department. But as a planned program with a definite end in view, functioning under the guidance of trained musicians, it is a new venture in our country. World War II restimulated activity along these lines, and since then progress has been made by leaps and bounds, culminating in the formation of the National Association for Music Therapy (1950), which is pledged to progressive development of the use of music in medicine, the advancement of educational and professional standards in music therapy, and the maintenance of a close working alliance and liaison with the medical profession.

Several universities have instituted in their music departments courses for the training of music therapists, in coöperation with medical-school and hospital in-service-training programs. The University of Kansas, the University of Michigan, the Musical Guidance Center for Functional Music (Boston), and the Long Island University are a few of those already well established.

As recently as 1945, when it was my privilege to make surveys of mental hospitals under the guidance of Willem van de Wall and Dr. Samuel W. Hamilton, most physicians declined to accept music as a therapy, primarily because of the lack of scientifically proven data. A few of these physicians who were openminded, or who had the time to go into the matter more thoroughly, were willing to make control-case trials. These experiments, too, were no doubt responsible for the rapid progress functional music programs have made within recent years. Now the cry is for properly trained personnel and funds and equipment with which to carry on a well-integrated program. The general public has been most hearty in its response to pleas for used equipment, but the supply is not enough to care for the thousands who need and want music in its various forms.

In a very short time the music-therapy department will stand side by side with other therapy departments as a necessary adjunct in the treatment of the mental patient. There will, of course, be some overlapping in the uses of music in the various departments, just as there is overlapping in the uses of food, medication, and activities. It is the close coöperation of departments, always with the aim of helping the patient to become a well-integrated personality, that makes for a well-rounded therapy program.

The music-therapy program at the State Hospital at Marlboro, New Jersey, was instituted by Dr. J. Berkeley Gordon, medical director, and Dr. David Wade McCreight, clinical director, who, in the fall of 1948, brought the writer to the hospital to organize such a department. The department opened officially on December 2, 1948, with one piano, one portable "White" organ—both badly in need of tuning—a few sheets of old popular music, some old records, a bass drum, and a record player that did not work. The best room available was one in the basement of a cottage, a fairly large, airy room with water facilities. Later, other necessary equipment was added, such as benches, a desk, and a cabinet in which to keep music when it arrived.

Twenty-two patients constituted the first group to sing carols on wards and in dining rooms that first Christmas. With the aid of an Antioch College student, a ward program was set up, so that within a given week most of the wards had at least a half-hour's program of music. In due time printed music was secured, and violins, a cello, two saxophones, guitars, and other fretted instruments were forthcoming, through the kindness of friends and an interested public. Later, additional pianos and a supply of records were also donated.

Meantime, we worked with the materials at hand, presenting an informal spring musicale early in 1949. By June we were ready to present the light opera, *The Pirates of Penzance,* which was a tremendous success from all points of view. Forty-seven patients and three employees took part. All props and scenery were made in our department. The Women's Auxiliary furnished materials and made up the women's costumes under our guidance. The men's costumes were developed from materials available at the hospital. This was not without its humorous side; the "pirates," for instance, were all labeled M.S.H. across the shoulders.

Patients worked with us on the recommendation of the nursing department or of attendants, or by personal request, all being approved by the chief of service before actually taking part in any way. A musician friend came to conduct the performance, leaving the director free to take care of the behind-the-scenes business, and the Elizabeth Musicians' Local 151 furnished several men for the orchestra.

[218]

Our leading tenor was a patient classified as dementia praecox, catatonic, with underlying psychopathic personality with pathological sexuality. He was discovered as a possible candidate for the rôle while he was residing on the men's disturbed ward. He always sang with the group and, when approached, expressed a keen desire to have lessons. Permission was obtained from the physician in charge of men's service to teach this man, but he had to be "specialed." He had a high, clear tenor voice. Shortly after he began his music lessons, he was placed on insulin treatments each morning; each afternoon we took him out and began all over again to teach him his part. But each day he remembered just a bit more from the previous day, so that eventually we made progress. This was evidenced in the fact that his voice no longer was a pure tenor, but gradually became heavier in texture and also not quite so high. By the time of production, he was able, by dint of interest and effort, to give an excellent account of himself as tenor lead. Within a few weeks after this performance, however, though he continued to sing regularly with us, he could no longer sing tenor, but began to develop his true baritone voice. Early in the fall he was released on parole; he returned to us in October as a guest to sing for a special musical revue, compiled and dramatized by the director, entitled, *In the Luxembourg Gardens,* at which time he was a definite full-voiced baritone.

Because of the heavy influx of new patients, in April, 1949, we had to turn over our studio to the nursing department to make room for twenty-eight beds, and we were given a room next door which is less than half the size of the first room—in fact, approximately only sixteen feet square—with no washing facilities. Its only recommendation is that it has an outside entrance and is dry. A shower-lavatory room nearby has to be used by both male and female patients; there are no facilities for employees. This was to have been a temporary arrangement, but it appears to be permanent at this writing.

Since the room is too small to accommodate the large group of patients—we now have ninety-six—we received permission to use an open cottage for afternoon rehearsal, which was later rescinded, and we now have morning rehearsals for the large group. The studio is used for small groups and individual work. Plans have been laid for the building of a larger studio in the basement of another cottage, with proper toilet facilities, which will ease our crowded accommodations somewhat.

Our ward programs progressed as per schedule. We added programs to the disturbed buildings twice weekly. Here music has proved to be of the greatest value in that it keeps down combative behavior, eliminates breakage and fights to a certain degree, and releases tensions through emotional outlets along constructive lines. These patients always welcome the therapist, even when they appear to be completely withdrawn. Such a patient, though he took no active part in the music program and appeared not to be listening, has come to us at the close of the music session, and said, "Thank you," occasionally extending his hand to show appreciation.

With the aid of two Antioch College students, we have been able to increase our service to our patients. Ward music programs are selected according to type of ward and the particular mood of patients on that ward. One cottage, for instance, is generally quite active, occasionally noisy. Here we begin with cheerful, lively tempos and sing loudly, paying little attention to those on the ward. Gradually they join us in singing, ask for favorites and repeats. If they wish, we have them sing or play solos. As the mood changes, we play softer and slower music, and by the time we leave, the ward is generally relaxed and happy.

Here is where the attendant or technician can be of great assistance. He can gently urge a patient to participate, or redirect his activity. When there are patients on the ward who like to sing or play, he can encourage them to release pent-up emotions through a stated period of music activity each day by himself or with other patients on the ward. This precludes a patient from monopolizing

an instrument, or annoying others on the ward with continual outbursts, yet gives him the activity he craves on an orderly, routine
basis. If no music is available, he can call upon the music department, which is only too glad to loan printed music for such
a purpose. Also, if he finds that record music is enjoyed and useful, he can borrow equipment, if and when it is available, and
have a brief music program daily at a time when the ward is apt
to be restless.

The attendant or technician can also be useful and helpful by
suggesting names of patients for the chorus, orchestra, individual
attention, or study groups to the department head, who in turn will
check with the physician for approval. He can also be most helpful
by encouraging the patient to attend regular sessions of the ward
and helping him to be ready at the appointed hour.

On senile wards strong, rhythmic music is most beneficial because it induces motor responses such as walking about, clapping
the hands, tapping the feet, or nodding the head, stimulating the
appetite and creating a feeling of general well-being. We frequently use our rhythm instruments here also to induce active
participation. Marches, waltzes, folk songs, and lively, familiar
hymns with hopeful messages are used most and with the best results. The same holds true in our deteriorated wards. Here we
frequently get more vocal participation as well as motor response,
but it takes a little longer. In this ward we have several good
drummers, a whistler, and a pianist who invariably plays the *St.
Louis Blues*. If he can stay at the piano long enough, he will modu-
late into *Prelude in C# Minor*, return to the *Blues* and back again
to the *Prelude*, completing it with a flourish, and then going on
to whatever piece may come to his mind. This is a regular procedure. The patient is a very deteriorated case of dementia praecox,
hebephrenic, institutionalized since 1934.

Also in this ward is a former excellent musician conductor,
who will play any composition requested, but he never completes
a given number, as a change in harmonic pattern recalls another

piece and he goes into that one. He will entertain others and himself for long periods of time in this way, never actually completing anything. For this reason one cannot sing with him. He also begins his part of the program by requesting every one to stand while he plays the *Star-Spangled Banner*. In order to keep him from monopolizing the program, we give him a time limit. He readily agrees to this, and when time is up, we ask him to come to a stop, so that others may take part. In this way he is not hurt and every one is satisfied. He always conforms—if we explain first.

Music on tuberculosis wards should be cheerful, soft waltzes and outdoor music. Bed patients always appreciate gay, familiar classics, especially hopeful hymns and folk songs, particularly in their native language. As they cannot participate too much, programs must be well-planned in advance to avoid periods of uncertainty during which the interest of the patient is lost. Reception wards need music that has frequent changes of tempo and mood as well as dynamics and rhythm. For a group of younger persons, popular music is suitable, but for older persons ballads, folk songs, and old-style popular music is best.

We have broadcast programs over the public-address system to various wards with gratifying results from the patient standpoint. However, as our monitor board gets very busy at times, the extra activity proved to be too much for the operator and we have had to discontinue this service until a proper public-address system can be added to our set-up. Occasionally, we present special record music in the patients' dining room while they have supper. Here instrumental numbers are best and such as are not too fast or excitable in tempo or rhythm. Again, care must be taken that the music can be heard without being too loud to be disturbing.

As printed music became available, we were able to plan and prepare additional programs by the chorus and soloists, and within a year had our orchestra and rhythm band well under way. *The Mikado, Epic of America* (an original, historic pageant), and several concerts were added to our repertoire. This last Christmas the chorus was divided into smaller groups with a few instrumentalists in each, and presented thirty-eight carol programs on wards, in dining rooms, and in the foyer of the main building.

Since Christmas, our program has been considerably curtailed for lack of assistance. Antioch College has had no music students to send, and others have not been forthcoming, though promised in the future. At this writing, a part-time worker, a Juilliard student, has begun his duties and a full-time assistant has been authorized. Now all we need do is to find one capable of doing the required work.

On the whole, these students have been a fine type of worker for institutions, though their youth, coupled with their lack of music training, has been a handicap in our special field. As young people interested in serving humanity, they have been keen and sympathetic. With a permanent, trained assistant, these Antioch students could be very useful in our work. Probably the greatest difficulty lies in the fact that they can stay only from two to three months at a time and are just beginning to be of use when they leave. Only the exceptional student can or cares to return for a second work period. We have, however, had two such fine young students.

Chorus rehearsals are divided into four sections for four-part harmony which patients can learn when properly taught and if the music is not too difficult for their particular group. The type of music is always determined by the educational background and mental ability of the patient. Anthems for Protestant services are not always sung in four-part harmony because they, of necessity, do not receive adequate rehearsals; hence, in these we make the necessary adjustments. For the Catholic services we use the Gregorian hymnary and a portable organ. Special music is always prepared for special holy days. Small groups are used to present programs on wards at stated intervals, to augment the regular ward-participation programs.

In addition to our ward, chorus, orchestra, and rhythm-band

programs, we also have music for electro-convulsive-shock therapy, and a music appreciation and study group. Classes in sight-singing and harmony are held when we have patients who are able to absorb such instruction. The music-study group is an outcome of patient request, and the patients themselves prepare the papers on a given subject, guided by the therapist. Interest in these sessions is very keen; discussion periods are lively and informative. A given composer's life is studied and his work discussed, particularly in relation to other composers of his day, but also in relation to other arts in the same era. Another patient, having prepared certain songs or piano selections, will present them during the discussion period, and we usually end with listening to recordings of sonatas or a symphony.

Whenever possible or advisable, we connect a composer's affliction with his determination to overcome it, bringing out the value of handicaps, disappointment, sorrows and so on as "stepping-stones" to integration and well-being. Time is always too short for these sessions. We believe that by preparing a paper himself, the patient derives greater benefit and it gives him an opportunity to express himself. It also enables the therapist to discover just what his reading abilities are, what materials he expects from the book, and which appeal to him most—trifles or substance.

Music before, during, and after electro-convulsive-shock therapy has been conducted on the disturbed wards since the early summer of 1949 when a record player was made available for that purpose, with sufficient records to carry out a properly prepared program. Before that we had presented music on all three wards of the male and female buildings on an active-participation basis with song sheets and organ. These programs were continued with the addition of the records used in electro-convulsive therapy. Through the efforts of Charles Morris, technician in charge of the male disturbed building, a large radio-record player was purchased, and this building now also has music during meals and at other stated intervals during the day when the music therapist is not there. The opinion of our medical staff of our electro-convulsive-shock program is that "this one use of music therapy justifies the existence of such a department." One physician has on several occasions made the statement: "Music provides the opening wedge which enables us to reach our patient better." At the Medical Center, New York, Rev. Dr. Hartley and Rev. Dr. Russell used to call us in to present emotional music to certain patients just before an intended visit because they found the patient more willing and able to discuss his problem after being conditioned through music.

In our electro-convulsive-therapy programs, we use music that is familiar and cheerful, but not agitating—relaxing rhythms, semi-classics, while the patients wait, and a slightly stronger rhythm when they begin to wake up. Primitive rhythms are rarely good, as they rouse baser instincts in an emotionally insecure person. Some popular music is used, if melodious. It is interesting to note that patients accept popular music without comment, but when we play light and semi-classics and familiar symphonies, they will ask, "What is it? I like that."

Attendants and technicians have told us that demands by patients for cigarettes, going to the toilet, or just wandering about, are considerably lessened when they have music. Patients themselves make pertinent comments, all on the favorable side of the ledger. Sometimes women patients will sing or dance to this record music. Workers are more cheerful, too. When the sessions have to be temporarily discontinued, as happened recently while the record player was in the repair shop, we are told at the next session that we were missed. During the actual treatment period, volume is kept quite low, so that the shock team can hear instructions as they work; music provides a pleasant undertone.

This department also provides music for picnics, parties, dances, fashion shows, and other programs presented at intervals by volunteer groups or other departments. With adequate and competent assistants, we have individual instruction in voice, piano, and other instrumental work, dependent upon the patient's needs, interests, and abilities.

A manic was assigned to us who was unable to concentrate on any given activity for more than a few minutes at a time. She was referred to us by her physician because of her previous interest in music. We tried her at the piano and found that she could not play more than two or three measures without jumping up to stretch her legs, dance about, request a drink of water or a breath of air. By constant recalling her to the task at hand, we managed after many sessions to get her to stay at the instrument for ten minutes, then longer, until a given piece was completed. Also, she gradually became able to play more accurately and to recognize errors in time, which were more frequent than errors in notes.

In time, we had her play with several other patients in a piano quartette. In this group her overactivity reacted favorably on an involutional patient and, under our guidance, each was able to help the other through a mutual medium. It took many hours, daily practice, gentle urging, and patience, but results were forthcoming. When our manic found that she could play again, she asked if she might sing, so we worked with her in this medium, helping her to memorize several numbers. She presented the *Habanera* (from *Carmen*) and *Giannina Mia* (from *Firefly*) at our spring musicale and took the audience by storm. Several weeks later she was released from the hospital.

One of our instrumentalists used to spend his time lying on the floor of his ward, coming out only to eat, shave, and for music. A former bank clerk, his appearance and deportment were quite changed from his normal pattern. His one joy was to play the saxophone. He would like to have had an "alto," but since we have none, he plays the "C" melody with equal delight. He reads music, but his rhythmic pattern was much distorted, so we insisted that he play everything as written at first, then let him play in his own style. Now he plays with excellent rhythm both ways. This patient has been in the hospital for some time and with us since early

1949. He is now working in the laundry and very proud of his job.

For community sings, we have printed word sheets, so that all can participate, even in the new songs which are becoming familiar through the medium of television and radio. Fun songs, rounds, and folk songs are alternated with old and new popular melodies and ballads, with constant change of mood and style. Those who like to perform as individuals can have the opportunity on these occasions even though they are not particularly capable. It gives them a chance for emotional release and the satisfaction of having performed in public—which they have always wanted to do— without disrupting a formal program presented by the more able patients.

One patient, aged forty-five years, who was over-shy, retiring, self-deprecatory, and classified as dementia praecox, paranoid, had always wanted to sing, but had not been able to study for lack of funds; also, her very nature precluded her taking part in our activities. Finally she picked up sufficient courage to ask us if she had a chance to learn. We tried her voice and found it exceedingly guttural, and she had no ear for pitch. However, we told her that we would see what could be done, but that she would have to help herself and be willing to put in much effort and work. This she was. First, we taught her how to listen to tone and reproduce the pitch that she heard. Next came tone-placement and proper breathing. Within three months of four-a-week half-hour sessions she was able to sing an Hungarian folk song as well as any one and she joined the chorus, singing in the alto section. A few months later she was released from the hospital. Through our help she found a sympathetic vocal teacher in her community, joined the local choral society and her church choir, and attended night classes to learn how to sew. We feel that this patient has made an excellent adjustment.

A patient who stuttered considerably came to sing with us and, through private assistance, has been able to overcome somewhat his speech impediment. Another patient who had gone through a lobotomy was inclined to read phrases in a very jumbled manner, sometimes even entirely backwards. We were able to get her to read much better by directing her attention to rhythmic singing, with constant repetition and always correcting even the slightest error. The therapist should at all times be sensitive to mood changes in the patient, should study his needs and try to help him in his thinking when the opportunity arises. Periodic reports are made to the physician in charge of the ward as to the patient's changes in behavior pattern, his interests, participation, and coöperation.

Musicians have volunteered their services and have also been sent by union locals as part of the welfare program through the record-transcription fund. Employees have volunteered to give of their time and talents to assist in our program, all of which is much appreciated. Since the turnover is great, we cannot always rely on such aid. Our department supplies the portable organ and the hymnals for a student nurses' weekly prayer service as well as record music for the mending room, and in general endeavors to coöperate with all departments and their various programs and services.

It is common knowledge that music changes moods even when the patient is entirely oblivious to his present surroundings, though it will take a hostile or very withdrawn personality somewhat longer to respond to the mood of the music than one who is more amenable. Repetition and the monotony of predetermined rhythm and melody will establish the desired mood. Occasionally well-planned programs do not produce the desired result because of personal associations, forgotten or remembered, with a particular piece, at odds with the general mood of that selection. Hence, it is essential to be aware of reactions at all times and to be prepared to make the necessary changes to more suitable music immediately. As in all other therapies, the aim is to rehabilitate, resocialize, and reëducate a patient through active and passive participation in music. As equipment and personnel are available, we plan to

[228]

include music with insulin therapy, and to work out an "applied-music" program for specific groups of patients similar in illness and in educational background, who need approximately the same type of treatment for changes in mood or behavior. It is through this type of service with "control cases" that much of our progress in music as a therapy has been made.

While working in a particular hospital for bone diseases, the nurse in charge of a ward stated, "When you come, I might as well throw out the sedatives, for my patients don't need them." It was my custom to present informal, light programs on this ward just before supper and medication time. The patients ate and slept better after these musical evenings.

During my in-service training at Allentown, one patient was assigned to me who was dementia praecox, hebephrenic, had certain compulsive patterns, and was over-religious, religion being the only subject on which he could talk intelligently; all other subjects had no meaning. His music education included choir work, playing the organ, and similar activities. He wanted a Bible, so we secured one for him, and then began our retraining program.

The first day we were introduced, he acknowledged the introduction in the following fashion: "Glad to meet you, Mrs. B——. Sit down. Begin on page one, first line," all the while crossing himself; then he sat down. I acknowledged the introduction and played the first note, and the same ritual began all over again. This kept up until I almost felt like getting up each time with him. However, we finally managed to get him to sit still for five minutes, then for ten, and later for an entire hour without ritualistic accompaniments. Meantime, we also had to retrain his "ear." Through lack of use, or because of his illness, he had lost his ability to sing a note as he heard it. Patience and complete coöperation from the patient were finally rewarded, and he was able to sing not only notes and words, but with accurate pitch. This man, once an accomplished musician, had to learn to hear tone properly just like any beginner. After several months' work, we felt that we had really accomplished something of value. He was able to join the chorus, hold his own part against the others, and learn other music more quickly than the first selection. During the summer he appeared as soloist in a concert. He had become so well adjusted that when he made an error in the ending of the first chorus section, it did not disconcert him. He covered up the slip, went into the second chorus, and no one, except those who had taught him, knew what had happened. Neither his deportment nor his singing showed that momentary lapse, such as can happen to the finest of musicians when performing from memory.

In order to acquaint the public in general and interested citizens in particular with this modern, yet old, form of therapeutic treatment, we have accepted many calls to speak before civic, church, and educational groups, presenting the work of music therapy as an adjunct to medical and psychiatric treatment in mental hospitals. We are also included in the regular teaching program of student nurses, technicians, and attendants. Despite all the handicaps, we find it most gratifying to know that this field of service is gradually coming into its own.

Through the foresightedness and progressive attitudes of the medico-managerial staff, Marlboro State is the first state hospital in New Jersey to set up a music-therapy department. We are fully aware of the many complexities that arise in developing any type of program in a state institution and we deeply appreciate the whole-hearted support of all concerned, but particularly that given by Dr. David W. McCreight and Dr. J. Berkeley Gordon, medical director of the hospital.

MUSIC AND THE GENERAL ACTIVITY OF
APATHETIC SCHIZOPHRENICS

CLYDE G. SKELLY and GEORGE M. HASLERUD

University of New Hampshire

Attempts to modify the activity of human beings by music have interested psychologists for many years. Tarchanoff (4) had early noted that "music exercises an influence on the muscular activity of man, increasing or decreasing it according to the nature of the melodic stimuli." On the introspective side, Weld (13) found that whatever visual imagery is present while listening to music is always imagery of movement. The earlier studies, however, did not lead to any consistent conclusion, based as they were on small samples, usually only a single case, little or no control of conditions, and general impressions rather than actual experimental evidence.

The last quarter century has brought more adequate experimentation on the motor side of the psychology of music, but these studies have largely involved the speeding up of such voluntary activities as handwriting and typing (5), delaying fatigue and increasing mental efficiency in industry (3), concentration and output in an architectural drafting room (6). Phares (11) showed that both gay and sad music markedly affected the psychogalvanic reflex. However, not until Altshuler (1) reported on two groups of four psychotic patients receiving hydrotherapy was music applied clinically in any sort of experimental setup. When programs arranged according to his iso-theory were played daily by an actual musician behind a screen, as much reduction in activity occurred with music as with hydrotherapy, and about 35 per cent reduction was observed as long as 15 minutes after the music ceased. He concluded, "Music seems a useful agent in decreasing output of disturbed and inaccessible mental patients both alone and in conjunction with various forms of hydrotherapy." Ogden (10), however, reviewing the entire field as portrayed in Schullian and Schoen's *Music and Medicine,* wrote, "Unhappily the content of the essays does little to demonstrate the value of music as a therapeutic agent or even to state 'the problems and institute a scientific approach to their solution.' "

THE EXPERIMENT

Purpose

The present experiment attempts to meet Ogden's criticism by securing the essentials of a scientific setup that can be duplicated anywhere:

1. Stimulation by music of objectively determined mood value with programs arranged according to a definite plan.

2. Adequate method of quantitative recording of level of activity.

3. Cancelling out of individual differences by making each subject his own control.

4. Sufficient stability of level of activity when without music to detect changes with music.

5. Sufficient numbers to use a statistical test of significance.

Altshuler's data are inadequate to support his conclusion about the value of music in therapy because of neglect of points 4 and 5. Moreover, to insure reproducibility of results, both the stimuli and the recording of activity need to be much more systematically defined than we find in Altshuler.

Subjects

Thirty-nine female mental patients, 19 to 56 years of age, who had been diagnosed as schizophrenics of apathetic mood (blunted emotionality, lack of feeling, and impassivity) were used in the present experiment. All had been admitted to the hospital within the past year and showed no signs of intellectual deterioration. Their unchanging, chronic inactivity seemed promising for point 4.

Stimuli

In order to remove the bias of music selected only by the writers, a group of 81 recorded musical selections which were fairly constant in melody, rhythm, and tempo were selected, ranging from classical to near-popular. They were played to various groups of a total of 402 college students untrained in music, each piece being rated by at least 60 subjects on a scale based on the work of Rigg (12), Hevner (7), and Campbell (2). These workers had found that college students could rate the general mood of a musical composition, that is, whether it is sad, gay, happy, lively, or the like. Hevner stresses the importance of rhythm and harmony in such ratings.

The rating scale consists of seven points with the following definitions: 1—stimulating, stirring, inciting, impelling, uplifting, elating, animated, tripping; 4—relaxing, restful, reposeful, tender, peaceful, gentle, sleepy, mellow; 7—depressing, oppressing, blue, dejecting, dismal, despondent, dispirited, despairing. Points 2, 3, 5, and 6 were left undefined but understood as moods proportional between the defined ones.

TABLE 1

Pieces Used in Programs During Music Sessions

No.	Selection	Composer	Scale Value	Q
1.	Tiger Polka	Uryga-Sandel	1.39	.59
2.	Perpetuum Mobile	Strauss	1.50	.56
3.	Helena Polka	Wladyslaw	1.55	.27
4.	Polonaise In A Major	Chopin	1.58	.73
5.	Jolly Coppersmith	Peter	1.60	.30
6.	Country Gardens	Grainger	1.62	.65
7.	Hail To the Spirit of Liberty	Sousa	1.62	.31
8.	Young Widow	Svec	1.64	.32
9.	Bumble Bee, The	Rimsky-Korsakov	1.78	.49
10.	Fiddle Faddle	Anderson	1.80	.50
11.	Etude No. 5 in G-Flat Major	Chopin	1.89	.66
12.	Second Movement, Organ Concerto No. 10 in D Minor—Allegro	Handel	1.94	.60
13.	Jazz Legato	Anderson	2.22	.62
14.	Zapateado	Sarasate	2.32	.51
15.	Ever Or Never	Waldteufel	2.51	.43

[233]

No.	Selection	Composer	Scale Value	Q
16.	Skater's Waltz, The	Waldteufel	2.68	.56
17.	Waltz In A-Flat Major	Chopin	2.79	.61
18.	Pizzicato Polka	Strauss	2.80	.43
19.	Wine, Women, and Song	Strauss	2.90	.57
20.	Southern Roses Waltz	Strauss	3.04	.65
21.	Voices of Spring	Strauss	3.12	.65
22.	Seamen's Waltz	Hellstrom	3.33	.65
23.	Missouri Waltz	Logan-Shannon	3.53	.72
24.	Gold and Silver Waltz	Lehar	3.60	.60
25.	Beautiful Ohio	Earl-MacDonald	3.64	.69
26.	Minuet In G	Beethoven	3.67	.61
27.	La Paloma	Yradier	3.69	.74
28.	Viener Blut	Strauss	3.69	.61
29.	Humoresque	Dvorak	3.71	.70
30.	Hear My Song Violetta	Bernier-Luckesch	3.82	.68
31.	First Love	Lehar	3.90	.63
32.	Trailing Arbutus, The	Friedman	4.07	.48
33.	Für Elise	Beethoven	4.56	.48
34.	Waltz In C-Sharp Minor	Chopin	4.69	.73
35.	Liebestraum	Liszt	4.75	.63
36.	Cradle Song	Brahms	4.82	.57
37.	On Wings Of Song	Mendelssohn	4.97	.62
38.	Barcarolle-Tales of Hoffmann	Offenbach	5.33	.65
39.	Sea Murmurs	Castelnuovo-Tedesco-Heifetz	5.52	.75

After all 81 selections had been rated by the groups of students, the median and semi-interquartile range were calculated and those with a Q of more than .75 discarded. The remaining 39 instrumental selections shown in Table 1 were then arranged into programs according to the iso-theory of Altshuler (1). This requires starting with music like the patient's mood and then gradually changing to a different one, in this experiment a gradual change from less active with high medians to more active with low medians. A sample program consisted of selections 38, 37, 31, 15, 6, 3, 13, 24, 37. These programs, lasting twenty to thirty minutes, came through the room's regular radio loud-speaker with the records played inconspicuously in an anteroom.

Recording

A quantitative measure of the general activity of Ss was obtained by time sampling, using a 7-point rating scale based on Newman (9) with these definitions: 1—overly active practically

[234]

all the time, extensive gross bodily movements, aggressive contacts with the physical environment, eager, animated bodily movements; 4—activity shown by Ss which one would expect to find in an audience listening to music, picking up a magazine, moving feet back and forth nodding head to music, rocking slowly back and forth in a chair, fixing clothes, turning pages of a magazine, wiggling back and forth in chair; 7—no overt activity, stationary, attitude of indifference, apathetic, no bodily movements. The intermediate points were left undefined as in the scale for selection of music. With each S observed for ten seconds on each rating, the group was sampled several times each session. At the 10:00 A.M. period the time samplings were made at the middle of the program when the livelier music was playing.

Controls on Recording

In order not to be influenced by them, previous ratings were kept covered. After the rating blank was completed, it was checked and filed by someone other than the rater and was not consulted until the end of the experiment.

To check the reliability of the ratings made by the experimenter, another observer (another psychologist) rated Ss for fifty samplings at the same time as the experimenter, both synchronizing their watches. The correlations between these ratings range between .70 and .88 for the various sessions.

Procedure

All samplings were made in an occupational therapy room to which the patients were accustomed. Before ratings were attempted, the experimenter became familiar with Ss and the Ss with the experimenter for a period of 12 days. When Ss came to the occupational therapy room, they were allowed to do as they wished—sit in a chair, look at books, or sew. The time samplings were not started until Ss had settled to their work. Because these patients were apathetic, many of them just sat in their chairs, looked at magazines— much the same activity that they would have shown on the ward. If for any reason an S did not want to come to the occupational therapy room, she was not forced to do so, and the sampling of the activity of that S was dropped for that day.

Sampling ratings were made five times a week at 8:00 A.M.,

[235]

10:00 A.M., and 4:00 P.M. In order to determine a base level of activity, before the main experiment began a total of 117 ratings were made at each of the three times on each S over a two-week period in the room where music would later be given. Then, for over a month a total of over one hundred experimental ratings were made at each time of day on each S. Music was played at the 10:00 A.M. period, with the Before-Music (8:00 A.M.) and the After-Music (4:00 P.M.) ratings to indicate changes and duration.

RESULTS

The group results are shown in Tables 2 and 3. Each S had six scores, each the mean of 99 to 117 samplings of general activity, which were the scores of base level at 8:00 A.M., 10:00 A.M., and 4:00 P.M. (preliminary No-Music period), and the experimental series 8:00 A.M. (Before-Music), 10:00 A.M. (With Music), and 4:00 P.M. (After-Music). Thus, the means in Tables 2 and 3 are actually the central tendency of 4089 to 4563 time samplings.

TABLE 2

DIURNAL SHIFTS IN ACTIVITY OF 39 APATHETIC PATIENTS

ACTIVITY	TIME OF SAMPLING	MEAN	SD	r	t
Base Level compared with	8:00 A.M.	5.12	.73	.95	1.29
Base Level	10:00 A.M.	5.07	.79		
Base Level compared with	10:00 A.M.	5.07	.79	.94	2.03
Base Level	4:00 P.M.	5.16	.69		
Base Level compared with	10:00 A.M.	5.07	.79	.88	10.63
During-Music	10:00 A.M.	4.41	.80		

The activity scores range from 4.29 to 6.44 for the various Ss, and the median standard deviation is .59 on the 7-point scale. Each S was remarkably stable in apathetic behavior during the several months of this study and even showed little diurnal change, as attested by the r's of .94 and .95 in Table 2. The only shift

TABLE 3

AMOUNT AND DURATION OF EFFECT OF MUSIC ON ACTIVITY OF 39 APATHETIC PATIENTS

ACTIVITY DURING PERIOD SAMPLED	M.	SD	r	t
Base Level	5.13	.72		
with			.93	.18
Before-Music	5.14	.89		
Before-Music	5.14	.89		
with			.96	17.86
During-Music	4.41	.80		
During-Music	4.41	.80		
with			.95	15.38
After-Music	5.10	.88		
Before-Music	5.14	.89		
with			.98	1.48
After-Music	5.10	.88		

was a slight but insignificant increase in activity at 10:00 A.M. ($t = 1.29$), which had been chosen as the time for playing music in the experimental series. Since, however, each S was her own control, the very great and significant change at 10 o'clock when music was played, shown by a t of 10.63 in the last column of Table 2, clearly differentiates the base level sampling from the experimental series sampling.

Table 3 indicates that only while music was playing was there greater activity. When the After-Music and Before-Music differences are compared, there is an insignificant t. In contrast, when the During-Music and After-Music, and the Before-Music and During-Music time sampling scores are compared, there are highly significant t's.

To check the findings from the group data an analysis of the individual records of each of the 39 Ss was undertaken. For each patient, the differences in pairs of ratings, e.g., the 10:00 A.M. minus the 8:00 A.M., were tabulated and the mean and standard deviation of the differences determined and interpreted for correlated samples according to McNemar (8). Meeting a t of 3.0 as the required level of significance beyond the 1 per cent point, all Ss showed significant increase of activity when music of such variety and in such programs as herein described was played to them. Further, a study of the individual records indicates that 35 Ss regularly went back to their previous base level, and six hours later (4:00 P.M.) the effect of the music was indistinguishable. Only four Ss had a t of greater than 3.0 when the activity at 8:00 A.M. was compared with that at 4:00 P.M. In two there was a slight persistence of activity, but this was counterbalanced by two who went below morning level; because of the high r, these differences were significant. For the majority, both the individual and group data indicate that music makes a difference in activity only while it is being played or shortly thereafter.

DISCUSSION

That the changes in activity during music were not due to diurnal rhythm nor to a conditioning effect of the experimenter's presence is demonstrated by the relatively narrow variability in all the nonmusic sessions, for all three times of day on the control base-level samplings and for the 8:00 A.M. and 4:00 P.M. periods of the experimental series.

Altshuler (1) found that music could decrease the activity of eight disturbed schizophrenic patients, and the present experiment shows that music significantly increased the general activity of 39 apathetic schizophrenics. This change in activity level of mental patients might give hope that music could be a form of psychotherapy. However, our results would cast doubt on such value of music by itself. When there is an insignificant carry-over of the effects of music for six hours and a continuing stable morning level of activity over several months during our experiment, one must conclude that music can probably be only an adjuvant to psychotherapy. For example, programs of the kind used in this experiment could be employed to regulate the activity of patients while in group psychotherapy, or in the dining halls of mental hospitals to increase the eating activity of retarded mental patients, or as a technique in occupational therapy to get patients to participate.

The music in this experiment was classical to near-popular. It should be determined whether modern popular music of the "Hit Parade" variety could give a more persistent effect with its simpler repetitive melodies. A check should also be made with excited patients to see whether the effect of quieting music would last the six hours from 10:00 A.M. to 4:00 P.M.

SUMMARY AND CONCLUSIONS

The purpose of this experiment was to study the effect of music, ranging from classical to near-popular, on the general activity of apathetic schizophrenics.

Music that had been calibrated on a 7-point scale for mood by 402 normal college students was played in programs arranged according to the iso-theory.

A 7-point rating scale was used to determine the general activity of patients with and without music. A check of their base level of general activity without music showed it, through high r's, to be very stable.

1. Both individually and as a group the patients showed significant increase in activity when livelier music was played to them.

2. For 35 of the 39 patients, there was no carry-over effect of the music after a period of six hours; two of the 39 patients showed slight persistence of activity and two a decrease slightly below morning level.

3. It is concluded that the therapeutic effects of music such as used in this experiment are temporary, and its probable main use would be as an adjuvant to other therapy.

REFERENCES

1. Altshuler, I. M. A psychiatrist's experience with music as a therapeutic agent. In D. M. Schullian, and M. Schoen (Eds.), *Music and medicine.* New York: Henry Schuman, 1948.
2. Campbell, J. G. Basal emotional patterns experienced in music. *Amer. J. Psychol.,* 1942, 55, 1-17.
3. Clark, K. *Music in industry.* New York: National Bureau for the Advancement of Music, 1929.
4. Diserens, C. M. Reactions to musical stimuli. *Psychol. Bull.,* 1923, 20, 173-199.
5. Diserens, C. M. *The influence of music on behavior.* Princeton: Princeton Univ. Press, 1926.
6. Gatewood, E. L. An experiment in the use of music in an architectural drafting room. *J. Appl. Psychol.,* 1921, 5, 350-358.
7. Hevner, K. Experimental study of the elements of expression in music. *Amer. J. Psychol.,* 1936, 48, 246-268.
8. McNemar, Q. *Psychological statistics.* New York: Wiley, 1949, 73-75.
9. Newman, F. B. The adolescent in social groups; studies in the observation of personality. *Appl. Psychol. Monogr.,* 1946, 9.
10. Ogden, R. N. Review of D. M. Schullian, and M. Schoen (Eds.), *Music and medicine. Amer. J. Psychol.,* 1934, 61, 595.
11. Phares, M. L. An analysis of musical appreciation by means of psychogalvanic reflex techniques. *J. exp. Psychol.,* 1934, 17, 119-140.
12. Rigg, M. The expression of meanings and emotions in music. *Psychol. Bull.,* 1940, 37, 556.
13. Weld, H. P. An experimental study of musical enjoyment. *Amer. J. Psychol.,* 1912, 23, 245-308.

A PHYSIOLOGICAL ASPECT OF EXPERIENCING MUSIC

MARTA GRUNEWALD, Ph.D.

New York, N. Y.

I

At all times attempts have been made to answer the old question of the essence of music, of the reason for its magic effect on the listener. Poets and musicians have written about it, philosophers, psychologists and physiologists have made it the object of their studies.

Most of the physiological contributions deal with the influence of music on bodily functions, such as breathing, heartbeat, blood pressure and others (1, 2, 3, 4). They examine the question of what *kind* of physiological reactions are produced by music, they do not, however, answer the question of the reason for the effects of music, of *how* it is that music affects the listener.

With regard to this problem, a neuro-physiological experiment may be described, the results of which will be applied to the conditions existing in music. The experiment is concerned with the psychosensory reactions of the pupil.

It is generally known, that the pupil of the eye contracts, when the quantity of light projected into it is increased, and that, vice versa, the pupil dilates, when light is followed by darkness. This pupillary reaction—the so-called "pupillary reflex to light"—is known to be due to the activity of the autonomic nervous system. It has been used for many years as a valuable diagnostic sign in

[241]

clinical examination, and it was for clinical reasons mainly that a special method has been developed for its study (6, 7, 8). This method, known as "pupillography" is applied in the above mentioned experiment, which is performed as follows:

The eye of the subject is exposed to a large number of light stimuli, up to one hundred or more. These stimuli follow each other at equal intervals (of, say, 4 seconds) and they are of equal duration (of, say, one second) and of equal intensity (say, 16 foot candles). By means of the "pupillographic apparatus," the main part of which is a specially constructed movie camera, the pupillary reflexes, elicited by the consecutive light stimuli, are recorded. Figures 1-4 show pupillographic pictures—"pupillograms"—as obtained by this method; they represent the pupillary reflex to light at various typical stages of the experiment.

Fig. 1 shows 4 of a series of 54 consecutive reactions to light. The first reaction (1) shows the fully developed reflex, which consists of a contraction (d), which is followed by a redilation (e). The following pictures show that the depths of the contraction diminish distinctly. This can be seen already in the third reaction. The 28th reaction is only half as deep as the first one; the 54th light stimulus is followed by a reaction which still shows in the pupillogram, but which is hardly visible to the naked eye. The reflex to light, hence, is seen to be fatigued and almost exhausted by means of a series of consecutive light stimuli.

If now, in this stage of complete, or almost complete indifference of the pupil to light, a single sensory stimulus, different from light—for instance an acoustic stimulus—is intercalated between two light stimuli—the series of which is continued uninterruptedly—the picture changes immediately. This is shown in Fig. 2: The 48th reaction is diminished by 1/7th of the first reaction, presenting the picture of the fatigued and exhausted light reflex. After a *sound stimulus* (s) has been given between the 48th and the 49th reaction, the pupillary reflex to light appears to be restored to almost the size of the first unfatigued reaction.

[242]

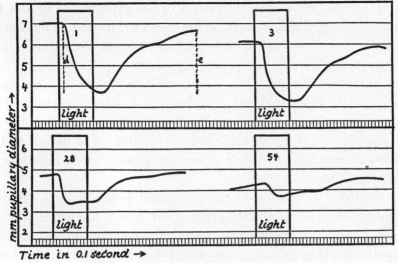

FIG. 1

STAGES OF FATIGUE OF THE PUPILLARY REFLEX TO LIGHT

(1) Reaction 1: The reflex to light before fatigue. It consists of a contraction (d) which is followed by a redilation (e).

(2) Reaction 3: The 3rd reflex to light already shows symptoms of fatigue. The contraction (d) is somewhat diminished in extent.

(3) Reaction 28: The contraction (d) is diminished to less than 1/2 of the first reaction.

(4) Reaction 54: The contraction (d) is diminished to about 1/8 of the first reaction. This stage of highly decreased reaction immediately precedes its exhaustion, such as it shows in reaction 73 in Fig. 3 and in reaction 100 in Fig. 4.

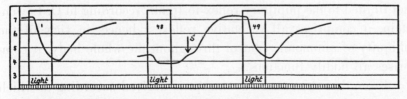

FIG. 2

RESTITUTION OF THE FATIGUED REFLEX TO LIGHT BY MEANS OF A SENSORY STIMULUS

(1) Reaction 1: The non-fatigued reaction to light.

(2) Reaction 48: The 48th reaction is diminished to less than 1/7 of the non-fatigued reaction.
    A sound stimulus (s) is introduced between the 48th and 49th reaction.

(3) Reaction 49: The 49th reaction appears restored to almost the size of the first reaction.

[243]

Figures 3 and 4 show the results of two experiments similar to that shown in Fig. 2, except for the fact that, instead of the interpolated sensory stimulus, psychological stimuli are given, after the pupil had become unresponsive to light.

In the experiment of Fig. 3, *a suggestion of fear* is given after the reflex to light is almost completely exhausted (reaction 73). In the following reactions a gradually progressing process of restoration is seen, from its beginning in reaction 74 to its full restitution in reaction 76, which shows the picture of an unfatigued reflex to light.

Complete restitution of the exhausted reflex to light can be obtained likewise, if other psychological stimuli are given. Fig. 4 shows the restituting effect of a *suggestion of joy,* which, in this experiment, is even more pronounced than that produced by fear as seen in Fig. 3.

These three experiments, then, show, that the function of a fatigued reflex can be restored, if the series of the fatiguing stimuli is interrupted by an interpolated new psychological or sensory stimulus.

O. Lowenstein derives from these data a physiological principle which he has called the "Psychosensory Restitution Phenomenon" (7).

It is one of the major features of this phenomenon, that it is not limited to the pupillary reflex to light. According to O. Lowenstein, it comprises all vegetative reflexes; hence, in view of the ubiquity of autonomic control throughout the whole body, it comprises all bodily functions.

From this observation a concept is derived according to which a far reaching general significance can be attributed to the phenomenon of psychosensory restitution. It is based on the fact, that the individual, while awake, is constantly exposed to sensory and psychological stimuli, coming from outside or originating within the person's mind. Each of these stimuli, according to the principle of psychosensory restitution, can be expected to be constantly

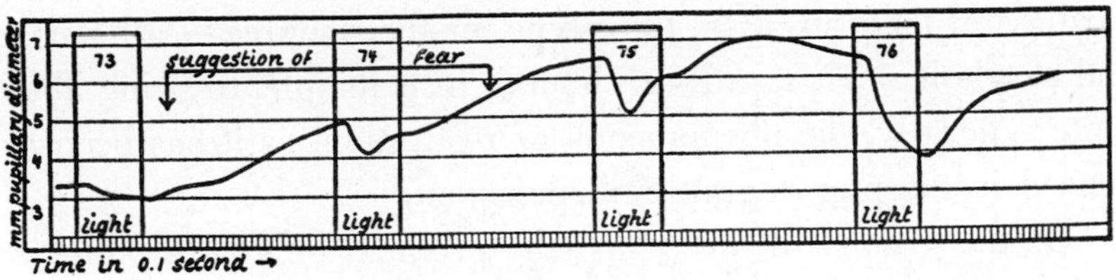

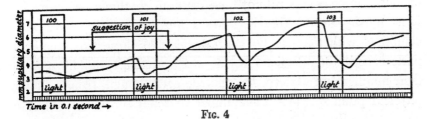

FIG. 3

RESTITUTION OF THE FATIGUED REFLEX TO LIGHT BY MEANS OF A PSYCHOLOGICAL
STIMULUS (SUGGESTION OF FEAR)

(1) Reaction 73: The 73rd reaction is almost absent.
　　A suggestion of fear is given between the 73rd and the 74th reaction.
(2) Reaction 74: Reaction 74 shows the beginning of a gradual restoration of the
　　reflex to light following the psychological stimulus. The pupil gradually dilates.
(3) Reaction 75: The phenomena seen in reaction 74 are more pronounced.
(4) Reaction 76: In this reaction the reflex to light is restituted almost *ad integrum*.

FIG. 4

RESTITUTION OF THE FATIGUED REFLEX TO LIGHT BY MEANS OF A PSYCHOLOGICAL
STIMULUS (SUGGESTION OF JOY)

(1) Reaction 100: The reaction to light is almost absent.
　　A suggestion of joy is given between the 100th and the 101st reaction.
(2) Reaction 101: This reaction shows the beginning of a gradual restoration of the
　　reflex to light following the psychological stimulus. The pupil gradually dilates.
(3) Reaction 102: The process of restoration is progressing.
(4) Reaction 103: The reflex to light is completely restored.

active in the sense of this principle, i.e., counteracting fatigue and
exhaustion in all vegetative functions—a process to which O. Lowenstein ascribes the important task of maintaining the overall
functioning capacity of the awake body. The stimuli involved in
this general restituting process comprise necessarily all possible
sources of stimulation—from the slightest sensory impressions to
the most powerful sensations, such as strong emotions, or the stir
of intense intellectual work, or the inspiration of the genius. Re-

[245]

gardless of their strength, their type, or their sources—all sensory and psychological stimuli are bound, in principle, to bring about, quite generally, the phenomenon of restitution, as it has been evidenced in the pupillographic experiment.

On the ground of these data the problem of the physiological basis of experiencing music shall be discussed.

II

Music, if looked at from a purely formal point of view, consists of two basic elements, which are common to all music, to the most primitive as well as to the most complicated: of rhythm and of tones (melody). A pile of tones without rhythmic configuration is no music, and rhythm becomes a musical creation only when combined with tones. It is characteristic of these two elemental parts constituting music, that there is practically no limit as to their number and variety. This is true even though, from a purely physical point of view, the number of tones, ordinarily used in music, is limited indeed, comprising about nine octaves. However, if one considers the innumerable possibilities of varying the quality of the tone——dynamically, or by varying the duration of the tone, or by changing the tone colors (timbre) as produced by the different instruments of the orchestra, the various "voices" of the organ, the individual character of the human voice (to mention but a few of these possibilities)—it is quite obvious that, in music, we are dealing with a number of tonal elements, which is quite unlimited. In combination with the (likewise unlimited) number of rhythmic elements present in music, they constitute an infinite multitude of "acoustic stimuli," i.e., stimuli which in the pupillographic experiment have been observed to produce the effect of psychosensory restitution.

Listening to music, then—in a purely physiological sense—is equivalent to being exposed to a great multitude of sensory stim-

uli, each of which can be considered capable of setting in motion the psychosensory restitution phenomenon.

It is a matter for special experimentation, however, to examine the degree to which this potential activity will be really effective. It will be necessary, first of all, to compare the restituting value of a multitude of acoustic stimuli present in music with the effect of a single acoustic stimulus in the pupillographic experiment.

Other questions to be examined in connection with the problem of the "restituting value" of the acoustic elements in music are concerned, for instance, with the effects of dynamic differences, of rhythmic changes, or consonant or dissonant chords, of simple musical phrases, and the like.

While the study of these problems must be left to future research, some of the results of O. Lowenstein's pupillographic studies on fatigue and restitution in general may be taken as answering some of these questions to a certain extent. It has been found, for instance, that the degree of restitution depends on the intensity of the defatiguing sensory stimulus (7, p. 52). This, in a preliminary way, bears on the aforementioned restituting effect of dynamic differences in music. Also observations such as that the restituted reflex usually refatigues more quickly than the unfatigued one, elicited at the beginning of the pupillographic experiment, will certainly have to be taken into consideration in this future research.

There is, however, also some direct experimental indication of the relationship between music and the psychosensory restitution. It has been noted, in some pupillographic experiments, that the normally developing symptoms of reflex fatigue failed to appear when music was played during the experiment. The number of these observations, however, is too small to draw from them more than preliminary conclusions.

III

It has been seen in the experiments shown in Figs. 3 and 4 that the restituting effect on the fatigued function is not limited to sensory stimuli, but that it can be produced by psychological stimuli as well. Psychological reactions were elicited, as has been mentioned above, by verbal suggestions which were either pleasant or unpleasant.

No verbal suggestions are given by music, to be sure, at least as far as "non-vocal" music is concerned. At all times, however, music has been considered to be a universal language, able to express *without words* all emotions—happiness, pain, joy and sorrow—with their innumerable moods and shadings. There can be no doubt, that this powerful language will be able to convey to a listener "psychological suggestions," i.e., psychological stimuli, potentially able to produce the phenomenon of restitution, much in the same way as it is done by the verbal suggestion of the pupillographic experiment.

Thus it can be safely assumed, that the psychological stimuli emanating from music—as well as the sensory ones—are able to produce a condition of continuously generated psychosensory restitution, a condition which subjectively is experienced as a feeling of physical and mental well-being and animation.

This experience is known to everyone. It is independent of the artistic level of the music by which it is produced. It is known to the man in the street, whistling the latest hit as well as to the thoroughly trained musician or the cultured music-lover listening to a concert conducted by Toscanini. Both are equally exposed to the sensory and psychological stimuli emanating from music. The sensory stimuli present in any kind of music affect them both. However, the effect of the psychological stimuli is necessarily determined by the type of musical "language" in which they are given; to produce psychological stimulation it must be understandable to the listener. Whatever psychological restitution, therefore, results from these stimuli, its degree depends on the degree of musical understanding.

In this connection a question may be discussed, which arises with respect to the concept of a "physiological basis" of experiencing music. "How is it possible"—it will be asked—"that there are people who are completely insensitive to music?" If there is such a thing as a "physiological basis" of experiencing music, everybody ought to be sensitive to music; a physiological principle should be generally valid by definition! It cannot be denied, however, that many non-musical people do exist, people who do not care about music in the least, who, on the contrary, consider music as a disagreeable noise.

There is no doubt, that these people must be subject to the purely sensory acoustic stimuli, emanating from music in the same way as those who enjoy music. Consciously or unconsciously they will experience all restituting effects produced in them by these stimuli. But the "non-musical" person is "deaf" toward the language of all music which, therefore, fails to produce any *psychologically elicited* restitution. The restitution effect produced by the sensory stimuli of music alone, however, frequently seems to be insufficient to bring forth a degree of restitution that could be sensed as such. This shows in every-day experience; for example, when in concerts, non-musical people are seen to be fast asleep. For them even the sensory stimuli of the music, after a short while, lose their restitutional value, become monotonous and indifferent from the adaptive standpoint, causing the individual to withdraw emotionally and to fall asleep. Such an individual can be awakened only whenever the smooth flow of noises is interrupted by a sudden loud sound, like that of the brass instruments or the kettle-drum.

The musical individual, instead, experiences the great variety of psychological stimulation which, changing from one moment to the other kaleidoscopically, excludes the tiring and lulling effect of monotony. It is for this reason that O. Lowenstein maintains that the defatiguing effect of music played during pupillographic experiments can be obtained in "very musical people" only (7, p. 84). This seems to indicate that, *with respect to their restituting value, psychological stimuli are superior to the purely sensory ones*. It is most likely that the restituting value of the multitude of sensory stimuli in music diminishes gradually, and that they fail more and more to elicit a defatiguing reaction. This corresponds to the fact that continuous light stimulation in the pupillographic experiment also becomes gradually inefficient in eliciting the pupillary reflex. This means that in spite of the great number of sensory stimuli in music (which is due to the great variety of tonal and rhythmic elements in music) the strength of these stimuli is not always sufficient to elicit a full restituting reaction. Their effect on the listener, then, is not different from that of a series of equal stimuli; the result is monotony of stimulation and, hence, fatigue and exhaustion of the reaction.

It has been mentioned above that it is necessary to compare by the pupillographic experiment the effect of a multitude of sensory stimuli, as present in music, with that of a single acoustic stimulus. The experiences in the pupillographic experiment of musical and non-musical listeners may be considered as capable of furnishing us with some preliminary material on this question, to which future experiments can refer.

On the basis of specific experiments it may be possible, in the future, to decide to which extent the principle of psychosensory restitution can be considered to be the physiological basis of all musical experience.

BIBLIOGRAPHY

(1) Washco, Alec Jr.: *The Effect of Music upon Pulse Rate, Blood Pressure, and Mental Imagery.* Philadelphia, 1933.
(2) Dogiel, J.: "Über den Einfluss der Musik auf den Blutkreislauf." *Arch. f. Psychologie,* 1880, 416-428.
(3) Schoen, Max: *Effects of Music.* Harcourt, Brace & Co., New York, 1927.

(4 and 5) Hyde, I. H. and Scalapino, W.: The Influence of Music on Electro-cardiograms and Blood Pressure. *Am. Journ. Psychol.* 1918, 36 and 1927, 46.

(6) Lowenstein, O. und Westphal, A.: *Experimentelle u. klinische Studien zur Physiologie u. Pathologie der Pupillenbewegungen.* S. Karger, Berlin, 1933.

(7) —————— *Der Psychische Restitutionseffekt.* Benno Schwabe & Co., Basel, 1937.

(8) —————— and Friedman, E. D.: Present State of Pupillography: Its Method and Diagnostic Significance. *Arch. Ophthalmol.* 27:969-993, 1942.

MUSIC IN MEDICINE

By GEORGE E. ARRINGTON, JR., M.D.

Huntington, W. Va.

PART I

MUSIC AS RELATED TO MAN

Although there have been references to the beneficial effects of music upon the sick throughout the recorded history of man, it was not until the turn of this century that serious, modern, scientific study of the subject developed. This was principally due to the need for a well organized system of mental measurement. By 1900 much had appeared in the field of psychiatry and psychology and the time was at hand to investigate music in the field of medicine. "Ethnological research, individual observation by competent naturalists and musicians, and psychological experiments have proven its influence beyond any doubt. The attention at present is being shifted to the study of the structural elements of music, the divergencies as to pitch, inflection and pause, and respective physiological and psychological influence upon the human organism" (1c). Unfortunately, the stigma of superstition has prevailed even until now to an extent and has dampened many serious, unbiased efforts to learn about and employ music in the care and treatment of the sick.

AN APPROVED THERAPEUTIC TECHNIQUE

The first purpose of this paper is toward dispelling this hesitancy in accepting music to the status of an approved therapeutic technique. It is felt that the surest way to do this is to give an honest evaluation of investigations thus far conducted and to present information pertinent to understanding the problem as a whole.

The healthy trend of interest in music on the part of physicians, especially those in administrative positions, is particularly encouraging. From the earliest known history of medicine, physicians have represented to the laity a special elevated segment of humanity. They are looked to for maintenance of health and guidance to happiness. They are expected to investigate all the means available to accomplish these ends and to employ them to best advantage. Further, physicians also represent a large number of those who support the arts as well as the sciences. There are several examples of physicians who have been either musical or acoustical geniuses or else world-renowned composers including Herman von Helmholz, Alexander Borodin and Theodore Billroth (37). Other eminent physicians have patronized the art of music and like many present day physicians were skilled in the art and found relaxation in its pursuit. These then are the men who shall principally stimulate employment of music with the sick, much as doctors with an eye to graphic art have guided the use of physiologically sound principles of decor in hospitals, operating rooms and offices.

The esthetics in man demand attention if we are really to treat the whole person. It is contended that because the effect of music varies somewhat from one patient to another, its use as a therapeutic agent is questionable or altogether invalid. However, these same critics would readily admit the variability of reaction to other medicaments. This paper deals with these variations in music therapy and the more significant consistencies. "One would expect that a medium which affects emotion, the endocrines, the circulation, respiration, blood pressure, mood, association, and imagery, would be worthy of further investigation" (1c). It behooves us then to scrutinize objectively and carefully this subjectively potent modality.

Music has many definitions. Some are fanciful, others are

analytical. We shall begin by clarifying the vocabulary of the subject.

"Music is an art of sound in time which expresses ideas and emotions in significant forms through the elements of rhythm, melody, harmony, and color." Longfellow said, "Music is the universal language of mankind," and Carlyle, "Music is the speech of angels" (47). Music then is a temporal art form whereas painting and sculpture are spacial art forms. Music is capable of expressing and affecting feelings and attitudes, and is, as we shall show later, akin to man and nature itself. It is well expressed that music is "the language of the soul."

Whether music should be called a therapy is purely an academic question. The important duty is to learn the effects of music and to use it to benefit our patients. Other than the primary irritants few agents known will give completely consistent results in biology. The variation in effects depends on such factors as the strength of the agent, resistances met, manner of administration et cetera. All this is true of the effect of music.

Little data have been reported concerning the consistency of effects of music on man, but many ideas have been expressed. The best authorities today feel that there is wide variation in effect from person to person, and in the same person at different times. Further, it is felt that reactions to music are more predominantly subjective (associative) than objective (physiological) and that, accordingly, there are as many reactions as there are associations.

But the counter opinion seems valid that within a given society, culture, and period of time, the gross associations developed in us are fairly consistent with some exceptions. By this is meant that an American living today will generally place the effect of Brahms' "Lullaby" in the category of a slumber song rather than call it a funeral dirge, and will respond to the "Going Home" theme of Dvorak's "New World Symphony" with nostalgia rather than be motivated to dance. In short, within certain limits music affects us all similarly, but with definite ideation based on associative content and background.

Beyond this similarity there seem to be three general types of response to music which are conditioned by mentality and personality. First, there are those who respond predominantly in an associative way, as mentioned, second, there are those who respond physically in a sensory-motor way and third, there are those who respond largely intellectually and analytically. These responses will be discussed later.

Why music? Why art at all? Few will deny the import of art and music on the lives of man now and always. The arts are a communicative medium first and foremost. They express the mind of their originator to the recipient—the hearer, in the case of music. This answers in small measure the "what" of art. But why? What motivates man to express himself at all? In the life of every man who lives fully there are many facets of personality which enhance the whole. One of these is his art. His participation in his art may be active (creative, original) or passive (appreciative, associative), but the fact that he participates is certain.

Perhaps the explanation lies in the idea of Max Schoen who said, "Music is the most moving of all arts, because sound moves all our senses, our muscles, and our minds. It moves us most deeply and most widely. Music can cause tension and relaxation and can create moods of joy, solemnity, melancholia, happiness, and bitterness. Music of all arts objectifies feelings the most completely by doing it most intensely and most purely, and for this reason music possesses healing powers in the greatest measure" (45).

The graphic arts (sculpture, painting, tapestry) were chiefly communicative formerly. Today this function has been dominated by photography so that the economic stimulus has been largely removed and many of those who would follow this art are detoured. Likewise in music the commercialization of the mechanical forms (recordings and movies), the artificially popularized "swing" music, and the "closed shop" of the music producers have detoured many of those who one day might have expressed themselves in this form. Chronicling of our times, once relegated to the artists and artisans, has left their domain.

But time and modern technological development have not altered human response to music or the human urge to participate in it in some manner. Where is the origin of this force? Suffice it to say that deep in us music strikes a resonance so that we respond, first on a rhythmic sensory-motor level and later in an associative, perceptual way or in an intellectual way. In brief, there is something in the listening to or the creating of music which is pleasant to us. Occasionally music may stimulate pain or uncomfortable associations so that we dislike the music, at least in part, but generally speaking participation in music is a deep-seated, pleasurable experience.

One writer who has studied the effects of music on the mentally deficient states that in "tests devised to investigate 'the perceptive aptitudes of mental defectives regarding music and more specially regarding musical rhythm,' mental defectives show in their behavior rhythmic aptitudes of children of their own mental age and are inferior to subjects of the same chronological age. The spontaneous rocking movements are manifestations of primitive auto-eroticism—they occur with greater frequency among those with the lowest mental ages" (27). Perhaps the fundamental explanation of the effect of music lies here—deep in our primitive nervous and psychic mechanisms.

The response to music may have little to do with the innate qualities of the music but rather be based largely on our reactions to associations which the music causes to arise. Thus, if we associate some happy experience with a certain composition, we are likely to enjoy the music and *vice versa*.

It is likely true that those who have little or no talent for playing or singing (by reason of motor incoordination, et cetera) can react emotionally and physiologically as strongly and satisfyingly as the talented. Is this not then the answer to music's universality;

that is, its power to touch us in one way or another and link us by a common bond of esthetic emotional experience? Music emerges as a great common denominator of man.

INDISPENSABLE TO MANKIND

But where does music fit in the structure of man's civilization? How potent a force is it?

Music is all around us. A mere cataloging of a week's contact with music will show the place of music in our civilization. Music is indispensable in a complete consideration of any level of human activity, be it personal, community, national, or even international.

Music is both a factor of society and a means of representing it. As a factor of society it is important to patriotism and nationalism in the official anthems and hymns of countries. These very songs along with folksongs are also elements of the nature and spirit of the people.

Music may not be designed to be representative of the period, but contemporary sociological influence is generally within it and can be analyzed. So-called ageless music is in nowise detached from this cultural influence. Its agelessness is due more to its directness of message about qualities and things which endure and are part of our own experience.

The technical form which the music takes may vary greatly depending on the ingenuity of the composer and the musical developments up to his time. Whether a certain musical form is attractive or not to us depends on personal inclination and background, but music of some sort is an enjoyable technique for participating in society whether it be as composer, performer, or listener. For example, one may delight in detail generally so that detailed music is particularly interesting. Or one may be meticulous, exacting, and enjoy symmetrical form, completeness, and convention, in which case music in the style of Bach, for example, would be attractive.

Music fits into the sphere of human activities in several different phases. Different functions, interests, and fields of thought and endeavor of society concern themselves with music, namely, science (particularly physics, biology, physiology, medicine and psychology), philosophy, and esthetics. The knowledge gleaned from all these sources can clear the way toward a sound evaluation of the service to which we can put music in the healing and alleviation of physical and mental suffering.

The personality consists of that organization of constitutional, affective, ideational, and conative capacities and tendencies which characterize an individual and largely determine his habitual pattern of behavior.

In music and throughout its history there are many relationships with nature and particularly with living creatures including man and his personality. In the whimsical and speculative field are to be found many interesting ideas concerning the origins of musical instruments, for example, the harp or lyre as beginning with the discovery of dried sinews stretched across a turtle shell; the drum as a hollow log; the flute as a reed broken and catching an adventitious breeze, and so on. Other relationships are apparently more serious and meaningful. These include the fact that *tempo moderato* is equal to the normal pulse, and that several of the elements of music are also elements of the physiological and psychological phases of man. Striking are the presence of rhythms in animals including the more obvious ones of respiration and pulse, and the less obvious hormonal (cyclic) patterns and the Berger brain waves. Even the motor and sensory and reflex reactions to electrochemical stimuli are rhythmical as are the peristaltic waves of the gastro-intestinal tract and the microscopic movement of the villi in the intestine and the ciliary action of the mucosa of the respiratory system. Many organs, it is said, cannot function for long without the presence of a rhythmic pulsation in the blood stream. These include the kidney and liver. The whole bodily function is related to and dependent on the maintenance of these rhythms. Obviously, any disturbance in these rhythms may be indicative of disease and the nature of the alteration may be the clue to diagnosis, prognosis, and therapy.

That music depicts or stimulates moods is one more kinship to human personality, that is, to man's psyche. Much argument is current concerning the possibility of music's containing mood. Many contend that the mood stimulated by music is a product of individual associative content and is not present objectively in the music, while others feel that certain effects will cause consistent results regardless of previous conditioning of the listener. Be that as it may, the fact remains that one's mood stimulates his desire to experience certain music which is compatible to his mood. We whistle a jolly tune when happy, and find solace, comfort and reassurance in more somber forms when sad.

Harmony is an element of music and in a sense there must be harmony of the various components of the physical and mental functions of man, so that ordered, purposeful and healthful ends may result. Bacon said in one of his essays, "The genius of music and medicine are alike. The function of the physician is to tune the lyre of the human body so that it shall give forth sweet and harmonious sounds." Plato also commented on this relationship.

The relationship of the art form of music to nature in general of which man is a part is apparent. Many sounds in nature are well depicted in musical form—the rippling brook, singing birds, wind in the trees, et cetera, and other elements of man's experience both within and without himself. The music of speech and singing are the closest and most personal connections. More subtle is the power of music to represent motion of various sorts. This, in fact, is more significant in music than in graphic art, for music is temporal in nature and so in part is motion. Whether it be the whir of a spinning wheel or the wild chase of children in play, music is the most emotionally and intellectually convincing single type of artistic representation.

Altshuler says, "Why does music affect human beings? Because tone and rhythm put into proper order appeal to the pleasure principle. Music has the property of attracting attention by appealing to the pleasure principle and arousing interest. Biologically, sound is used to lure, to convey, and to warn, and to challenge and appears far down in the evolutionary scale" (1c).

Psychology of Music

The psychology of music differs from the philosophy of music. This difference lies in the more exact nature of psychological knowledge. The effects of sound, says Licht, may be physiologic or intellectual; related to intensity, quality, or direction on one hand and to past or present mental associations on the other. Sound serves as a warning of approaching danger and may thus incite fear. The reaction varies from "reflex panic produced by an air-raid siren to the soothing effect of a softly sung lullaby" (42). Conscious mental images may arise in profusion or be entirely absent following musical stimuli. "It is undoubtedly possible to influence the mood of healthy trained musicians by the use of selected compositions but to assume that all listeners will react in similar fashion or that the moods of the mentally deranged can be changed at will by prescribed music is to ignore the nature of mental disease and the scientific findings of psychologists" (42).

According to Licht, the following are the effects of the elements of music:

"Pitch: High pitch calls forth happy, bright feeling and low pitch characterized by gloomy or melancholy in Western minds. The reverse is true in Orientals.

"Intensity: Softness is soothing and holds attention. Fatigue results from great intensity over long periods.

"Timbre: Certain instruments emit prejudicing tones. Chomet (The Influence of Music in Health and Life, New York, 1875) considered the bassoon mournful, the flute tender, and the trombone harrowing. The clarinet expresses grief, the oboe suggests reverie, but the violin 'seems suited to express all sentiments common to humanity.' Low tones are dull and high tones cutting. The French horn is smooth, piccolo sharp, oboe stringent, cello velvety, and the bassoon rough. Gundlach (An Analysis of Some Musical Factors Determining the mood characteristics of music in the Psychological Bulletin, 1934, 31:592) finds the brasses triumphant and grotesque, never melancholy or tranquil, delicate or sentimental; the woodwinds mournful, awkward, uneasy, never brilliant or glad. In the human, voice has emotional ties with its timbre, that is, the virility of the basso and the sparkle of the coloratura.

"Duration: A single long note will attract attention, but after some time if unaltered it becomes monotonous, annoying, and finally exasperating.

"Rhythm: This probably was the first primitive state in the evolution of music. There is also strong evidence that this is the most primitive reflex type response. (See above.) It is difficult to walk deliberately out of time to a well accentuated march. With the aid of the electromyograph, Jacobson (Electrophysiology of Mental Activities in the American Journal of Psychology, 1932, 44:677) has shown that in complete relaxation mental activity results in fleeting but specific muscle contraction invisible to the eye and unknown to the subject. Singing or chanting overcomes laziness and facilitates synchronous expenditure of energy by individuals engaged in a common task. Rhythm gives us a certain pleasure because of its orderliness to which the mind is sensible.

"Melody contributes chiefly to restfulness. If simple and recognizable it recalls other times and rests the mind from thoughts of present problems. More complex melody distracts the more musical people but has less desirable effect on the uninterested.

"Mode: Mode refers to the arrangement of whole and halftones in the musical scale construction. In our society two are commonly used—major and minor. The argument of the effect of mode on the psyche has an interesting history. Rameau, in 1722, in a treatise, prejudiced us first against the minor mode and in favor of the major as more pleasing and beautiful. Hauptman strengthened this and then Helmholz introduced the idea that the foreign element of the minor mode which is introduced, though not strong enough to destroy the harmony, does add a mysterious, obscure effect almost unaccountable to the ear because the weak combinational tones are concealed by the louder conventional ones. Gurney (The Power of Sound, London, 1880) disagreed and pointed out the perpetual occurrence of minor triads of D and A in the harmonics of C major does not convey a pathetic impression, which it would do if the mysterious effect were simply due to slight degrees of dissonance as in the minor triad. In 1944, Valentine published in the British Journal of Psychiatry, 1944, 6:190, his experimental findings in this regard. He found that 'Major intervals are described as sad or plaintive twice as often as minor.' Henlein (Journal Comp. Psychologists, 1928, 8:101) substantiated this and found that intensity is the dominant modifier of feeling. He also showed that children are first indoctrinated by the titles of piano pieces in the minor mode, which are invariably weird, mysterious, sad and gloomy. In adults, Beaunis has shown that among European composers, the major mode is used for bright, gay passages while the minor is reserved for uneasy, stirring ones. Hevner (American Journal of Psychology, 1935, 47:103 and 1947, 49:621) concluded that 'All of the historically affirmed characteristics of the two modes have been confirmed," but that "in producing its effects on the listener, the mode is never the sole factor." He maintains also that modality is effective in the dimensions of sadness and happiness but quite useless in the dimensions of vigor, excitement, and dignity. Of course, the mechanism for the production of psychic stimulus is important to know with a view to complete understanding of the possibilities of control, but in using music with those of already well established reactive patterns it is these patterns and not knowledge of scientifically derived insight into the nature of music which must guide our decision of what music is indicated in a given situation.

"Key: Gurney (*ibid.*) has shown why music is written in certain keys, namely, that the composers conceive it in a given key because of their facility in that key. They then set it down and we become used to its appearance in that form. Only the few with perfect pitch can detect the difference in a piece played up or down one semi-tone and the emotional effect remains constant. We hum or whistle in a key comfortable to us, not in a key 'colored' suitably to the mood of the piece. In short, it is felt that key has little if any specific, innate ability to stimulate the psyche.

"Tempo: Gundlach (Psychological Bulletin, 1934, 31:592) and Hevner (American Journal of Psychology, 1937, 49:621) find that speed stimulates excitement, and Hanson (American Journal of Psychiatry, November 1942) shows that as tempo is accelerated above *tempo moderato* (that of the normal pulse) the greater the emotional tension. Regular rhythm is exhilarating but not disturbing. Rhythmic tension is heightened by the extent to which dynamic accent is misplaced in terms of metric accent, and the emotional effect of off balance accents is greatly heightened by an increase in dynamic power.

"Sonority: (Dissonance, Hanson feels, produces a sense of tension and conflict, but Licht feels that to the musically uncultured it may just as often create boredom or annoyance).

"Composition: The effect of the piece as a whole may be due to environment or association with the situation in which the selection was first heard. Mood effect may be altered by unanticipated contrasts of intensity, unusual patterns, rhythm, or tempo. This meeting of the unexpected affords pleasure of a kind. The story telling value is of importance to full enjoyment by some and not at all important to others. As regards imagery, there are some who 'see' colors with music. Sir Isaac Newton first compared the diatonic scale with the seven colors of the spectrum beginning with C as red. Kawarski and Odbert (Color Music, Psychological Monographs, 1938, No. 50) showed that a rise in pitch or quickening of tempo increases brightness. Gilman (American Journal of Psychology, 1892, 4:42) has pointed out that without benefit of title or program notes there is no consistent story interpretation of music. Without emotional conditioning music cannot paint blue skies or green pastures."

What can music excite in us emotionally? Schoen states the following:

"The data show that rest, sadness, joy, love, longing, and reverence appear most frequently as the effects produced" (45). Music produces a mood change in every listener or intensifies the existing mood. The tendency for the same composition to produce the same mood in every listener is very marked. The degree of enjoyment derived from the musical composition is in direct proportion to the intensity of the mood effect produced.

According to van de Wall in *Music In Hospitals* (p. 22), "The physiological effects of music fall under the category of physiomotor and sensory reactions." These reactions are listed by Burris (7) as follows:

1. Metabolism increased.
2. Breathing accelerated and regularity retarded.
3. Variable effect on blood pressure, pulse, and blood volume.
4. Fatigue reduced or delayed; therefore, increased muscle endurance.
5. Various sensory stimuli thresholds increased.
6. Volume of activities (typing, writing) speeded.
7. Attention facilitated.
8. Muscle reflexes used in writing and drawing are increased.
9. Increased electrical conductivity of the body. Increased psychogalvanic index fluctuation.
10. Certain music with certain people can sustain attention to prolonged psychomotor performance above and beyond the effects of drugs.

Another interesting and uncommon physiological response to music is a peculiar effect which is quoted by Shakespeare in the *Merchant of Venice*, Act IV, Scene I, Line 50, namely, the reflex urination by Scotch men upon hearing the bagpipes play.

Etiological Relationship

Since 1884 twenty-seven cases of illness etiologically related to music have been reported. These are, of course, musicogenic epilepsy. Stubbe-Teglbjoerg reviews these in his article, "Musicogenic Epilepsy" (32). The last four cases from Sweden and Denmark are of cryptogenic, arteriosclerotic, traumatic, and psychogenic origin. The EEG is like that of other epilepsy and one case in which the patient was operated upon showed a typical traumatic process in the temporal lobe.

Shaw and Hill have found "definite and unequivocal examples of musicogenic epilepsy (that is, epilepsy induced by musical sounds which are clinical rarities). It was accepted from the evidence and description of these cases that hysteria is no explanation, and an opinion was expressed that a conditioned reflex to certain musical sounds may be present" (30).

What then is known of this rare medical oddity? Musicogenic epilepsy occurs later than idiopathic epilepsy. Many such patients are keenly interested in classical music. Both the nature of the attacks and the stimulus required to initiate the attack vary greatly. In one case reported by Shaw and Hill the patient was tested with pure tones from an electronic oscillator. At 512 cycles per second (about middle C) she became overtly emotional but did not convulse until the tone was musically modulated at which time she would suffer an attack within five minutes. The EEG was taken during the experiment and it was shown that prior to the seizure there was no change in rhythm and that cortical discharge began six to seven seconds after the clinical onset. This patient also responded adversely to musical stimuli other than the type used experimentally.

Another case reported to me verbally and as yet without authentication concerns a patient in California who suffers attacks only upon hearing a specific musical stimulus, namely, the sound of Bing Crosby's voice singing "Home on The Range." Regardless of

[265]

the validity of the latter, it serves to illustrate the diversity of musical stimuli which may occasion a *grand mal* convulsive seizure.

In one case reported, the blood pressure, heart rate, and respiration rate increased while the patient was listening to music. Some cases have a history of head injuries, and most cases show an epileptogenic area in the left temporal lobe on EEG made between seizures.

This rare entity serves to demand adequate investigation of music and its meaning to well being. It is to be hoped that wider study of fundamentals of music and experimentation will be excited by this condition, so that music in its complete significance will be better understood and applied.

Music and Preventive Medicine

Preventive medicine refers to the application of sound principles of physical and mental hygiene in the lives of well persons with the hope of avoiding needless illness. Thus, any measure which tends to keep us well is important to preventive medicine.

Music serves in this capacity daily, sometimes subconsciously, sometimes with intent and by application. The simplest example of this is relaxation and diversion from the cares and tempo of life. Music does this by virtue of its power to hold attention and to recall pleasant memories and associations. Many people turn to musical pursuits either actively or passively for these purposes plus the pleasure obtained from the esthetic experience involved. The modern generation is studying to the accompaniment of radio and TV music. Some writers (like Howard Hanson [29]) are fearful that unless an immunity to the power of highly dissonant and rhythmic popular music to build up psychic nervous tension is developed we may find ourselves a nation of neurotics. Then music may become an antidote for itself. Others (Licht, especially) belie this trend. Nevertheless, the power of music in our lives must not be disregarded if we are to practice good preventive medicine.

Properly chosen music can be applied in the home to serve good health. For example, proper background music with meals can enhance appetite and aid digestion. The popularity of the so-called "clock-radio" which lulls one to sleep to comfortable orchestral arrangements and then turns out the light certainly makes insomnia difficult; and by awakening one gradually to suitable themes it spares the sleeper the traumatic experience of a shattering alarm which initiates the day on an unpleasant basis. Radio producers are becoming increasingly cognizant of the particular types of music indicated at various hours of the day.

MUSIC IN INDUSTRY

The use of music in industry came to the fore during World War II when it was applied to increase output. The success of this is attested to by the fact that its use has been continued and expanded on the basis of experimental knowledge. Today many cities have private systems available to industry, offices and public places by which various suitable types of background music can be "piped" in by telephone wire, reamplified, and used to enhance working conditions or environmental atmosphere. The programs to doctors' offices, for example, differ much from those to an industrial factory. The former is designed to soothe while the latter is designed to stimulate, especially during slump periods of the day. By making work and life more pleasant, much disgruntlement and dissatisfaction along with their ill effects on personality and physical well being are obviated.

Music, when properly applied, can be used in industry and institutions to aid in accident prevention. Whiting (38) states that there was almost 27 per cent reduction in patient injuries in a controlled experimental trial of the use of music in a hospital. Moreover, the general improvement of atmosphere on the wards was marked.

The active pursuit of music, that is, singing or playing, is

[267]

exhilarating, satisfying, and may serve as a good hobby or avocation.

After the life situation is established, that is, when thirty to forty years of age is reached, many return to the pleasures of one art or another, including music, which they pursued as children and adolescents but laid aside for awhile. In music this may manifest itself in renewed activity in a church choir, amateur choruses and orchestra, et cetera. Others may develop record libraries and read about the subject to become authoritative if their bent is more on the intellectual side. There is an immense value in such activities for older people, especially for women in menopause and for older men, in bolstering self-confidence and making life worthwhile. There is pleasure in the doing and pleasure in the knowing that accomplishment is appreciated and well received.

Summary of Part I

It has been shown that the art of music is closely akin to man and nature. As such it can have strong physiological and psychological effects upon man. Furthermore, the effects, along with the various elements of music, can be subjected to analysis now that means of physiological and psychological measurement are available.

The disease of musicogenic epilepsy has been discussed, and the possibilities of music in preventive medicine have been presented.

PART II

Music as a Therapeutic Modality

The role of music in acute illness is principally that of sedation and reassurance. Of course, all of the principles of good application previously mentioned apply here, but certain types of music seem particularly appropriate because of their calming, soothing, cheerful qualities. In acute illness, the most important application is by way of background music.

In the case of the patient who is chronically ill, music can divert the mind during long periods of convalescence and enforced rest. Patients suffering from tuberculosis, rheumatic fever, malignancy, heart disease, neurological diseases, orthopedic disorders and a host of other conditions find that music can help to while away the hours and remove the thoughts to more pleasant spheres. This can be accomplished by good use of background music and records, books, musical instruments and singing activities.

Music can be utilized also as an adjunct to physical therapy. The active participation of patients with limbs which need remedial exercise is often invaluable. The piano provides a contraction-relaxation pattern scarcely equaled by any other instrument for strengthening the upper extremities. Even patients in arm casts can play if their casts are properly supported. Joint motion in contractures from burns can be markedly improved by the use of the piano. Mistakes need only be erased from the memory, unlike an error in weaving or writing. Precise exercises for the various digits are available on pages 51 to 57 of the book, *Music in Medicine* by Licht. Other instruments are useful also in this respect.

Children love music, especially music they know, with simple words and catchy tunes. Music can be used with children even more extensively than with adults, for their learning and experiencing capacity is so much greater that they seldom tire of it. They like their music to be loud and to tell a story. Music can be used also as an adjunct to games with children and is useful in lowering the ill effects of the noise or of crying on pediatric wards. It can be utilized for slumber music or mealtime music, as elsewhere. It is of particular value with chronically ill children who are required to stay in bed for long periods of time.

Recent evidence has shown that mental defectives are more easily handled when soothing, rhythmic music is played to them.

Study of this group has opened new ideas concerning the basic effect of music on the human mind. Rhythm bands have been used with good success in these cases (27).

In dentistry the application of music is designed to allay anxiety, raise the pain threshold and improve doctor-patient relationship. Like physicians, many dentists are using background music in their offices as well as special music with local anesthesia for painful procedures (19).

In obstetrics and gynecology music is used to allay anxiety and raise the pain threshold, and has the added value of helping the patient pass the hours in the labor room with more ease.

"In surgery, besides the use of background music on the wards, music has been applied in the operating room as an adjunct to local, spinal, or regional anesthesia to lessen apprehension and avoid operating room sounds and conversations which increase the patient's fears" (22). The history of this is reviewed by Light and dates from 1892, when Fenter placed a piano in Helensburg Hospital in Dunbartonshire, Scotland. Even at that time he could write, "Cessation or at least diminution of pain is marked in many cases and in seven out of ten cases fever was lowered" (22). Dogiel conducted a series of laboratory experiments using both animals and men and concluded that listening to agreeable music improved the circulation of the blood, increased the cardiac output, and produced changes in the respiration. He believed also that fatigue was increased by sad music and relieved by lively and soothing music.

In 1948, in Light's experiment, a tape recording device was located outside the operating room and grounded, with the anesthetist and the patient having earphones and the anesthetist controlling the volume. The surgeon was often interested and permitted the music to be heard by way of a loudspeaker in the operating room. The patient was permitted to request the type of music desired from five classifications. One hundred ten patients took part and the following musical requests were made:

Classical	9 —	8.2%
Semi-Classical	61 —	55.4%
Popular	35 —	31.9%
Children's Records	3 —	2.5%
Stories	2 —	1.8%

The educational and cultural levels were as follows:

Very High	High	Average	Poor	Normal
10	26	64	7	3

The operations included vagotomy, cholecystectomy, gastric resection, exploratory laparotomy, splenectomy, colon resection, ileostomy, appendectomy, herniorrhaphy, nephrectomy, bladder fulguration, miscellaneous minor surgery, thyroidectomy and major and minor orthopedics. Major surgery equaled 78%, and minor, 22%. The reactions of the patients were as follows:

76.4% Enthusiastic
13 % Mildly enthusiastic
6.4% Indifferent
5.4% Disliked it

In conclusion, it is important that the selection of music calm and soothe, and possess a quality that will hold the patient's attention.

MUSIC AND THE MENTALLY ILL

According to Fultz (14), the realm of the effect of music on the patient is used as an area of normality from which to spread and extend operations to affected parts of the personality. This is the "psychobiologic approach" of Adolf Meyer. Music is a common ground for rapport between the doctor and the patient, especially if the doctor is musically inclined, in which case it can be a center of discussion of imagery and associations. Altshuler believes that music is the only "medicine" which helps to convert

[271]

instinctual forces into socially acceptable forms. He writes, "Stimulated by music, man can still offer his lowly instincts free expressions, camouflaged by jitterbugging and boogie woogieing. Indeed there is therapeutic action acumen to an agent which is capable of reconciling the instinctual with the social, and the sensual with the spiritual."

Licht presents the following outline for the application of music in psychiatry:

1. By listening
   a. To improve attention
   b. To maintain interest
   c. To influence mood (to produce acceleration, etc.)
   d. To produce sedation
   e. To release energy (by tapping of foot, etc.)
2. By participation (in group singing, dancing, etc.)
   a. To bring about communal cooperation
   b. To release energy
   c. To arouse interest
3. By the creation of sound (the playing of instruments)
   a. To increase self-respect by accomplishment and success
   b. To increase personal happiness by ability to please others
   c. To release energy

Psychoneurosis is a "part reaction" in which the personality is well preserved and the patient has some insight. The various types of psychoneuroses include conversion hysteria, hypochondriasis, anxiety, asthenia and obsessive-compulsion. The usual treatments include psychotherapy, persuasion, suggestion and psychoanalysis.

Levine (41) states, "Many individuals achieve a feeling of self-confidence if they develop such hobbies as music. Learning to play musical instruments may compensate for a feeling of inferiority, especially when the individual has ability which he underestimates."

Group therapy in the form of mass singing has therapeutic

[272]

value according to Harrington and Kraines who believe that recreation and hobbies are important energy release techniques. This applies also to listening in which the passivity is also only seeming. Subconscious activation of muscles either as contraction or relaxation occurs and this relaxation and harmonious appeal to the senses produces a "feeling tone" which causes the patient to realize that peace and harmony exist outside himself and will continue despite his own troubles, so that he puts aside his own conflicts for a while. Conversely, stimulating music will excite and exhilarate the patient and serve as an outlet for energy release and give him enjoyment (17b).

In psychoses, including general paresis, alcoholism, arteriosclerotic disorders, senility, involutional melancholia, manic depression and schizophrenia, the use of music often is very effective.

The diagnosis of the etiological factors of the psychoses and the psychoneuroses can be aided by the use of music. Through the medium of conscious self-expression in music, elements of the patient's conflict may become manifest. Under hypnosis music has been found to have a particularly beneficial effect. The following is an abstract by this writer of an article concerning this investigation in "Music and Psychotherapy," by Eugen Frey, Zurich. It is taken from the Swiss Archives of Neurology and Psychiatry.

Frey reports his findings during a year's study of a psychotherapy technique in which he employed music and loud auditory stimuli with patients under hypnosis. He discovered that during hypnosis a sudden, shocking, acoustical stimulus would result in strong, optical, subjective perception by synesthesia. Thus the sounding of a bell would manifest itself as a dazzling, shining light. Moreover, the subconscious was dynamically activated, resulting in very productive, symbolic dreams and profound fantasy development. Recordings of certain compositions of Bach performed on the pipe organ and recordings of Beethoven performed by a string trio were unexpectedly played in the hearing of a patient under hypnosis. The patient was then awakened, and her verbatim account of her dream experience was reported. The hypnotic dreams are beautifully colored and symbolic, and contain a strong redemption motive. Frey contends that through this method of using music with hypnotized patients "the unconscious is influenced immediately and very dynamically, and can be clearly and arrestingly explained," and its symbolic structure subjected to analysis. The working of beautiful music in hypnosis presents a question of music psychotherapy as a theoretical fundamental and a psychologically reasonable answer.

Thus music with hypnosis may become another technique in the diagnostic and therapeutic armamentarium of the psychiatrist.

Altshuler (1c) believes that the first appreciation of music occurs in the thalamus, the seat of all sensations, emotions and feelings, and that this property is the basic factor in music therapy. Schizophrenia results in a "functional decerebration" in which feeling and perception replace reason and the subcortical centers are the only levels accessible. The automatic reaction to music is increased. He speaks of a "thalamic reflex" or a noncortical response to music. By virtue of the free flow of impulses between the thalamus and the cortex, mental patients, difficult to reach through the spoken word which requires cortical evaluation, are still accessible rhythmically and tonally via the thalamus. Patients who respond unconsciously at first later begin to respond consciously. In his selection of music, Altshuler uses what he speaks of as the iso-principle in which music identical to the mood or mental tempo of the patient is used, i.e., depressed patients receive sad music and manics "allegro" music. He has analyzed music and classified it according to the psychological level of appeal as follows:

A. Rhythm
   1. Most Primitive
   2. Useful with a child, the feeble-minded and the psychotic

This stresses the duration and pause so typical of musical rhythm, acts as an isolated, shorter stimulus in contrast to melody, for instance, which evokes a more prolonged response.

B. Melody. "A succession of musical tones felt as a psychological entity. Its capacity for holding attention in this is thus much greater. It is prepotent in the consciousness, for it forces itself upon it because of its continuity."
C. Mood modifying music. "Its purpose is the arousal of emotion and modifying the mood."
D. Harmony. "Higher form . . . A change in orientation to harmony occurs at about the age of twelve. Harmony has also a general integrating influence."
E. Pictorial associative music. "Stimulates the imagery and association. This is a higher intensity of mood modifier." Thus music is represented alphabetically as the RMHMP principle.

Altshuler utilizes the tone color of a string trio (violin, cello and piano) feeling that mental patients are more susceptible to this. In his work at Eloise Hospital, in Detroit, he found that familiar tunes revive an engram, a basic reality, and help to relieve emotional tension.

The nationality of music's origin is altered percentage-wise according to the nationalities represented in the hospital. In his technique a theme song suggests that the patients come to the music activity. They are not forced to do so.

Mitchel and Zanker (25) present the following data:

1. Romantic music produces emotional release but does not facilitate group cohesion.
2. Serious contemporary music has more integrative effect and with inhibited schizophrenics brings repressed forces into consciousness.
3. The formal structure of classical music provides security for patients of all types and tends to increase group cohesion.
4. Comic music is of no value due to the egocentricity and consequent lack of humor of mental patients.
5. Traditional and folk music fosters integration of individual personalities and increases harmony of the group as a whole.

Altshuler (1a) states that the application of music in quieting excited patients is 35 per cent more effective than the wet sheet pack as a sedative when the isoprinciple is utilized.

Conversely, early morning music can gradually arouse the lethargic and start the day on a vigorous, interesting note. The use of increasingly stimulating music is beneficial in patients of slowed response. Stimulating music such as march or dance music serves not only the purpose of stimulation but can act as a mode of energy release. The psychological benefits of this are discussed elsewhere.

Price and his co-workers (29) describe the favorable results obtained by using music with electroshock therapy. This technique for allaying fear and anxiety prior to shock and for enhancing the recovery period afterwards is described. The patients are placed in one room where the soft music is presented over a loud speaker. This preparatory music is serious but not depressing and is designed to reassure. The patients then are shocked and removed by another door to a recovery room. Care is taken to avoid letting the patients see another who has been treated and is unconscious. During the awakening period music of a type which elicits pleasure and stimulates is presented by loud speaker and under careful supervision. It is mainly melodic and sentimental and free of strong rhythms. After recovery to consciousness, highly stimulatory music of the dance type with strong rhythms is utilized. Throughout, lyrics are avoided to obviate possible unwanted associations.

Music with hydrotherapy has been shown to facilitate this mode of therapy and to render it more effective by virtue of music's sedative effect.

Van de Wall states: "The appalling evil of medieval times was 'smell,' that of our present day is 'noise.'" Noise abatement and sound regulation is a regular problem of hospital administrators. Though it may seem that the addition of music to the atmosphere would tend to increase the annoying sounds, the happy fact is that music tends to detach the attention to other pleasant associations and stimulate us favorably in spite of the noise. Further, the desire to hear restrains would-be noise makers who ordinarily do not think about their disturbances.

Music in Hospitals

The following material is taken largely from the book, *Music in Medicine,* by Licht, and *Music in Hospitals* by van de Wall, and from an article "Music Therapy: Boon or Bane," by van de Wall. We quote from the last mentioned.

"The most rigorous control of the sources of noises and sounds and prevention of all avoidable noises are imperative to give purposeful sound including music its constructive function. This function will be enhanced by such measures as the following:

1. The use of sound absorbing material for construction of rooms, wards and service halls and soundproofing of such spaces intended to be used for music and other entertainment.
2. Reservation or construction of a special room or building for music and related purposes.
3. Music activities limited to these areas.
4. The most discriminating use of public address systems for musical purposes. The jarring and grating noises produced by these systems too often defeat the purpose for which they are used, namely, to inundate the rooms and wards with sounds pleasing to the patients.
5. Exclusive use of earphones for radio listening in rooms and wards.
6. Limitation of personally owned radios, phonographs, etc., to certain hours and spaces.
7. Acquisition of musical instruments and supplies of standard quality only and a definite assigned control in care of these materials.
8. Supervision by especially assigned staff members.
9. Inclusion of notes on patients' responses for determining treatment value of musical activities.
10. Utilization of the active interest of staff members, auxiliary committees and friends of the hospital for the development

of ideas and practices for the provision of music talent and materials.

11. The use of good musicians exclusively.
12. Systematic introduction to the hospital routine and objectives and continuing supervision of the musicians while they are in the hospital" (36).

It has been shown that the value of a well integrated music program in hospitals is manifold. Aside from the more special "therapeutic applications," there are certain rationales for the use of music for purely diverting and entertaining purposes. The patient suffering from the discomfiture inherent in certain therapeutic measures or from painful illness can well afford to be spared the additional pain of anxiety, boredom and loneliness often present in hospitalized patients, particularly those with long, confining illnesses. Music has proven its worth in dispelling these detriments to speedy return to well being.

Though hardly necessary to say, it is true that in cases of patients suffering terminal illnesses, humanitarianism prompts us to fill their final days, in so far as possible, not only with freedom from physical pain but with cultural and esthetic interest as well, in an effort to maintain the integration of personality as long as possible.

Music may be presented in one of two ways: that is, in the form of so-called "canned" music (music reaching its audience by mechanical means, such as radio, movies, phonograph, or TV) or "live" music in which the audience is in the presence of the performer. Each is important and has particular applications. Passive participation in music by patients includes such subjects as background music, mealtime music and slumber music.

Background music, as the name implies, is used to improve the qualities or pleasures of activities in living. It must be emphasized here that a small minority dislike music, and for them background music is especially contraindicated. Background music is secondary to some other activity. Its value has been proven in the diminution of the ill effects of noise; as a counterirritant, that is, the raising of the pain threshold (especially by virtue of diversion); and as a means of raising the efficiency of the hospital personnel (including decreased number of hospital accidents); as a sedative and hypnotic for irritated and insomniac patients.

However, background music must never be incessant, obvious or loud, or consist of highly dissonant or rhythmic forms. It is not the purpose of hospital music (and especially background hospital music) to educate the listeners or lift their standards of music appreciation. Its chief purpose is the stimulation of pleasure, and to achieve this, the musical tastes of the patients (however different from our own) must be the index of judgment in selection of repertory along with any sound principles of therapeutic effect which may be desired.

Background music is generally "canned" music, and as such reaches the patient via either a loudspeaker or earphones. The evidence is strongly in favor of the use of earphones or pillowphones rather than the loudspeakers which may serve to the detriment of some patients. This can be accomplished relatively inexpensively by wiring separate phonejacks to each bed and supplying simple earphones to those interested.

Background music should be presented at specific times of the day and should consist of programs lasting from 15 to 30 minutes. An early morning program around seven o'clock, before breakfast, is appreciated by many and should consist of fairly rousing, rhythmical music designed to initiate the day on a happy, joyous, co-operative basis and to stimulate the appetite. It has been found that a fifteen minute period should elapse between this program and the serving of breakfast. A midmorning program in the nature of a special request program often is successful and somewhat more than passively participated in by patients.

Some people do not enjoy music during breakfast but find it pleasant during lunch and dinner. Mealtime music must be unobtrusive. "The hesitant legato style of Eddie Duchin is particularly desirable." The listener should not be able to recall the piece heard five minutes previously. Pieces with particularly distinctive lyrics are better avoided, as are pieces with striking and syncopated rhythmic patterns (as in "jive" and some examples of South American Latin music). The volume should be low, and strange instruments avoided.

Music should be built around special holidays. The patients will look forward to and enjoy these special occasions.

Music for slumber is in a special class and requires careful supervision. Most hospital patients require extra sleep during the day. It is possible to make this time pleasant by use of a nap period theme of quiet, restful music over a public address system to announce the time for sleep. However, it is felt that music during sleep is contraindicated, so, following the induction period it should be dispensed with. An exception is in the case of children with whom lulling slumber music is often useful. In this case, music of loud, high-pitched type can be gradually reduced to music of low-pitched, soft quality. Children are attracted by music they know and especially by music with lyrics.

The second classification of music for diversion is music for listening. Here the music assumes a place of greater importance and is designed to attract and hold the attention of the patient. This is an active pursuit. For this purpose the use of a much different type of music is applicable. The midmorning program of request music is of this type. Here the use of LP (or 45 rpm) records is highly indicated in order that the requests be organized into entertaining programs and then the same records reshuffled at some later date or used for some other purpose. Of course, these programs may be worked out in advance and copied on tape recording for consumption in the near future if tape is more easily handled in the hospital situation. In order to meet requests reasonably well, either a fairly large record library must be maintained or some source such as a library or a radio station must be available.

Another interesting program of the music for listening type is the mystery tune program in which the patients actively participate by trying to guess the names of several unannounced selections rendered. At the end of the program, or perhaps the next day, the names are presented and the listeners check their lists. Many variations of this type of program can be used to good advantage.

Music for listening also includes filling the cultural needs of those of higher musical tastes and training. To do this, portable record players with a small selection of records are useful. The player may be put in a soundproof room where a small group may enjoy a self-controlled program, or else brought to the bedside and used with earphones. Supervision of the type of music included should again embrace a regard for the tastes of the patients that they may listen to music they enjoy.

Musical community sing movies tend to overcome inhibitions of people and serve as useful outlets for those who like to sing. Playing instruments and singing may also serve to help certain less debilitated patients while away the hours during recuperation.

The bedside radio and TV should be rigidly controlled to prevent annoyance to other patients unable to enjoy their programs. Specific periods should be allotted, earphones employed, and volume kept down. Programs occurring late at night that are of great interest may be transcribed on tape and used to good advantage the following day.

The use of organized programs with live talent is most valuable. A program with the living presence of the performer is many times more popular than "canned" music. Of course, here again control must be imposed and the haphazard use of inexperienced or poorly qualified performers avoided. The performer must be oriented as to the aims and the purpose of music in the hospital; he should be excellent in his field and have a specific program planned; he should furnish an accompanist, if necessary, with whom his program is already well rehearsed. The program should be short enough to avoid boredom or fatigue (usually 20 to 40 minutes) but encores should be prepared so that the desires of the audience may be fully met. The performer should be under constant escort by competent staff members while in the hospital and every effort made to make him feel welcome and useful. The performance should be in a place (preferably sound-proof) which will not annoy other patients too ill to participate.

In his article, "Boon or Bane," van de Wall qualifies medical music personnel as follows: the musician must be a master of his craft in the sense that he has a wide repertory, good standards of music production and leadership and insight into the physiologic reactions and psychologic responses of the patients; he must be capable furthermore of guidance by physicians and other hospital staff members. However, it is possible that the musician may be employed to oversee the program through a competent volunteer especially trained to assist.

This music aide may be of either sex and of any age. He should be mature, patient, well informed and have the urge but not have pre-formed opinions about the handling of patients. He should be able to play at least one instrument, preferably the piano. He should be devoid of "artistic temperament." Previous experience in teaching music is a valuable asset to the music aide. It is of great value for the music aide to be familiar with the use of the various public address and phonograph systems and in the maintenance of record libraries, musical instruments, sheet music, and so on.

A complete listing of ideal qualifications for the musical director of the hospital will be found in the book, *Music in Medicine,* on page 123 (42).

CONCLUSION

This paper has called attention to the many varied and interesting applications of music to medicine. The implications of the subject excite the imagination today as they have for centuries. However, in our present state of knowledge and technological advancement, we are better prepared to investigate the fundamentals more effectively. To date, the most serious interest has been shown in the fields of psychiatry and occupational therapy, but those in other fields including medicine and surgery are developing a curiosity sufficient enough to stimulate limited investigation and experimentation. Many of the beliefs about music and its effects have been clarified, while others still need to be subjected to analysis. Certain universities are devoting time to courses in training of hospital personnel for music supervision and are offering opportunities for study in the field.

Many large hospitals have music (and radio programs) presented over the public address systems. But unfortunately, the manner of presentation is such that often even fundamental principles of practice are disregarded and the effect is almost more detrimental than constructive. For example, the use of loudspeakers on open wards bespeaks lack of consideration for the patient too ill for this treatment, and availability of the programs to the patient when he is receptive often is missing. Other defects are apparent to the observer.

However, these same hospitals do not make the most of their music program, and other hospitals take no advantage of it at all. Public address systems often are ineffectual because of the reasons mentioned above, but are better than nothing. Many situations could be greatly improved if pillowphones were substituted for loudspeakers, especially on open wards. In many large cities, there is background music of various types available for rent commercially via telephone wires. The waiting rooms and treatment rooms of the senior staff would be enhanced by the use of music. This same sort of music would improve the atmosphere of the halls of the operating room floors. An electronic type organ might be highly effective for short concerts in the hospital.

Finally, it is recognized that the application of music to the sick is perhaps most efficiently utilized in large medical centers and mental institutions. However, we feel that on a more limited scale smaller institutions and even private physicians may utilize music to benefit their patients.

Lists of recordings suitable for the various applications mentioned in this paper are available.

REFERENCES

1. Altshuler, I. M.: (a) Music's Part in Resocialization of Mental Patients, Occup. Therapy 20:75-86 (April) 1941; (b) Music Aid in Management of Psychotic Patients, J. Nerv. & Ment. Dis. 94:179-183 (Aug.) 1941; (c) Four Years' Experience with Music at Eloise Hospital, Am. J. Psychiat. 100:792-794 (May) 1944; (d) A Psychiatrist's Experiences with Music as a Therapeutic Agent. Music & Med. 22:266-281.
2. Beardsley, G. L.: The Medical Uses of Music, New England M. Monthly 2:214-216, 1882-3.
3. Benton-Mednikoff, P.: Music Therapy Used for Post-operative & Correctional Work in Orthopedics, Occup. Therapy 22:136 (June) 1943.
4. Bernaerts, A.: Medical Significance of Music, Bruxelles-med. 26:40-43 (Jan.) 1946.
5. Blackwell, E., & Neal, C. A.: Music in Mental Hospitals, Occup. Therapy 25:243-246 (Dec.) 1946.
6. Bowers, M.: Music with Mental Defectives, Am. J. Mental Defic. 50:520 (April) 1946.
7. Burris, B.: The Place of Music in Healing, J. Acoustical Soc. Amer. 17:232-235 (Jan.) 1946.
8. Chenowelth, R.: Music for Convalescent Children, Occup. Therapy 25:241-242 (Dec.) 1946.
9. Cherry, H., & Pallin, I. M.: Supplement to N₂O Anesthesia, Anesthesiol. 9:391-399 (July) 1948.
10. Cornell, E. L.: Am. J. Obst. & Gynec. 56:582-583 (Sept.) 1948.
11. Critchley, N.: Musicogenic Epilepsy: Two cases, J. Roy. Nav. M. Serv. 28:182-184.
12. Davison, J. T. R.: Music in Medicine, Lancet 2:1159-1162 (Oct. 28) 1899.
13. Donais, D.: Music Sets Stage for Recovery from Mental Disease, Mod. Hosp. 61:68-69 (Dec.) 1943.
14. Fultz, A. F.: Music as a Modality of Occupational Therapy, War Medicine 5:139-141 (March) 1944.
15. Gatewood, E. L.: Is There Evidence for the Therapeutic Use of Music, Abstr. Arch. Occup. Therapy 1:433 (Oct.) 1922.
16. Gilliland, E. C.: (a) Music in Treatment of the Sick, Hygeia 22:896 (Dec.) 1944; (b) Making the Most of Music, Occup. Therapy 25:238-240 (Dec.) 1946; (c) The Healing Power of Music, Music Ed. J. (Sept.) 1944; (d) Apollo the God of Music & Healing, The Wheel of Omicron Delta (May) 1945; (e) Music Therapy, Nelson Encyclop. 1947.
17. Harrington, A. H.: (a) The story of the State Hospital Pipe Organ, Abstr. in Occup. Therapy 6:170 (April) 1927; (b) Mental Hygiene 23:601, 1939.
18. Hanson, H.: (a) Musician's Point of View Toward Emotional Expression, Am. J. Psychiat. 99:317-325 (Nov.) 1942; (b) Objective Studies of Rhythm in Music, Am. J. Psychiat. 101:364-369 (Nov.) 1944.

19. Jacob, J. F.: Music in Dental Education, Dent. Digest 58:22.
20. Kane, E. O.: The Phonograph in the Operating Room, J. A. M. A. 62:1829 (June 6) 1914.
21. Lehermette, J. L.: Music Hallucinosis, Rev. Neurol. 75:37-38 (Jan.-Feb.) 1943.
22. Light, G. A.: Use of Magnetic Recorder, Anesth. & Analg. 28:330-338 (Nov.-Dec.) 1949.
23. Mann, C.: Music and Exercise as a Form of Therapy, Psychoanalyt. Rev. (April), 1950.
24. McGlinn, J. A.: Music in the Operating Room, Am. J. Obst. & Gynec. 20:678-683 & 727 (Nov.) 1930.
25. Mitchell, S. D., & Zanker, A.: (a) Music in Group Therapy, J. Ment. Sc. 94:737-748 (Oct.) 1948; (b) Music Styles and Mental Disorders, Occup. Therapy 28:411-422 (Oct.) 1949.
26. Paparte, F.: Music in Military Medicine, Ment. Hyg. 30:56-64 (Jan.) 1946.
27. Pichot, F.: Effect of Music on Mental Defectives, Ment. Health, London, 9:6-10 (Aug.) 1949.
28. Pallin, I. M., & Chiron, A. E.: Indications for Music in Anesthesia, Current Researches in Anesth. & Analg. (July-Aug.) 1950.
29. Price, H. G., Mowntrey, V., & Knouss, R.: Selectional Music to Accompany Electroshock Therapy, Therap. Rehab. 29:147-156 (June) 1950.
30. Shaw, D., & Hill, D.: Musicogenic Epilepsy, J. Neurol. & Psychopath. 10:107-117 (Aug.) 1947.
31. Schoen, M.: Conclusion: Art the Healer, Music & Med. 22:387-405.
32. Stubbe-Teglbjoerg: Acta. Psychiat. 24:697-698, 1949.
33. Taylor, S.: Musicogenic Epilepsy, J. Roy, Navy M. Serv. 28:394-395 (Jan.) 1947.
34. Tilly, M.: Masculine and Feminine Principles in Music, Am. J. Psychiat. 103:477-483 (Jan.) 1947.
35. Underwood, R.: The Human Response to Music, Proc. Music Teach. Nat. Assn., 1946, pp. 356-359.
36. Van de Wall, W.: Music Therapy: Boon or Bane, Modern Hospital (June) 1945.
37. Vincent, E. H.: Doctors Look at Music, Quart. Bull. Northwest. U. M. Sch. 20:240-246, 1946.
38. Whiting, H. S.: Effect of Music on Hospital Accident Rate, Am. J. Ment. Defic. 51:397-400, 1947.
39. Diserens, C. M.: Psychology of Music: The Influence of Music on Behavior, Cincinnati Col. Music (c 1939) 405 pp.
40. Feibleman, J. K.: Anesthetics: A Study of the Fine Arts in Theory and Practice, Duell, Sloan and Pearce, New Jersey, 1949.
41. Levine, S.: Psychotherapy in Medical Practice, New York, 1942.
42. Licht, S.: Music in Medicine, Boston, New England Conserv. Music, 1946.
43. Marmelszadt, W.: Musical Sons of Aesculapius, New York, 1946.
44. Seibelman: Therapeutic and Industrial Uses of Music, New York, Columbia Univ. Press, 1948.
45. Schullian, D. M., & Schoen, M.: Music in Medicine, New York, Henry Schuman, 1948.
46. Van de Wall, W.: Music in Institutions, New York, Russell Sage Foundation, 1936.
47. Webster's Dictionary.

GEORGE E. ARRINGTON, JR.

APPENDIX TO "MUSIC IN MEDICINE"

W. Va. Medical Journal, June, 1953. George Arrington, M.D.

Following are lists of musical selections on modern phonograph records suitable for various medical applications:

MUSICAL TONICS:

a. *Tchaikowsky*—3rd Movement 6th Symphony—Colum. ML4506; London LLP257B; Vic LM 1036; Lon LL33
b. *Beethoven*—Egmont Overture; Vic 49-0304; Vic LM6001
c. *Chopin*—Prelude Opus 28 No. 1—Col ML 4420
d. *Liszt*—Hungarian Rhapsody No. 2—Col AL 2

e. *Bizet*—Toreador Song (Carmen)—Vic LM 1069
f. *Sousa*—Military Marches—Decca LP 5075, 5076
g. *Offenbach*—Gaite Parisienne—Col. ML 4233
h. *Bach*—Prelude and Fugue in E Mi. Vic. LCT 1000 or WCT 69

MUSICAL SEDATIVES:

a. *Mascagni*—Intermezzo (Cavalleria Rusticana)—Vic 49-1445
b. *Schubert*—Ave Maria—Vic. 49-1447
c. *Saint Saens*—The Swan—Vic 490474; LM1187
d. *Brahms*—Lullaby—Vic 49-1434
e. *Beethoven*—2nd Movement 6th Symphony—Col. ML 4506; ML 4510; Lon LL33

f. *Chopin*—Nocturne G Mi.—Col. ML 2143
g. *Debussy*—Clair de Lune—Cap. H8156
h. *Schubert*—Westmin.—WL 5110 Andante from Quartet in B Flat Mi.
i. *Beethoven*—Moonlight Sonata—Col. ML 4432

Among those orchestras which habitually use arrangements suitable for MEAL-TIME MUSIC are the following:

Wayne King
Marek Weber
Andre Kostelanetz
David Rose

Frankie Carle
Carmen Cavallaro
Eddie Duchin
Guy Lombardo

Percy Faith
New Mayfair
Eaton and Paramount
Victor Salon

Victor Continental
Salinski String
 Ensemble
Paul Weston

MEALTIME MUSIC:

Southern Roses Waltz—Vic LK 1021
Sweethearts—Vic LK 1015
Holiday for Strings—Vic. 27-0034
Voices of Spring—Vic LMP 17
None But the Lonely Heart—Vic LM 96
Lover Come Back to Me—Vic LK 1011
Indian Love Call—Vic LM73; LK 1012
Come Back to Sorrento—Vic LM 65
Zigeuner—Vic 24609B
Begin the Beguine—Col V-LPM 32
Easter Parade—Col V-LPM 2
With a Song in My Heart—Col V-LPM 27

The Touch of Your Hand—Col V-LK 1007
Somebody Loves Me—Col 4291M
Falling in Love—Col LK 1006
Tea for Two—Col V-LPM 27
Estralita—Col V-LPT 8
Swan Lake—Col V-LM 1083
Rosalee—Col V-LPT 28
Speak to Me of Love—Col V-LM 62
Pavanne—V-P 189
Minute Waltz—Decca 18066A
Blue September—Decca 15050A
Lost Louette—Decca 15049B

MUSIC IN MEDICINE

Certain Recording companies have released albums of records for background music, music for relaxing, and mealtime music. See the catalogs of these companies for these lists.

MUSIC FOR USE WITH ELECTROSHOCK: (May be applied elsewhere with good effect also)

Before Treatment: (Serious, reassuring)

Awakening Period: (Pleasurable, stimulating, melodic, sentimental, no strong rhythm)

Largo Concerto in A—Bach—Vic M1017
Symphony in B Flat—Vic 7484A
Suite for Orchestra—Vic 7484B
Beethoven—Moonlight Sonata—Vic 16250A
Symphony No. 7—Vic DM 317
Intermezzo in E Flat—Brahms
Chopin—First Piano Concerto 2nd
 Movement—Vic DM 418
Italian Symphony 2nd Movement—Mendelssohn—Col M 538
Rachmaninoff—Second Concerto 2nd
 Movement—Vic DM 58

Time on My Hands—Adamson—Col C32-1
Eddie Duchin Album—Berlin—Col C32
Rhapsody in B Mi.—Brahms—Vic M893-8
Waltzes in A and C—Chopin—Vic 863-4
 and 7
The Way You Look Tonight—Fields—
 Col 43-8
Lover Come Back to Me—Col 32-8
Show Tunes—Kern—Col C 34
Sleeping Beauty Waltz—Vic 11932B

After Treatment: (Stimulating, dance Music)

Use modern swing music and Latin rhythms. Also very effective are Gershwin recordings.

Personal ingenuity can add many other examples to this nucleus of effective music. Of course, in many situations where music is purely for diversion and entertainment (e.g. with chronically ill patients) the tastes of the patient must be considered and complied with.

MUSIC IN MILITARY MEDICINE

FRANCES PAPERTE

Music Research Foundation; Director, Department of Applied Music,
Walter Reed General Hospital, Washington, D. C.

Physicians and musicians alike have desired more accurate
knowledge about the value of music as an accessory therapeutic
tool. Extravagant claims have been made regarding its efficacy, but
few claims have been substantiated by carefully measured and
controlled conditions. The present world conflict has added impetus
to this desire to know, since no tool that has any value should be
left unused in the restoration or improvement of the thousands of
war casualties.

Music as medicine is by no means a recent discovery. Many
examples of the use of music as therapy are recorded in history.
Probably the first written observation on the influence of music
upon the human body is that in Egyptian medical papyri, discovered at Kahum by Petrie in 1889, dating back to 2500 B.C.

Music has been purveyed to hospital patients for many years.
In some instances patients are free to go where music is applied,
and in others music is brought to a ward either by radio or phonograph or by a musician in person. The groups involved have been
heterogeneous, however, and recorded data concerning the effects
of the music have been minimal.

On authority from the Surgeon General's Office, a study in the
controlled application of music according to a predetermined plan
was undertaken at Walter Reed General Hospital. The present
paper is a report on this six-month study. It is hoped that it will

[288]

answer some of the hundreds of inquiries concerning the project that have come from colleges, hospitals, organizations, and individuals in nearly every state in the Union as well as in Great Britain and Canada.

The primary objective of the study was to determine whether music presented according to a specific plan could temporarily or permanently bring about such changes in the individual as to hasten his recovery. Possibly the simpler approach would have been to focus research activities on cases commonly recognized as psychosomatic, such as the endocrine dysfunctions or gastrointestinal or hypertensive disturbances, in which the measurement of results can be more objective. However, since the pathway of action of music is by way of the emotions, psychiatry—the branch of medicine concerned primarily with emotional states and deviations —was the department selected in which to initiate the study.

In this pioneer work the following technique was employed: The medical officers selected patients for the study who presented certain symptoms. These patients were classified according to their predominant symptoms and their level of musical intelligence. The medical officers indicated on the prescription form not only the classification, but the mood and behavior change that was desired.

The psychiatric diagnoses obtaining in these patients were almost wholly in the psychoneurotic group rather than the psychotic. This choice was deliberate because the psycho-neurotics were in the majority, and also because, for the first time in our history, large numbers of people officially classified as psychoneurotic were gathered together in one place, and no better opportunity would be likely to present itself for studying this group. As the medical officer in charge stated, "The psychotic we have with us always."

Control cases were selected by the medical officers and were given identical treatment except that they received no musical applications. After selection and classification, each patient was then interviewed by the musical director to determine his "musical level," and was classified on the basis of this evaluation into one of four groups: (1) little or no familiarity with any music; (2) moderate familiarity with the simpler forms and expressions of musical composition; (3) educated musical taste or preference; (4) some degree of experience in participation.

This interview was conducted quite informally, but with definite direction and plan, so that when it was terminated, all manner of pertinent data on the individual were available for use by the musician. These data included background information, the patient's home state and home town, his occupation, the nativity of his parents, the schools he had attended, the places he had been or wanted to go, his branch of service, whether he had been overseas, and where. The things that lay close to his heart might often be brought to him through music.

Patients who fell into similar classifications—*e.g.*, "Restlessness—educated musical taste—soothing therapy," or "Depression—moderate familiarity with music—stimulating therapy"—were then assigned to small groups of from three to six members. A specific hour for the application of the music was arranged for each group and it met regularly at the same hour, five days a week. The duration of the treatment varied greatly, but was basically determined by the length of hospital residence, an average of twelve days before transfer or discharge.

The physical environment of the sessions was carefully ordered so as to predispose to a feeling of comfort, relaxation, and informality. The predominant color was subdued, but not somber. Chairs were upholstered and there were facilities for reclining. The musical instruments were in the room and plainly visible, but were not given dominant position.

The piano was the instrument chiefly used, although violin, cello, harp, and solovox attachments were also employed. An expanded study might well include the comparative value of the various instruments.

The musical-treatment sessions were divided into three parts:

1. The introductory or mood-determination and development period. Compositions selected with the aim of meeting the patients at the mood level that they brought to the sessions were played in order to establish a basic rapport between the patients and the music. Then, gradually and without any abrupt transition, music designed to develop the feeling tone prescribed by the medical officer was presented, simply and without obtrusion of the musician into the picture. The duration of this part of the session varied according to the patients' span of attention as carefully observed by the musician or session manager.

2. A brief interim period for establishing verbal rapport between patients and musician should the patients feel so inclined.

3. The period of patient participation. No direct invitation was issued, but the informality of the environment was conducive to this goal. Participation might be in the form of comments, queries, requests, or through humming, beating time, singing, whistling, or following the score. Whenever any patient showed especial desire or aptitude to express himself through music, he was encouraged to do so through arrangement for private instruction as well as through participation in group sessions. The results obtained in the limited number of cases that received such special instruction in music served to verify our expectations that this was an important aspect of therapy.

In the beginning, our ideal was more nearly achieved than at any other time because, although we could not add a full-time psychiatrist to our staff, an interested medical officer offered to devote all his spare time to our project, seeing and interviewing our patients daily and charting reactions. We also had an extremely gifted staff pianist, experienced in the use of music and deeply interested in the potentialities of the situation. She coöperated closely with the director, playing selected and planned programs daily, and teaching such individuals as were referred to her as well as assisting in the keeping of records.

This plan originally called for no continuity of musical personnel, but rather that musicians of merit and outstanding talent be recruited and give of their time and skill to the project without remuneration. This was actually done, but experience led to the opinion that this plan was neither desirable nor feasible, since it is not practicable to instruct fresh talent daily in the special art required in such a project. Likewise, in any research endeavor, the variable factors should be reduced to a minimum, and, therefore, the constancy of the musician or musicians is of great importance.

The personality qualifications of the musicians were of paramount importance. Especial difficulty was encountered in getting musicians to understand that the sessions were not intended to present opportunities for their own emotional expression or demonstration of the brilliance of their techniques, and that the spotlight was on the patients rather than on themselves. The extent and degree of their adaptability to the project was the most important consideration. Whereas they needed the skill of true artists, this alone was insufficient recommendation. The personality of the performer seemed to exert a definite influence upon the response of the patient.

The classification of the music presented was a never-ending task. A committee of musicians prominent in national musical life devoted a great amount of time to placing all the musical selections used into a practical classification.

The criteria for this first general classification were as follows:

I. All music for use in hospitals, as per the Institute of Musico-Therapy's plan, should be first generally classified as follows:
    A. Music of solely rhythmic interest.
    B. Music of solely harmonic interest.
    C. Music of solely melodic interest.
II. Of the first group (I), each subheading (A, B, C) should then be divided into two groups each (slow, fast), as follows:
    A. Music of modal nature—slow, fast.
    B. Music of classic nature—slow, fast.
    C. Music of romantic nature—slow, fast.
    D. Music of impressionistic nature—slow, fast.
    E. Music of modern modal nature.
III. Of the second group (II), each subheading (A-E) should finally be subdivided as to key, length of piece, tempo, and character (program of absolute-music).

The repertoire of the musicians was submitted in advance and selections that were applicable to the group to be treated were made.

Records were kept on all patients and on all sessions. The session record included the name of the composition, the key, the tempo, the instrument, and the comments of the musician on the patient's reactions. The session manager also recorded on another sheet her impressions regarding each patient after every session. Between sessions the medical officers kept progress notes on patients' reactions, using the form shown on page 294.

The final evaluation was a composite of the total recorded evaluations.

At the conclusion of the first six months, a condensed report on our first one hundred cases was submitted, in accordance with a request from the Office of the Surgeon General. Representative samples of these first case histories are given in abridged form on page 295.

The period of hospitalization of all patients was so unpredictable that control cases might and often did receive transfer orders immediately after selection or long before the case under treatment had his musical sessions, and this constituted a serious drawback to an accurate evaluation.

The lack of a directing psychiatrist present at the sessions was another handicap that was keenly felt, since he would have been the liaison officer between the medical department and the institute. He would have been familiar with the patients and their case histories; he would have been the person to whom the medical officers would have communicated any important information relating to patients' reactions or experiences between sessions. He would have observed patients during sessions with a trained eye, and he would have communicated silently with the musician throughout the sessions in regard to the timing of the development of the desired mood, since this timing cannot be determined *a priori*. This close coöperation between the psychiatrist and the musician would have

[293]

FRANCES PAPERTE

Department of Applied Music—W. R. G. H.

Progress Notes   Date.....................

M. T. will chart daily the kind of music played, length of period, and patient's reaction.

Name.................................   Ward...................

		M.	T.	W.	T.	F.
Initial Reaction	1. Resentful	....	....	....	....	....
	2. Sullen	....	....	....	....	....
	3. Apathetic	....	....	....	....	....
	4. Indifferent	....	....	....	....	....
	5. Apprehensive	....	....	....	....	....
	6. Anticipatory	....	....	....	....	....
	7. Interested	....	....	....	....	....
	8. Cheerful	....	....	....	....	....
	9. Excited	....	....	....	....	....
Immediate Response During Session	1. Sleeps	....	....	....	....	....
	2. Reads	....	....	....	....	....
	3. Converses with others	....	....	....	....	....
	4. Listens attentively	....	....	....	....	....
	5. Requests a piece	....	....	....	....	....
	6. Participates	....	....	....	....	....
	7. Restless, walks about	....	....	....	....	....
	8. Objects to particular pieces	....	....	....	....	....

Changes during period: From...   ....
                         To ....

Patient's Remarks
M. ....
T. ....
W. ....
T. ....
F. ....

existed not only during the sessions, but prior to them, when the musical selections to be presented were determined.

There was still another reason why the lack of a psychiatrist was deemed a handicap. It not infrequently happened that the music stirred something within patients and made those who had been silent or sullen or withdrawn suddenly begin to talk or to cry or to express other feelings. Only a psychiatrist would have been in a position to make intelligent use of these pathways into the patients' lives, and it is believed that important leads were thus lost.

In conclusion, it is hoped that this brief report of a six-month

CASES FROM FIRST 100 TREATED WITH MUSIC

Age	Diagnosis	Recommendation	Number of sessions	Medical evaluation
22	Psychoneurosis, conversion hysteria	Stimulating music	16	Definitely benefited.
33	Psychoneurosis, anxiety type	Relaxation	2	Inconclusive.
21	Psychoneurosis, anxiety type	Soothing, relaxing music	8	General sense of well-being was improved.
21	Head injury	Soothing music	7	Definite evidence of improvement shown.
35	Dementia praecox, paranoid	Soothing music	14	The effect of the music on his general emotional tone was of value.
19	Dementia praecox, hebephrenic	Stimulation	7	Only objective datum was change in personal appearance. No longer had to be urged to keep himself neat.
50	Manic-depressive psychosis	Soothing music	18	Contributed to his improvement.
32	Paranoid condition	Stimulation	15	Patient's participation in appropriate music contributed to his ability to socialize.
32	Complete paralysis, median and musculocutaneous nerves, right	Relaxing music	20	Complete response with active participation.
28	Paralysis of nerves, partial	Relaxation	18	Musical therapy has been of benefit.
34	Psychoneurosis, mixed type	Relaxing music for marked tension	15	Helped to socialize.
30	Post-traumatic syndrome	Relaxing music	23	Definitely benefited.
28	Psychoneurosis	Need for stimulation	13	Derived considerable pleasure.
49	Psychoneurosis, unclassified, paranoid	Sedation	20	Sessions undoubtedly of value.
20	Psychoneurosis, conversion hysteria	Stimulation	12	Great deal of benefit derived from sessions.
20	Psychoneurosis	Stimulation	11	Active participation and expressed great interest.
22	Psychoneurosis, anxiety	Stimulation	12	Some temporary benefit.
22	Dementia praecox, hebephrenic	Stimulation	17	Benefit derived. Tendency to socialize.
27	Psychoneurosis, anxiety state	Relaxation	7	Derived much benefit. Tenseness markedly lessened.
23	Psychoneurosis, neuralgia, trigeminal, right, severe	Relaxing music	7	Beneficial effect.
27	Psychoneurosis, anxiety type	Relaxing, soothing	5	Inconclusive.
19	Psychoneurosis, anxiety type	Relaxing therapy	8	Lessening of tension to noticeable degree.

[295]

study of the rôle of music in military medicine may serve as a stimulus to further investigation and that from factual data accumulated, there may be evolved a standard method of procedure which will develop fully the potentialities of music as an aid to medicine.

HIGH FIDELITY AND MUSIC THERAPY

By GEORGE E. ARRINGTON, JR., M.D.

Huntington, W. Va.

The advent of commercially available high fidelity sound reproducing devices has demanded the attention of physicians and music therapists interested in the use of music with the sick.

High fidelity is the term applied to loud speaker amplification systems which reproduce sound faithfully from electrical, physical, and optical sources. They include disc and magnetic tape recordings, radio broadcasts (especially frequency modulation), television, and motion picture film sound tracts.

The importance of these systems lies in the simple fact that for the first time since Thomas Edison discovered the principle of recorded sound in 1877, we are at last able to hear realistic reproductions of the original sounds when and where we want them. So real are these sounds, in fact, that in tests in which recordings were alternated with the live performing artists, it was impossible to distinguish the difference. The reason for this lies in the removal to the inaudible point of distortion, foreign sounds, and false emphasis. Now real, life like, musical sounds are available to millions of persons who live in remote areas where live concerts and performances are not available.

The music therapist, likewise, need no longer fret at the expense and trouble of presenting large, live music ensembles. Now all the thrilling, stimulating, or sedating and soothing sounds are available to him by means of high fidelity recordings presented on high fidelity equipment. By virtue of the "living presence feeling" of this technique, the therapist has all he desires in the way of well performed music and excellent sounds plus the complete control of volume, time and dates of presentations, repetition of performances and repertory available. Such sound systems are space saving, time saving, and economical.*

Anyone who has attended live music performances and has felt the excitement of them must have also experienced the disappointment in listening to the same music by conventional sound reproducing techniques. To these people, high fidelity music has opened the door to renewed enjoyment, for it is possible by these techniques to hear all the music without distraction.

What is the problem and how has it been solved? The problem revolves around the difficulty of inscribing the full audible sound range necessary to realism plus the avoidance of introducing undesired, factitious sounds.

In order to understand, we must recall that the human ear normally can perceive sounds from roughly 20 cycles per second to 20,000 cps. If the sounds at either end of this spectrum are cut off, the result is immediate awareness that something is false. For example, a conventional table radio sounds from 150 to 5000 cps. Small home type tape recorders at 7 inches per second speed record only 50 to 7000 cps. The reasons for this low fidelity are manifold. In some instances it is due to physical limitations innate in the mechanics involved. In other instances, it may sadly be due to lack of demand on the part of listeners who are not aware that improvement is possible.

In the case of disc recordings, it was not until the development of commercially available vinylite plastic and microgroove cutting and 33⅓ RPM that surface noise could be limited so that the upper frequencies could be heard. Once this was accomplished, it became possible for record manufacturers to successfully utilize sufficient pre-emphasis of the treble end of recordings; thereby,

* A representative set including amplifier suitable for the average listening room, matched speakers, steady turntable, magnetic pickup with diamond stylus currently costs between $200.00 and $300.00, or no more than a good radio or TV.

the remaining surface noise can be relatively subdued. This permits the upper musical tones and overtones so essential to brilliance and life like quality to become distinct and free of noise. High fidelity amplifiers contain phono preamplifiers with equalization controls or tone controls to compensate for treble pre-emphasis.

A second defect in recorded sound is in the bass end where, due to mechanical difficulties encountered in cutting the wide amplitude notes of 20-200 cps, it is necessary for the record manufacturers to introduce an artificial bass droop. This is to prevent these low notes' waves from cutting into adjacent grooves. Thus, a second compensatory factor becomes necessary in high fidelity amplifiers: namely, bass boost.

The next problem is hum. Hum is the term used to describe unwanted low frequency sounds (60 and 120 cps) not present in the original music and introduced accidentally because of poor electrical shielding or other faulty techniques. It should be inaudible, that is, reduced to the order of 1000 times less than the softest musical sounds to be heard.

The next problem is the avoidance of faulty emphasis. To have taken a well recorded, wide range record, and, by means of a good amplifier to have created a perfectly balanced, distortion free electrical signal is no assurance of hearing the original sounds unless the speaker is perfectly matched to the amplifier. The speaker is the actual physical source of the sounds that we hear and must be of high quality equal to the rest of the system. Care must be taken also to see that the enclosure or cabinet is exactly suited to the speaker. A faulty speaker may resonate to certain pitches, giving a false emphasis to these tones, which is unlike the original.*

The next problem has been the fact that the human ear normally has less acuity at the extreme ends of the audible spectrum.

* To obviate this danger, we believe it advisable to purchase a package unit including *matched* turntable, amplifier, and properly balanced enclosed speakers. This unit should be guaranteed to function at the highest efficiency together. We hear that many who are putting together alien units which are excellent alone, but not matched to each other, may still not possess true high fidelity.

If a flat frequency response persists as the volume of the amplifier is turned down, the ear would hear only the middle tones with the highs and lows becoming more and more attenuated. Since we wish to hear music at a quiet level occasionally (for example as background music) it is desirable to have a system whereby the highs and lows can be emphasized as the volume is lowered. Certain systems have this built into the volume control and others expect the listener to adjust the tone controls to compensate for this loss.

The last mechanical problem is related to the listening room. Room acoustics can play a large role in whether we hear what is actually in a record or broadcast. In order to prevent the room from adding to or taking away from the sounds on the record, it is necessary that there be as little reverberation as possible. This can be accomplished by using heavy carpets, thick drapes, soft furniture, or ideally, by the use of soundproofing. The latter serves not only the listener, but also the other patients by preventing them from being disturbed. It must be remembered that the maximum number of people who will be listening must be considered when deciding what power is needed in the amplifier, for people tend to absorb sound also.

Practically speaking, for small groups, an average sized room (15 x 20 feet approximately) which is well carpeted and curtained and, with five to ten listeners, will need no alteration.

The final problem is a purely aesthetic one. It is the selection of suitable recordings. Many excellent wide range recordings have become available during the last year and more are on the way. They represent the best parts of many performances recorded on tape, edited and spliced together so as to represent outstanding total performances. These composites often surpass any single live performance. Try to learn the serial numbers which represent late releases which are more likely to be high fidelity. Of course, the final test is listening. Many critics also write reviews of new releases which help in selecting highest quality recordings.

Much of recording technique remains experimental and variable. Microphone placement, for instance, is very critical and accounts at times for such dramatic differences between recordings. The amount of hall characteristics (echo) included will likewise color the sound. All of this allows you freedom of personal taste and is a healthy trend, we believe.

For the fastidious therapists who wish to create the "live" illusion even further, there is binaural or stereophonic sound. Here, two recordings are made simultaneously on disc or tape from two microphones picking up the right and left sides of the sound "picture." These two recordings are then played back, being amplified and presented through right and left speakers corresponding to the original relationship. The result is one of remarkable depth and placement projection by the mind of the listener. While listening to binaural sound, one is convinced that the strings of a symphony are at the left before him, the brass and woodwinds in the center, and the tympany up and to the right. In choral music, the voices spread out before the listener so that he can literally turn to the predominant part.

Although binaural is somewhat more expensive, it is likewise more authentic and entertaining. Of course, the individual systems for each ear must be high fidelity from microphone to speaker in order that its capabilities may be fully appreciated. The two systems must be perfectly balanced in order to recreate the sound in a perfect illusion.

Disc recordings must be played on a good turntable which is free of wow and flutter. Wow and flutter refer to variations between the speed of different revolutions of the turntable. When this is sufficiently marked, disturbing changes in pitch will occur. This is most marked in long sustained notes.

The pickup cartridge should be magnetic or capacity in type. Inexpensive crystal cartridges are unsuitable because of the low fidelity and because they tend to wear the records unnecessarily. Magnetic cartridges require a preamplifier which is a part of all good high fidelity systems.

The stylus tip (needle) should be a diamond. These styli cause the least damage to records and wear more than a hundred times longer than the next best material which is sapphire.

Besides disc recordings, there are now available wide range tape recordings (both monaural and binaural) for those who have tape reproducing machines. The repertory is ever increasing, and, at present includes some very fine performances of symphonies, organ selections, and soloists. It should be carefully understood that although tape suffers little wear with long use and has little surface noise compared to discs, only certain machines are capable of reproducing high fidelity. Several machines from $250.00 up advertise 40 to 15,000 cps. This is a good range of sound; however, it is important to select a machine in which this represents a flat frequency response with no dropping off at either end, and is plus or minus no more than five decibels volume throughout. In tape machines it is the mechanism as much as the electronics that counts. They should also have quick stopping, fast forward, and fast reverse mechanisms to facilitate prompt location of desired passages.

Of course, the amplification systems must be high fidelity for tape the same as for other sound sources.

Frequency modulation programs are often excellent and can be copied directly onto tape to build a library for future use. Selection of an FM tuner (receiver without audiopower amplifier and speaker) must be governed by certain important qualifications. First of these is high sensitivity of the order of five microvolts for 30 decibels quieting. Second is an automatic frequency control (with on-off) without which the receiver is likely to drift from the station. Third is response from 20 to 15,000 cps in order to hear high fidelity sounds. Fourth is care to see that the output from the tuner does not exceed the allowable amplifier input so as to avoid overloading the amplifier tubes with resultant distortion.

FM radio broadcasts *can* be very wide range if they are from locally originating shows or if high fidelity recordings are being ·

broadcast from the local station. However, network programs are generally sent over telephone wires which are limited to 50 to 7000 cps. Even television sound, which could be high fidelity is often sent over phone wires instead of over the high fidelity coaxial cables with the pictures, as is possible. Even special high fidelity wires are available in certain localities, but are seldom used for some reason. Enough demand for good sound by discriminating listeners might remedy this.

Once high fidelity equipment is in use, the therapist will notice how much easier it is to detect flaws in recordings. Many record shops will permit owners of high fidelity equipment to check records on their own machines. Of course, care should be exercised to avoid scratching or otherwise damaging these records.

Long playing records are made of a vinylite plastic which is softer than the old shellac 78's. This means that special attention to avoid sliding the records against anything is necessary. The cardboard container should be buckled open before sliding in the record, and a flap should be affixed over the opening to keep out dust. Special detergent liquids are commercially available and should be applied to the surface of the records periodically to break the static electric attraction for dust. Any foreign bodies such as dust (and even fingerprints) can be heard when played on high fidelity reproducers. Handle the records by the edges and centers only to avoid fingerprints on the grooves. Settle the needle carefully on the leading edge and use great care to prevent its sweeping over the record.

The use of high fidelity recordings should be expected to produce more intense responses in patients than other forms of recorded music.

The music of high fidelity is clearly defined—moving and clean cut. It is capable of concert hall volume without injury to sensitive ears, for it is devoid of distortion and hum which are the distracting and annoying elements of most "canned" music at high volumes. Sibilants are defined. The sound "s" is never confused with "f." The inhaled breath of a flutist may be discerned between notes. Instruments retain their individuality even in the upper registers, because their distinguishing overtones can still be heard by virtue of the extended upper range. Great pipe organ pedal notes and kettle drums rumble and roar to the pit of the stomach with astounding realism, while low plucked strings are distinct and ringing. The delicate tinkle of treble piano passages as well as celestes, harps, and triangles retain their lustre, nearness, and brilliance. The 'cello with its tremendous range of overtones can at last be fully reproduced.

At present, many therapists may be using defective sound equipment, unaware of its defects. In many cases, noise, hum, and distortion may actually serve to alienate patients, rather than to win them.

This seems unfortunate in the light of the simplicity and economy involved in obtaining a high fidelity sound system. Many of these systems are acceptable, but certain ones are outstanding. The therapist should ideally try to hear several various units in order to note the difference and to select what suits his needs best. Certain dealers in larger cities maintain listening studios equipped with various combinations to demonstrate sound equipment to prospective buyers. If none of these is available, the author will forward data regarding various units upon request.

SOME OBJECTIVE STUDIES OF RHYTHM IN MUSIC

By HOWARD HANSON

Mus. Bac., Mus. Doc., LL.D., F.A.A.R., Rochester, N. Y.

It is not necessary to point out the emotional attributes inherent in rhythm. The mass hysteria present in recordings of the rhythmic chants of primitive peoples and the similar mass hysteria of the modern "jam-session" indicate—at times, all too clearly—the emotional tension producible by subjecting groups of people to concentrated doses of rhythm. The reasons back of this rhythmic excitement, however, are not always clearly understood and require some explanation.

In the same way that tones of definite pitch constitute the raw material of which harmony and melody are made, so equal divisions of time constitute the raw material of rhythm. To pursue the analogy further, as there are theoretically an infinite number of different tones and combinations of tones, so there are also an infinite number of combinations of rhythmic patterns. Here the similarity ends for, though the infinity of pitch-tones has been reduced to a finite number through arbitrary agreement, the infinite number of possible rhythmic relationships persists.

To begin we must distinguish between beat, tempo, meter and rhythm. All written music presumes division of time into *equal* pulse or beats. These beats may be slow or fast, expressed or only implied, but they are always *equal* divisions.

The variation of the speed of the recurring pulse is generally referred to as the *tempo* of the music. In other words *adagio* simply means a *slow* beat, a beat of long duration, and *allegro* means a *fast* beat, a beat of short duration. For the sake of easy reference we may think of a moderato tempo as the tempo of the normal pulse—approximately 72 beats per minute. This is also the tempo of a leisurely walking gait, the *andante* tempo of music, as illustrated, for example, in the Wedding March from Wagner's "Lohengrin," (written *alla breve* for purposes of comparison).

A tempo twice as fast as the normal pulse—144 beats per minute—is at the rate of a fast march, as in Bagley's famous "National Emblem" march.

A tempo three times as fast—216 beats per minute—is approximately the tempo of the Italian Tarantella, the dance which is supposed to have originated from the excitement induced by the bite of the tarantula. It is also the tempo of the half-beat of the jitterbug rug-cutter who has been bitten by one of our deadlier swing bands!

The mind refuses to consider each beat as a separate, independent entity but proceeds to group them. The grouping of beats produces meter. The most elementary metric grouping is the natural grouping by twos, possibly suggested by the natural grouping of foot-steps in walking. By instituting a slight accent on every other beat this duple meter becomes readily apparent. This is the fundamental meter of marches and of the great mass of popular music.

[306]

♪ ♩ ♪ ♩ ♪ ♩ ♪ ♩
1 2 1 2 1 2 1 2

By accenting in groups of three rather than two we produce
the second basic meter, triple meter. This is the meter of the waltz
and of many graceful and charming folk-dances.

♪ ♩ ♩ ♪ ♩ ♩
1 2 3 1 2 3

This is an over-simplification of the subject of meter as there
are also compound duple rhythms and compound triple rhythms
formed by the grouping of basic units within a larger compound
unit. There are also in contemporary music complexes of duple
and triple rhythm in combinations of groups of three and two within larger units of, for example, five or seven.

♪ ♩ ♩ ♪ ♩   or   ♩ ♩ ♪ ♩ ♩
1 2 3 4 5   1 2 3 4 5

♩ ♪ ♩ ♩ ♪ ♩ ♩   or   ♪ ♩ ♩ ♩ ♩ ♩ ♩
1 2 3 4 5 6 7   1 2 3 4 5 6 7

In the main, however, this simplification serves our purpose.

When we have discussed tempo and meter we have, however,
not yet discussed rhythm itself for rhythm is essentially the combination or subdivision of time units within fixed metric patterns,
and to these temporal relationships of notes within a metric design does music owe a large part of its ability to produce effects
which are soothing or exhilarating, quieting or disturbing.

Now, in proceeding to the consideration of the effects of
rhythm, we may lay down a few simple principles. First, everything else being equal, the further the tempo is accelerated from
the pulse rate toward the upper limit of practical tempo the greater

becomes the emotional tension. Second, as long as the subdivisions of the metric units are regular and the accents remain strictly in conformity with the basic pattern, the effect may be exhilarating but will not be disturbing. Third, rhythmic tension is heightened by the extent to which the dynamic accent is misplaced in terms of the metric accent. Fourth, the emotional effect of "off-balance" accents is greatly heightened by an increase in dynamic power.

Let us begin our illustrations with a duple meter with subdivisions of two. This is an English folk-dance of ancient vintage. It will be noticed that the *dynamic* accent is in complete accord with the *metric* accent producing an effect of smooth rhythmic balance.

Here is a similar case, but with a slight variation in that the stronger dynamic accent is shifted from the first to the second beat.

Our third dance is also in duple rhythm but with a subdivision of three, giving an increased rhythmic vitality.

The stately court dances of the 17th and 18th centuries were for the most part conceived in this balanced form. The style is beautifully illustrated in, for example, the Minuet from the C major, or "Jupiter" Symphony of Mozart

and persists in the early works of Beethoven as illustrated in the charming Minuet from the G major Sonata.

A beautiful illustration—one so theoretically perfect as to constitute what we might call a clinical example—is found in a Gigue of Handel where the dynamic stress in a triple meter is on the first beat, the harmony is repeated in the second beat without accent, and the third beat receives no stress at all as half of the beat is occupied by a rest. The result is a rhythm of superb grace and elegance, again with the metric and dynamic accents in complete accord.

Even the classic composers, however, were intrigued by the disturbing effects of off-balance rhythms and we find "Papa" Haydn in the Minuet of his "London" Symphony deliberately disturbing the regular rhythmic flow of the dance by placing a dy-

namic accent on the third beat of each measure—a mild disturbance it is true, but a forerunner of later developments.

As dissonance began creeping into the music of the 19th century composers in their search for the expression of emotional
tension, so the introduction of rhythmic unbalance was used for
the same purpose. The first movement of the "Eroica" symphony
serves as an excellent illustration. The movement is in a basic
three meter but in the most exciting part of the movement Beethoven introduces a duple dynamic accent into a triple meter. In
other words, the dynamic and metric accents are thrown violently
off-balance.

As I attempted to point out in my previous paper, the composers from the 16th century to the 20th were highly conscious of
the possibilities of dissonance for the arousing of emotional excitement. The older composers were equally conscious of the power
of rhythmic displacement to create similar tension, and the 16th
century theorists established numerous "rules" to keep music on
the straight and narrow path of rhythmic regularity as well as
consonance. The increase in the use of disruptive dissonance and
rhythmic irregularity from the 16th to at least the middle of the

19th century was slow and gradual. With the advent of the 20th century, however, caution was generally abandoned and music proceeded rapidly on the path to greater harmonic dissonance and greater rhythmic irregularity.

The development of rhythmic irregularity found its most fertile field in contemporary popular music. It began mildly enough in early American "rag-time" by the simple device of a shifted accent in the melodic line, a device which had long precedent in classical music. See, for example, Braham's famous "Limehouse Blues."

From this it proceeded, more subtly, through the use of the classic device of the super-imposition of a three-beat rhythmic figure upon a basic two-beat meter (as previously illustrated in the Beethoven example) in Zcz Confrey's "Stumbling."

It finds its ultimate development in the current "Boogie Woogie" craze. A short technical explanation of this queer atavistic manifestation is, I believe, in order. Popular music has in large measure discarded the more graceful three meter for the more "square" and angular two beat measure. Now it is apparent that if eight beats follow one another in two beat meter there would normally be four groups of two beats with a slight accent on the first of each group, that is, *1* 2, *3* 4, *5* 6, *7* 8. It is apparent, however, that, arithmetically, eight may be divided into unequal groups of three and two, for example, 3 3 2, in which cases the accents fall *1* 2 3, *4* 5 6, *7* 8.

In "boogie-woogie" a repeated figure in the bass—the classic basso ostinato—continues indefinitely in regular rhythm.

Above this the harmonies are placed on accents at variance with the basic meter.

When the ostinato is played by a vigorous pianist and one or more violent slap-bass artists, and when the harmonies are played by six leather-lunged trumpets and trombones intent on mayhem on the ears, the effect can be devastating.

There is a particularly—to me—nerve-wracking variety which I understand is called "Indian Boogie-Woogie"—the title apparently constituting the white man's crowning insult to the noble Indian. In at least one version a little crass dissonance is added to the usual ingredients with the following results.

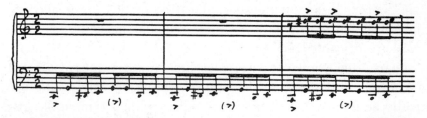

In conclusion may I say a word about contemporary popular music in general since it has been the subject of wide controversy and has even been singled out by some critics as a contributory cause to juvenile delinquency.

Popular music, like any other kind of music, may be good, bad or indifferent in quality. Much of it is harmless, some of it is over-sentimental, some contains at least a modicum of fantasy and beauty. The popularity of Frank Sinatra has caused his name to be mentioned frequently in connection with the deleterious effects of popular music but I can find no evidence to support this view. Most of the music which he sings is sentimental and nostalgic. He sings with sincerity and sensitivity and not infrequently artistry. If young girls are moved to squeal with delight I do not believe any harm has been done.

The music to which I am objecting—the violent boogie-woogie —is something quite different. It is frequently crass, raucous and commonplace, and could be dismissed without comment if it were not for the radio whereby hour after hour night after night American homes are flooded with vast quantities of this material. To its accompaniment our youngsters dance, play and even study. Perhaps they have developed an immunity to its effects—but if they have not, and if the mass production of this aural drug is not curtailed, we may find ourselves a nation of neurotics which even the skill of your profession may be hard-pressed to cure.

THE EFFECTS OF PERSONAL INSECURITY ON REACTIONS TO UNFAMILIAR MUSIC

By SEYMOUR FISHER and RHODA LEE FISHER

Elgin State Hospital, Elgin, Illinois

A. Introduction

Past research (1, 2, 3) concerned with the determinants of musical preference has indicated that reactions to musical compositions are markedly influenced by degree of familiarity with them. Dynamics of response to familiar music seem to be different from the dynamics of response to unrecognized music. In reacting to familiar music the individual is not only influenced by the pattern of sounds, as such, but also by the context in which he previously heard the music and the context of what he knows other people whose opinions are important to him think about that music. Response to unfamiliar music seems to be much less influenced by such factors. It has in the past been shown (2, 3) that educational background, economic status, and age correlate significantly with character of preferences for familiar music; whereas preference patterns for unfamiliar music fail to show such correlations (1). When responding to unfamiliar music the individual has only a restricted opportunity for referring his judgments to the conventional frames of reference associated with his rôle in the culture. Unfamiliar music requires the individual to respond outside of the framework usually provided by conventional social "props" and demands a more spontaneous self-involving attitude. Since this is

[314]

true, one would anticipate that individual differences in personality makeup would have a greater opportunity to influence reactions to unfamiliar music than reactions to familiar music. There has been much general speculation in the past with regard to the question of influence of personality differences on musical preference, but it has been difficult to carry on objective study of this question because of the "covering over" complications introduced by generalized cultural variables. However, since general cultural influences appear to be minimized in judgmental situations involving unfamiliar music, study of responses to unfamiliar music would seem to be a potentially valuable means for evaluating the kinds of personality variables that may affect musical preference.

B. Purpose

The present study was an exploratory attempt to determine if it was feasible to demonstrate the influence of a significant personality variable on musical preference. The specific personality variable chosen for study in this regard was degree of personal insecurity. It was the intention to demonstrate that individual differences in personality security may strongly affect reactions to unfamiliar music varying widely in degree of excitement and dramatic feeling. It was postulated that if an individual were internally disturbed by feelings of instability or expectations of threat that these feelings would significantly influence his response to different kinds of music varying in their degree of dramatic climax, excitement, and swelling crescendo. It appeared likely that the insecure individual would find in dramatic, exciting music certain reminders of his inner disturbance and would probably find fewer such reminders in calm restrained music.

C. Procedure and Subjects

The procedure used in testing this hypothesis was as follows:

1. Two contrasting musical selections were taken from the

music of each of four composers. These contrasting selections were jointly chosen by two judges with the criterion in mind that one of each of the two selections taken from each composer should be a very subdued, unemotional passage and the other selection should be a rousing, emotionally dramatic excerpt. Furthermore, an attempt was made to choose passages which were relatively infrequently played. Thus, there were four exciting passages and four quiet passages chosen. These passages were taken from the following sources:

(1) Richard Strauss
    (a) "On the Shores of Sorrento" from *Aus Italien*
    (b) *Ein Heldenleben*
(2) Manuel De Falla
    (a) *The Three Cornered Hat*
    (b) *El Amor Brujo*
(3) Modest Moussorgsky
    Pictures at an Exhibition
(4) Ferde Grofé
    The Grand Canyon Suite

Each of the selections was represented by a 45-second recorded excerpt. From these eight excerpts eight pairings were set up, each pairing consisting of an exciting composition and a quiet composition. Thus, one of the excerpts in a given pairing would be played and then the other excerpt; and subjects were asked to indicate which of the two they "liked best." The presentation of the pairings was such that first and second positions of exciting and quiet compositions in the pairings varied randomly. Altogether, each subject expressed eight choices with regard to the musical compositions.

2. In order to obtain a measure of degree of personal insecurity existing within each of the subjects a semi-projective technique was employed. A series of eight pictures were drawn, each depicting an ongoing activity or event. Each picture was so drawn as to give some potential cue or basis for assuming that the ongoing activity was one in which an individual had lost control over him-

self or in which some object had in a dangerous fashion become uncontrolled. Illustratively, one picture depicted a man riding around a racetrack and certain cues were put into the picture which made it possible to see the man as falling off of his horse. Similarly, another picture depicted a woman sitting on top of a tall object and cues were inserted which made it possible to see her as falling off of that object. All of the pictures were structured in this fashion. Each of the drawings was presented to the subjects on a screen by means of slides. Subjects were to indicate their interpretations of the pictures by checking various listed alternative descriptions. That is, for each picture a group of five alternative interpretations was listed; and these interpretations varied so that at one extreme they depicted an activity in which a person or object was completely out of control and at the other extreme they depicted a very controlled undisturbed kind of activity. Subjects were to indicate for each picture the interpretation they considered to be most likely and also the interpretation that was their second choice. Furthermore, they were to indicate the one interpretation they considered to be least likely or least possible. Since a preliminary testing out of these pictures had shown that they were amenable to a wide variety of interpretations, it was considered that any unusual positive or negative concern with "loss of control" alternatives was a sign of internal insecurity. In other words, the theory underlying this measure was that if an individual were moved by feelings of insecurity and expectation of threat from the environment that he would be more likely to perceive and become disturbed by the themes of loss of control in the pictures than would the more secure individual.

3. Another procedure was employed for measuring feelings of insecurity. Each subject was asked to draw a picture of a person "doing something"; and he was further asked to write beneath his drawing a brief description of what the person in his drawing was doing. The assumption behind this procedure was that subjects

who were insecure would draw a very restricted kind of picture involving a very hemmed in inhibited kind of movement. It was felt that the more secure individual would draw a picture in which the movement expressed was freer, less inhibited, and more truly exemplifying real spontaneity.

The subjects used in this study consisted of 41 boys and 56 girls varying in age from 12 through 18. They comprised all of the students from the ninth through the twelfth grades in a small community about 40 miles from Chicago. The population of this school is of a mixed "small town" and rural composition. As indicated in Table 1, there is a fairly equal sex representation in the group. The majority of the subjects fall in the age range 12 to 14.

TABLE 1

SEX AND AGE DISTRIBUTION IN THE EXPERIMENTAL GROUP

Sex			Age (Years)		
Male	Female	$N = 97$	12-14	15-16	17-18
40	57		54	28	15

Subjects were tested in groups of approximately 50. During the test sessions there were three observers present to clarify instructions for subjects who had individual questions. The whole procedure was introduced as "a study of your interests, the kinds of things you like." The first task to be presented was that which required the subjects to indicate their interpretations of the picture series depicting "loss of control" themes. They indicated their interpretations on a printed form which listed various alternatives. Secondly, as described above, subjects were asked to draw on sheets of paper of uniform size a picture of a person doing something and to describe what the person was doing. Finally, the various musical excerpts were played and subjects were to indicate on a printed form which member of each of the given pairings of excerpts they liked best. During this last procedure subjects were frequently asked if they recognized the compositions being played. None of the subjects expressed recognition of any of the compositions.

D.   RESULTS AND DISCUSSION

Initial inspection of the data indicated that there was no simple relationship between degree of personal insecurity, as indicated by the picture measure, and the character of the subjects' reactions to the two contrasting types of music. Thus, the subjects were classified into three groups in terms of the number of exciting musical selections they preferred. These three groups comprised those who had preferred 0 to 2 of the exciting selections; and at the other extreme those who had preferred 5 to 8 exciting selections; and a middle grouping of those who had preferred 3 to 4 exciting selections. It was found that the percentage of times subjects designated loss of control alternatives for the picture measure as their first choice, as their second choice, or as their least likely choice did not vary significantly among the three groups. Table 2 shows how approximately similar the percentage of each type of "loss of control" choice is in the various musical choice groupings.

However, a more complicated form of analysis did reveal a significant difference in the reactions to the "loss of control" pictures of those falling into different musical preference groups. It became apparent after inspection of the data that disturbance in reacting to the "loss of control" pictures would not reveal itself in any simple index (e.g., number of "loss of control" alternatives selected as being the most likely interpretation). Rather, it was hypothesized that disturbance in reaction to these pictures could best be detected in terms of marked disparities in the proportions of loss of control alternatives designated as first choice, second choice, and "least likely." The indications were that piling up of "loss of control" alternatives in any of these three categories was a sign of disturbance; whereas a smooth equal distribution of "loss

[319]

TABLE 2

PERCENTAGE DISTRIBUTION OF DESIGNATIONS OF "OUT OF CONTROL" PICTURE ALTERNA-
TIVES AS FIRST, SECOND, AND LEAST LIKELY BY SUBJECTS DIFFERING IN
NUMBER OF EXCITING SELECTIONS PREFERRED

Choice positions assigned to "out of control" alternatives	Number of exciting musical selections preferred		
	0-2 ($N = 41$)	3-4 ($N = 32$)	5-8 ($N = 24$)
Number of times chosen as first alternative			
0-3	58	47	48
4 or more	42	53	52
Number of times chosen as second alternative			
0-3	42	59	60
4 or more	58	41	40
Number of times chosen as least likely alternative			
0-3	78	81	84
4 or more	22	19	16

of control" alternatives was a sign that such alternatives had not had a disturbing influence. That is, if the pictures were not disturbing there would be no reason for showing any form of extreme reaction to the "loss of control" alternatives. Consequently, the final scoring system worked out for evaluating each individual's degree of insecurity was based on the following formula:

Degree of insecurity = Difference between number of "loss of control" alternatives designated as 1 and those designated as 2, plus the difference between those designated as 1 and those designated as "least likely," plus the difference between those designated as 2 and those considered as "least likely," plus the one largest disparity existing between any two of the categories of choice.

When each individual's profile of "loss of control" choices had been scored in this manner, it was found that internal insecurity did have a significant relationship to differences in reaction to the exciting as contrasted to the calm musical selections. As shown in Table 3, insecure persons tended to prefer either a very few or

TABLE 3

Percentages of Subjects in Three Musical Choice Categories Manifesting
Insecurity Reactions Toward the Picture Series

0-2 Exciting compositions preferred ($N = 41$)	3-4 Exciting compositions preferred ($N = 32$)	5-8 Exciting compositions preferred ($N = 24$)
45*	15	29

* When Group 3-4 was compared with the combined 0-2 and 5-8 groups, it was found that there were 28 per cent more insecure persons in the combined extreme groups than in the middle group. This difference was significant in terms of a critical ratio of 3.3.

a great many of the exciting musical selections. A significantly lower percentage of those persons who preferred a moderate number of the dramatic selections were insecure persons than of those who preferred either an extremely few or an extremely large number of the exciting selections. It would appear from such results that over-restrictiveness or over-enthusiastic freedom in response to the dramatic excerpts was for many of the subjects a function of feelings of insecurity. These two extremes in mode of reaction to the musical stimuli which were apparently disturbing is strikingly analogous to the extremes in reaction often displayed by neurotics in real life situations when they are reacting to disturbing demands. Of course, it is not being suggested that all of the extremes in reaction to the unfamiliar exciting music were a function of internal insecurity, but only that insecurity was in many cases an important influence in producing such response.

In order to relate the character of the figure drawings produced by subjects to their musical preferences it was necessary to devise a scoring system for evaluating the drawings. The method of scoring finally devised took into account only the subject's own description of what the figure was doing. Each subject had been asked to write beneath his drawings a description of what the figure was doing; and it was this description which was evaluated. The movement expressed in the description was categorized under one of the following subdivisions.

1. Freely expressed movement in which the figure spontaneously undertakes some activity usually considered to involve personal satisfaction. An example of this type of movement is provided by such a description as "A boy playing basketball."

2. Movement which is spontaneous and freely expressed but which has temporarily not yet gone to completion or which is temporarily in the process of being blocked. "Boy *trying* to catch a ball" is an example of this type of movement.

3. Passive movement in which the figure is described as engaged in such activities as "sleeping," "lying down," or merely "walking along."

4. Movement in which the subject is engaged in an activity that is usually regarded as work, labor, or a task imposed by someone else. "Someone mowing the lawn" or "Someone building a chicken house" are examples of this kind of movement.

5. Movement in which the figure is described as being in an insecure position, getting into an insecure position, or losing control. "Girl sitting on the edge of her chair" or "Boy falling into the water" are examples of this category of movement.

Table 4 summarizes the distribution of these different kinds of figure drawing movement among those subjects falling into the various categories of musical preference. Once again it is clear that of those who express either an unusually small or an unusually large number of preferences for the exciting musical compositions a larger percentage are insecure persons than of those who express only a moderate preference for such compositions. Eighty-eight per cent of those in the middle or moderate category of musical preference drew figures in which the movement was either freely expressed or freely expressed but temporarily not complete. But in the 0 to 2 musical category 66 per cent drew figures in which the movement was of the freely expressed type;

TABLE 4

PERCENTAGES OF SUBJECTS IN THREE MUSICAL CHOICE CATEGORIES EXPRESSING
DIFFERENT TYPES OF MOVEMENT IN THEIR FIGURE DRAWINGS

Type of movement	0-2 Exciting compositions preferred (N = 41)	3-4 Exciting compositions preferred (N = 32)	5-8 Exciting compositions preferred (N = 24)
Freely expressed	59*	72	58
Freely expressed but incomplete	7	16	4
Passive	7	3	0
Work	17	9	25
Insecure	10	0	13

* When Group 3-4 was compared with the combined 0-2 and 5-8 groups it was found that the percentage of freely expressed types of movement was higher in the 3-4 category than in the other combined category. There was a difference of 23 per cent. This difference was equivalent to a critical ratio of 2.8.

and in the 5 to 8 musical category 62 per cent drew figures expressing free movement of this type. Furthermore, 10 per cent of those in the extreme 0 to 2 musical category drew figures in which the movement was of an insecure, losing control type. Thirteen per cent in the extreme 5 to 8 musical category drew figures expressing the same kind of insecure movement. None of the subjects in the middle 3 to 4 musical category drew figures expressing insecure movement. When the 0 to 2 group is combined with the 5 to 8 group and compared with the 3 to 4 group, the difference in the percentage of the freely expressed type of movement between the combined first two groups and the 3 to 4 group is significant at the one per cent level. Thus, there is additional confirmation that personal insecurity has a significant influence upon reaction to dramatic unfamiliar music.

The results of the present study imply that musical preference is not some abstracted aesthetic response, but a reaction which is influenced by personal needs and difficulties in the same way that most other reactions are. There has been a tendency to think of the determinants of musical preference in terms of rather impersonal categories like "socio-economic status" or "educational level." But when one studies the reactions of the individual to music in situations where he does not have the usual social cues from guiding his preference expressions, one can see in a rather direct fashion that insecurities, anxieties, and fears frequently do have an influence on response to music. A musical preference may be a very personal expression which is the dynamic outcome of an attempt to deny certain fears and to compensate for certain fears. The data here obtained show distinctly that both undue rejection and overly enthusiastic acceptance of given kinds of music may both represent defensive responses to musical stimuli which are disturbing.

E. SUMMARY

1. The reaction of 97 subjects to two kinds of unfamiliar music contrasting sharply in their degree of excitement and dramatic effect were obtained.

2. The degree of insecurity and internal anxiety of these subjects was measured by means of two separate techniques. One of these techniques was based on the degree of disturbance shown by subjects when asked to describe vague pictures with potentially disturbing themes. A second technique for detecting insecurity was based on an evaluation of human figures drawn by the subjects.

3. It was found that of those who reacted to the unfamiliar excitingly dramatic music with either unusual favorableness or unusual unfavorableness that a larger percentage showed signs of marked personal insecurity than of those subjects who expressed only a moderate number of preferences for the exciting compositions.

4. In general, it was demonstrated that personal insecurity may have an important influence on individual reactions to unfamiliar dramatic music.

[324]

REFERENCES

1. FISHER, R. L. Preferences of different age and socio-economic groups in unstructured musical situations. *J. Soc. Psychol.* (In press.)
2. RUBIN-RABSON, G. The influence of age, intelligence, and training on reactions to classic and modern music. *J. Gen. Psychol.*, 1940, *22*, 413-429.
3. SCHUESSLER, K. F. Social background and musical taste. *Amer. Sociol. Rev.*, 1948, *13*, 330-335.

LIMITATIONS OF RESEARCH IN MUSIC THERAPY

By ABE PEPINSKY, Ph.D.

Head of Department of Psychology, Haverford College, Haverford, Pennsylvania

Consideration of the limitations imposed upon research in the use of music in therapy was provoked by inquiry and the discussion of a paper presented by the writer at the Third Annual Meeting of the National Association for Music Therapy in October of 1952. The paper was entitled "Applications and Mis-Applications of Research Techniques in Music Therapy." It is admitted that music therapy is not entirely a virgin field; that it has been practiced for many centuries if we are to believe accounts found in the literature. The Bible makes more than casual mention of it; Carl Engel devoted a whole chapter to "Music and Medicine" in his "Musical Myths and Facts"; and Max Schoen et al gave us a comprehensive survey of the use of music in medicine in a book by that name. It seems obvious that a belief as strongly held as is the beneficent utilization of music in therapy would eventually have to be evaluated and interpreted by research techniques. It is moreover evident that such research techniques must necessarily involve consideration of the application and mis-application of the procedures used and in the design of experiment. The paper referred to attempted to show that inasmuch as mental patients respond either favorably or unfavorably, or are indifferent to exposure to music, scientific research is vulnerable to the verdict of intellectual dishonesty if only the favorable responses are brought into the limelight. Far too many reports of research contain sweeping statements in the evaluation and interpretation of their findings. It

would be a desirable limitation placed on research if certain qualifications might tend to reduce their generalities to a more particular or restricted form. Such a restraint within bounds would be
very desirable at this stage of our knowledge of music in therapy.

We would do well to pattern our research techniques after that
of the physicist, making simplifying assumptions to insure a
keener, more positive analysis and verification of hypotheses. Yet
we have always to remember that such assumptions were made
deliberately and that the ultimate solution is no more valid than
were the assumptions. However, such procedure makes for basic
research and we must be grateful to the physicist for showing us
the way to the "grass-roots" level of sophistication.

I am always intrigued by the block-diagram used by the modern
physicist in presenting his experimental set-up. Each block represents a little black box which has a well defined imprint and a
measurable output. Often the physicists' block-diagram contains a
whole train of these little boxes, sometimes in "series," sometimes
in "parallel," and sometimes in "series-parallel." These may
illustrate an electrical circuit including various types of electronic
gadgetry or they may represent an equivalent circuit defining a
situation in mechanics as an analogue. It is not too difficult to
stretch our imaginations a bit and represent our mental patient in
therapy in such an analogue. Consider, for a moment, just one
little black box representing our patient. Vectorial forces, having
direction as well as magnitude, impinge upon the box and it looks
for all the world like a stylized pin-cushion. Physically speaking,
this would be quite a simple problem because the resultant force
would be the vectorial sum of the various forces acting on the box.

Poincaré and others observed that every phenomenon in nature
is capable of a mechanistic explanation and that dynamical laws
alone are sufficient to account for every possible situation. Our
little black box is not very different from Kurt Lewin's "Dynamic
Theory of Personality" with his naïve drawings of the topological

geometry of a person's "life space," his "valences" and "barriers," his goals and conflicts. Lewin's topology represents the person as he sees himself or herself, whereas our little black box in the physicists' block-diagram would show the person as the therapist sees him. Furthermore, you and I now see the therapist as another little box in the diagram. Now permit the retina of your mind's eye to picture the innumerable forces of the environment and of the patient's heredity as arrows of various lengths and directions, going toward the little box representing the patient. These arrows depict forces acting on the person. The dynamics of the situation are necessarily a function of the changes wrought in the person as a result of the forces acting upon him.

There are many possible meanings ascribed to the word force. The dictionary lists terms ranging all the way from strength, or vigor, to moral power, and even "a body of men trained for action in any way, as in a police force or military force." People generally associate a kind of technical significance with the word force as in the movement of a body when force is exerted on it. There is conveyed the notion of a muscular push or pull which can be extended to inanimate objects as well, so that one speaks of the force of a locomotive pulling on a train, or the force which a house exerts on its foundation, and the like.

The forces impinging on our patient may be the thousands of genes acting as catalysts to direct the growth of specialized tissues, influencing the size and shape of bodily features, reactivity of muscles and nerves, and even susceptibility to disease. They may be the external restrictions or nutritive deficiencies preventing fulfillment of the germinal possibilities. They may be the results of learning and acculturation. They may be the effects of frustrations and loss of status. They may be the emergence of traits, values and attitudes. They may be constitutional changes, ego changes, sexual behavior, socio-cultural determinants, or cultural influences. They may be vocational adjustments or love relationships, or familial

[328]

relationships. Thus you begin to see what I mean by innumerable forces represented by those arrows whose lengths indicate the order of magnitude, and whose directions give indication of the component influences on the personality.

All of these forces make up the input which the physicist could easily have replaced by a single vector, the resultant of all the many forces we indicated. At the other end of the box the physicist would draw another force vector, not necessarily of the same magnitude and direction as the input vector. Something must have happened within the little black box! We might be tempted, as was Pandora, to open the box just a little to see what it contains, what could account for the change in input to output. Maybe we'd find just another smaller box, and it in turn contain another box, ad infinitum. Perhaps it would be more profitable to examine the boundary conditions and assume the laws of probability as does the physicist in formulating his kinetic theory of gases. Or we may be sufficiently sophisticated to insert a probe and attempt to measure what occurs at some particular point in the inclosure. Indeed we may be so successful that we reduce our sphere of observation to the order of magnitude of an electron. Now we're getting somewhere, learning more and more about less and less! Surely this must be the ultimate in research.

We merely require to determine the position and the momentum of our little electron. Now, however, because of its smallness only radiation of very short wave-length can be used to measure the electron's position because radiation of wave-length larger than the electron's diameter would not be reflected by it and fail to betray its presence. But if we do this, the electron will experience a recoil because of the great momentum of short wave-length radiation. This resultant recoil would completely change the initial state of the electron's motion and thus preclude every possibility of determining it. If only we had not been so pre-occupied with the neatness and cleverness of our approach to the problem, the technical beauty of our gadgetry, the power of the tools available, we might have taken time to consider the "uncertainty principle" of Heisenberg with its far-reaching and fruitful system of analogies, known as "indeterminacy relations" in the treatment of quantum mechanics.

This is a limitation, indeed, but we must know about such limitations. Perhaps we'd have gotten further if we had treated the little black box as a unit, together with its input and output, subject to observation and measurement. Even the musical therapist can be represented by such a little box. He is implicated as one of the force vectors of the patient-box input. However, he in turn is subjected to a grand array of forces even as was the patient. In "parallel" with the music-therapist-box is another one representing the musical sounds produced. Possibly in "series" with the therapist-box and the one representing the patient may be interpolated another box representing a "live" musical instrument rather than the "canned" music from a phonograph or radio. Then, too, we might in our block diagram, further contain boxes pertaining to the musical composition with its stimulus values, and possibly even another for the composer and his creative urges. And we must not neglect to include a box to represent the room in which the music is performed. This room may possess distinctive qualities of selective absorption and reverberation. The masking effects of other sounds present at the time of the musical performance should also be represented.

Each one of these boxes that were added show forces acting upon them just like those we discussed acting on the patient. We have a few boxes left over which may be used to represent the psychiatric aid, the nurse, and the psychiatrist. The diagram might be simplified by including the attendant, nurse, and doctor, all in one box, the function of which would be the making of observations, measuring and recording them. But the circuit doesn't just come to a dead-end there. We discover a "feed-back" forming a "loop-circuit," first between the psychiatrist and the patient, then one between the psychiatrist and the nurse, the psychiatrist and the music therapist, as well as between the nurse and the patient, another between the nurse and the attendant, and the attendant and the patient. And, now, let us include one last little box.

This one will represent the research worker. The way he "plugs" into the circuit is very important to the interpreter of the diagram. We won't be tempted to represent the interpreter himself by a block in the diagram although it might be wise; but there are too many different kinds of interpreters. Even if we put all such possible interpreter-blocks together we would still have quite a bumpy pavement on which to ride to ultimate understanding. You will note, also, that we purposely omitted a number of blocks which might have represented the other adjuvant therapies. We must not ignore them in our thinking, however, because the music-therapist is not solely responsible for the patients' well-being. The research worker must not ignore the other therapies either because they also influence the patients' behavior. Our block-diagram is now quite complicated and the researcher must probe with his measuring instruments very carefully.

If the dynamics implied by the block-diagram can be represented by our equivalent electrical circuit, Kirchhoff's Network Laws may give us a lead toward possible solution, i.e: 1) that the algebraic sum of the currents at a junction equals zero, and 2) that the algebraic sum of the potential differences around any closed path in an electric circuit equals zero. If we substitute the word drive for currents in the first law we get some notion of the interaction between the musical therapist and the patient during treatment. The second law, likewise, has "dimensional" notation significance for us if we realize that potential difference is equivalent to electromotive force. In our case we would speak of the motivational forces in the patient. Then if we remember the relationships between electromotive force, current, and resistance, we would infer from the second law that the sum of the electromotive forces are equal to the sum of the products of the currents and resistances. Such an analogue guides us to the possibility of gauging the degree of equilibrium of the patients' emotional state. This makes sense qualitatively but we have made very little progress quantitatively as yet. The engineer has definitely established an equality between the electromotive force and the product of current and resistance. If any two of these can be measured the third can be calculated. We cannot hope to accomplish as much with our pseudo-dimensional notation. We can only establish a sense of proportionality. The exact coefficients are as yet wanting.

Our research workers hope to accomplish this with the fine instrumentation available today, impatiently eager to make use of the beautiful gadgetry devised by the electronics engineer for the physicist, the physiologist, the psychologist and the acoustician, but we have yet to know how to interpret the graphs obtained. For example, what shall we measure in the encephalograph? Should we measure the number of peaks per unit time or their relative amplitudes, their degree of periodicity or the integration of the areas under the curve? Or should we just refer to the Gibbs Atlas and match our waveform with the stereotypes contained in the atlas? Is not this very much like cutting a "2 x 4" with a cross-cut saw, using a micrometer to measure the desired length? We feel so dignified in being permitted to play with scientific apparatus that we begin to think that we are scientific also. It might be well to reflect on Lloyd Morgan's Canon to the effect that one should not approach a problem with a higher level of sophistication when a simpler approach is adequate. It would seem that our researcher in music therapy is finding himself between the horns of a dilemma, limited at both extremes. Clinical observation without controlled experimentation is certainly open to question, whereas basic research without consideration of the interaction of the total personality and the environment of the mental patient would be righteously frowned upon by the Gestalt psychologist.

BIBLIOGRAPHY

ALTSHULER, IRA M. 1939. Rational Music-Therapy of the Mentally Ill. Music Teachers National Association. Proceedings. XXXIII: 153-157.

ALTSHULER, IRA M. 1941. The Part of Music in Resocialization of Mental Patients. Occupational Therapy and Rehabilitation. XX:75-86 (April).

ALTSHULER, IRA M. 1944. Four Years Experience with Music as a Therapeutic Agent at Eloise Hospital. American Journal of Psychiatry. C:792-794 (May).

ALTSHULER, IRA M. 1946. The Case of Horace F. Music Teachers National Association. Proceedings. XL: 368-381.

ALTSHULER, IRA M. and B. H. SHEBESTA. 1941. Music as an Aid in the Management of Psychotic Patients. Journal of Nervous and Mental Diseases. XCIV: 179-183. (Aug.).

BENEDICT, MILO E. 1924. What Music Does to Us. Boston, Small, Maynard.

BENNETT, C. 1942. Music and Emotion. Musical Quarterly. XXVIII. 406-414 (Oct.).

BLACKWELL, ETHEL and GORDON A. NEIL. 1946. Music in Mental Hospitals. Occupational Therapy and Rehabilitation. XXV:243-246 (Dec.).

BURRIS-MEYER, H. and R. L. CARDINELL. 1946. The Place of Music in Healing. Journal of the Acoustical Society of America. XVII:232-235 (Jan.).

CAWSTON, NORMAN. 1932. Music and Medicine. South African Medical Journal. VI: 119 (Feb.).

CHAMBERLIN, H. E. 1942. Mental Hygiene and Music. California State Department of Social Welfare. Pamphlet.

CODELLAS, P. S. 1930. The Evolution of Melotherapy, Music in the Cure of Disease. California and Western Medicine. XXXII: 411-412 (June).

CORIAT, I. H. 1945. Some Aspects of a Psychoanalytical Interpretation of Music. Psychoanalytical Review. XXXII:408-418 (Oct.).

DAVIS, FRANK A. 1929. Music as a Part of the Occupational Therapy Program in a Mental Hospital. U. S. Veterans Bureau Medical Bulletin. VI:23 (March).

DISERENS, CHARLES M. 1923. Reactions to Musical Stimuli. Psychological Bulletin. XX:173-199 (April).

FULTZ, A. FLAGLER. 1944. Music as a Modality of Occupational Therapy. War Medicine. V:139-141 (March).

GARDINER, B. BELLAMY. 1944. Therapeutic Qualities of Music. Music and Letters. XXV:181-186 (July).

GROTHE, E. W. 1926. Music in Medicine. Occupational Therapy and Rehabilitation. V: 353-358 (Oct.).

HAMPTON, PETER J. 1945. The Emotional Element in Music. The Journal of General Psychology. XXXIII: 237-250 (Oct.).

HARMON, FRANCIS L. 1933. The Effects of Noise Upon certain Psychological and Physiological Processes. Archives of Psychology. XXIII-81 (Feb.).

BIBLIOGRAPHY

Harrington, A. H. 1939. Music as a Therapeutic Aid in a Hospital for Mental Diseases. Mental Hygiene. XXIII: 601-609 (Oct.).

La Master, Robert J. 1946. Music Therapy as a Tool for Treatment of Mental Patients in the Hospital. Hospital Management. LXII: 110 (Dec.).

Larson, B. H. 1928. Music in Medicine. Journal of the Michigan State Medical Society. XXVII. 252-256 (May).

Licht, Sidney H. 1946. Music in Medicine. Boston. New England Conservatory of Music.

Miles, J. R. and C. R. Tilly. 1935. Some Physiological Reactions to Music. Guy's Hospital Gazette. XLIX: 319-322 (Aug.).

Montani, Angelo. 1945. Psychoanalysis of Music. Psychoanalytic Review. XXXII: 225-227 (April).

Mott, Frederick. 1921. The Influence of Song on Mind and Body. The Journal of Mental Science. LXVII: 162-167 (April).

Pierce, A. H. 1934. The Therapeutic Value of Music for Psychotic Patients. The Medical Bulletin of the Veterans Administration. XIII:142-147 (Oct.).

Podolsky, Edward. 1919. Some Astonishing Effects of Music on the Body. Etude. XXXVIII:411 (June).

Podolsky, Edward. 1922. The Influence of Music Upon the Human Body. Illinois Medical Journal. XLII: 410 (Nov.).

Podolsky, Edward. 1925. The Physical Influence of Music. Etude. XLI: 710 (Oct.).

Podolsky, Edward. 1925. Singing for Health. Etude. 63:127 (Feb.).

Podolsky, Edward. 1926. The Influence of Music on the Circulation. Western Medical Times. 46:66 (Sept.).

Podolsky, Edward. 1930. How Music Exerts its Favorable Influence on the Body. Medical Herald. XLIX:328 (Sept.).

Podolsky, Edward. 1931. The Doctor Looks at Music. Northwest Musical Herald. VII:9 (Nov.).

Podolsky, Edward. 1931. Influence of Musical Stimuli on the Body. Trained Nurse and Hospital Review. LXXXVII: 613 (Nov.).

Podolsky, Edward. 1933. Music's Role in Healing. Etude LI:442 (July).

Podolsky, Edward. 1935. Music and Health. Virginia Medical Monthly. 710 (March).

Podolsky. Edward. 1936. Music Keeps the Mind Healthy. Modern Living. 227 (Feb.).

Podolsky, Edward. 1939. The Doctor Prescribes Music. N. Y. Stokes.

Podolsky, Edward. 1939. Music as an Anesthetic. Etude. 707 (Nov.).

Podolsky, Edward. 1940. Music Can Work Miracles. Etude. 514 (Aug.).

Podolsky, Edward. 1941. Some Aspects of Musical Therapy. Tomorrow 33 (Nov.).

Podolsky, Edward. 1942. Music in Military Strategy. Etude. 382 (June).

Podolsky, Edward. 1943. Music While You Work. Liberty. 71 (Feb. 8th).

Podolsky, Edward. 1946. Music Rhythm Affects Brain Rhythm. Etude. 604 (Feb.).

Podolsky, Edward. 1948. Change Your Mood with Music. Journal of Living. 19 (June).

PODOLSKY, EDWARD. 1948. Music and Warped Personalities. The Stigmatine. 2 (Oct.).

PODOLSKY, EDWARD. 1950. Music as a Hobby. Recreation. 100 (May).

RICHTER, W. G. 1934. The Beneficial Effects of Music for the Mentally Ill. Medical Bulletin of the Veterans Administration. XI:148 (Oct.).

ROBERTSON, ENID. 1934. The Emotional Element in Listening to Music. Australian Journal of Psychology and Philosophy. XII:199 (Sept.).

RUEGNITZ, MARJORIE J. 1943. Applied Music on Disturbed Wards. Occupational Therapy and Rehabilitation. XXV:203 (Oct.).

SCHOEN, MAX. 1927. The Effects of Music. N. Y. Harcourt, Brace.

SCHOEN, MAX. 1941. Doctoring with Music. Etude. LX:166 (March).

SCHRIEBER, LUCILLE. 1943. Music Hath Charms. Occupational Therapy and Rehabilitation. XXII:77 (April).

SEAR, H. G. 1939. Music and Medicine. Music and Letters. XX:43 (Jan.).

SEAR, H. G. 1942. Cure by Music. West London Medical Times. LI:9 (April).

SEARLE, W. F. 1933. Musical Experiment with Patients and Employees at Worcester State Hospital. Occupational Therapy and Rehabilitation. XII: 341 (Dec.).

SEYMOUR, HARRIET AYER. 1920. What Music Can Do for You. N. Y. Harper.

SHEEHAN, VIVIAN M. 1946. Rehabilitation of Aphasiacs in an Army Hospital. Journal of Speech Disorders. XI:149 (June).

SIMON, WERNER. 1945. The Value of Music in the Resocialization and Rehabilitation of the Mentally Ill. Military Surgeon. XCVII:498 (Dec.).

TINDALL, G. M. 1937. Rhythm for the Restless. Personnel Journal. XVI:120 (Oct.).

UNDERWOOD, ROY. 1946. The Human Response to Music. Music Teachers National Association. Proceedings. XL: 356.

VAN DE WALL, WILLEM and EARL D. BOND. 1934. The Use of Music in a Case of Psychoneurosis. American Journal of Psychiatry. XLC: 287 (Sept.).

VINCENT, SWALE and J. H. THOMPSON. 1929. Effects of Music upon Human Blood Pressure. Lancet. I:534 (March).

WALDEN, S. 1945. Music for the Mentally Disturbed. Etude. LXIII:263 (May).

WARD, MILTON H. 1945. Note on Psychomusic and Musical Group Therapy. Sociometry. VIII: 238 (Aug.).

WASHCO, A., JR. 1933. The Effects of Music Upon the Pulse Rate, Blood Pressure, and Mental Imagery. Philadelphia. Temple University.

YEAGER, R. P. 1945. The Use of Music in Neuropsychiatric Service Proceedings of the Neuropsychiatric Conference. Sixth Service Command. War Department. Chicago, 103-109.

YEARSLEY, M. 1935. Music as Treatment in Elizabeth Medicine. Lancet. I:415 (Feb.).